FOR CARLOS BAKER

Dear Scott/Dear Max

THE FITZGERALD–PERKINS CORRESPONDENCE

Edited

by

JOHN KUEHL

and

JACKSON R. BRYER

CASSELL · LONDON

CASSELL & COMPANY LTD.

35 Red Lion Square, London WC1R 4SG
Sydney, Auckland
Toronto, Johannesburg

First published in Great Britain 1973

ISBN 0 304 29150 1

PRINTED IN GREAT BRITAIN BY A. WHEATON & CO., EXETER
F 1272

Preface

The editorial procedures adopted in this book have grown out of our conception of it as a *narrative* involving two principal characters: Maxwell E. Perkins and F. Scott Fitzgerald. Consequently, we have included only letters between the two men and only those that sustain the interest and continuity of their story. The use of linking footnotes numbered sequentially at the back has enabled us to eliminate much tiresome material and to quote from letters with other correspondents who figure in the collection. Our view of this book as a *narrative* rather than a group of isolated documents has led us to exclude several letters included by Andrew Turnbull (*The Letters of F. Scott Fitzgerald*, 1963) which seemed to bog down. We have also felt free to cut within letters, supplying five dots for the deletion of an entire paragraph and three for an elision inside a paragraph. It should be noted, however, that the letters appear here exactly as they were written – typographical errors and all. *Sics* have not been employed, but wherever the text would be otherwise unintelligible, brackets have been inserted to express what was intended. We have, however, silently corrected obviously careless errors, such as uncrossed t's and the like. All salutations, addresses, and closings have, for stylistic purposes, been set in italics; and, for the same reason, the first paragraph of each letter has not been indented. In the case of undated letters, we have followed Turnbull's dating when we could agree; his biography (*Scott Fitzgerald*, 1962), Mizener's biography (*The Far Side of Paradise*, 1951) and internal evidence proved helpful as well. The reader will notice a second kind of footnote positioned at the bottom of the page. It is designed to provide immediate identification of persons, places and things without interrupting the flow of the story. Because the linking footnotes are numbered sequentially, these identification footnotes are designated by symbols: * stands for [1], † for [2], ** for [3], †† for [4] on any given page.

We wish to thank Dean David S. Sparks (the Graduate School of the University of Maryland), the General Research Board of the University of Maryland, and the Arts and Science Research Fund of New York University for their generous financial assistance. The human assistance rendered by Mr. Alexander P. Clark and Mrs. Alden Randall of The Princeton University Library and those who aided in the preparation of the manuscript – Mrs. Carolyn Banks, Miss Mary Lou Ference, Mr. Steven Stosny – is deeply appreciated. We are also grateful to our publisher, Mr. Charles Scribner, Jr., and our editor, Mr. Burroughs Mitchell, who were invariably patient and kind.

Introduction

On May 6, 1918, Shane Leslie, the Irish novelist and critic, wrote his publisher, Charles Scribner II, that he was sending him a manuscript which expressed "real American youth" by "an American Rupert Brooke." This young man, who had been Leslie's pupil at the Newman School and was now at Princeton, turned out to be F. Scott Fitzgerald. His future editor and friend, Maxwell E. Perkins, liked the book but asked for revisions, so Fitzgerald requested that *The Romantic Egotist* circulate among other publishers. When he had received their formal rejections, he rewrote it, first as *The Education of a Personage* and then as *This Side of Paradise*. Perkins accepted the novel during September, 1919, saying that the last version, like the original, abounded "in energy and life" while showing "much better proportion." The Fitzgerald-Perkins relationship began here.

Their correspondence, which covers the period between the two World Wars or the second American literary renaissance, also covers the most crucial professional period in the lives of the correspondents. It takes Fitzgerald from age twenty-one when he was composing *This Side of Paradise* to the year of his death at forty-three when he was composing *The Last Tycoon*, and Perkins from age thirty-three, a few years after he had given up the position of advertising manager to become a Scribner editor, to fifty-five, a few years before his death at sixty-one. Consequently, the letters reflect several kinds of history: that of two decades in the lives of a major American author and an incomparable American editor; of their friendship; of an important literary epoch and some of its significant figures – Ernest Hemingway, Thomas Wolfe, Edmund Wilson, Ring Lardner; of the genesis of a writing talent; and, above all, of the interaction between this talent and creative editing.

Fitzgerald, whose original phrases "The Jazz Age" and "emotional bankruptcy" aptly characterize certain aspects of the Twenties and Thirties and whose novels are steeped in cultural history, embodied a society and an era. In "Pasting It Together" (*The Crack-Up*, 1936), he equated early happiness and late despair with the country's boom and depression: "my happiness . . . was . . . unnatural as the Boom; and my recent experience parallels the wave of despair that swept the nation when the Boom was over." During the Twenties Fitzgerald soared, marrying Zelda Sayre, becoming a father, traveling and publishing widely. But during the Thirties he declined: his wife was in and out of sanitariums, he grew increasingly alcoholic, experienced a number of illnesses, spent considerable time in Hollywood, and published only one novel and one volume of stories. Earlier a celebrity both for his life and for his work, he wrote Perkins during 1938: "Since the going-out-of-print of 'Paradise' and the success (or is it one?) of the 'Fifth Column' I have come to feel somewhat neglected. Isn't my reputation being allowed to let slip away? I mean what's left of it."

During these same two decades, Perkins divided most of his time between New Canaan, Connecticut, where he lived with his wife and five daughters, and New York City, where he worked, making occasional visits to Windsor, Vermont, where he had grown up, and Key West, Florida, where he fished with Hemingway. Perkins' life was as steady as Fitzgerald's was not. *You Can't Go Home Again* (1929) provides an insight into the domestic part: The Fox awakes at eight o'clock; starts into the shower wearing pajamas and hat; nearly forgets to dress; rejects a gay tie for a modest cravat; and passes the doors of wife and daughters reiterating the expletive, "Women!" Interior decorators have torn things up; the female French poodle appears ridiculous; a mulatto maid argues with him. There ensues a tenderly awkward scene over breakfast between father and youngest offspring; then she leaves for school and he picks up the newspaper. Though Perkins often rejected Wolfe's caricature, he was unquestionably a person of set routines. Arriving at Scribners at ten o'clock, he would check correspondence, dictate letters, look over manuscripts, accept callers. At one o'clock he would eat lunch in Cherio's, ordering the same dishes for weeks on end. Back at Scribners, he examined more manuscripts and interviewed more callers from 2:30 until about 5:00, when he would meet an author or an agent in the men's bar of the Ritz before catching the 6:02 train to New Canaan, his briefcase full of additional manuscripts.

Once Fitzgerald remarked that Americans "should be born with fins, and perhaps they were." He knew what he was talking about, for by the time Scribners accepted *This Side of Paradise*, he had – thanks in part to his father's failure as a businessman – already resided in many cities and states. The return addresses of the letters to Perkins indicate that this pattern of rootlessness soon became one of restlessness. During the Twenties, he went abroad four times, twice for extended periods, while in his native land, he led a peripatetic existence. But just as the nomadic aspect of Fitzgerald's life was prefigured by adolescent experiences, so too was Perkins' stationary life. He lived in Plainfield, New Jersey, spent vacations in Windsor, attended St. Paul's School in New Hampshire and Harvard, worked in a Boston settlement house, and became a reporter on the *New York Times* in the city of his birth. Both early and late Perkins, like his ancestors, alternated between New York and New England, and consequently knew neither rootlessness nor restlessness. Malcolm Cowley has said that "the Manhattan Yankees, among whom the Perkins and Evarts families belong, are a small but recognizable tribe." (*The New Yorker*, "Profiles," April, 1944) Such security was lacking in Fitzgerald's life. He mentioned the dilemma of his split background during 1933, saying, "I am half black Irish and half old American stock with the usual exaggerated ancestral pretensions. The black Irish half of the family had the money and looked down upon the Maryland side . . . who had . . . 'breeding' . . . So being born in that atmosphere of crack, wise crack and countercrack I developed a two cylinder inferiority complex."

Fitzgerald's exhibitionism might be attributable to this inner turmoil. An unpublished autobiography marked "Outline Chart of My Life," but commonly called "Ledger," shows him to have been an actor from the age of seven; his childhood diary, "Thoughtbook," reveals him as a kind of proprietor, founding "the gooserah" and "the white handkerchief" clubs. Fitzgerald characters often have the need to perform or run things. At its least complicated, exhibitionism takes the form of showing off, as in the case of Basil Duke Lee, and at its most, that of self-destructive "charm." Fitzgerald says about Dick Diver: "the old fatal pleasingness, the old forceful charm, swept back with its cry of 'Use me!' He would have to go fix this thing that he didn't care a damn about, because it had early become a habit to be loved." Not until the time of *The Crack-Up* could Fitzgerald say of himself, "There was to be no more giving of myself." Meanwhile, from the publication of *This Side of Paradise* (1920) to the publication of *Taps at Reveille* (1935), the compulsion toward self-advertisement was frequently manifested through his obsessive consternation over the physical appearance of his books. There are innumerable references in the letters to dust jackets, uniform bindings, blurbs, photographs, titles, illustrations and tables of works. That he took such matters "personally" may be deduced from a comment to Perkins concerning *The Beautiful and Damned*: "The more I think of the picture on the jacket the more I fail to understand his drawing that man. The girl is excellent of course – it looks somewhat like Zelda but the man, I suspect, is a sort of debauched edition of me."

In contrast, Perkins, knowing who he was, developed a penchant for anonymity. He avoided professional gatherings, booksellers' conventions and publishers' cocktail parties; he refused to address the public through speaking engagements or articles, and he tried to dodge interviews. Perkins once warned Fitzgerald, "Don't ever defer to my judgment," implying a philosophy of editing that reflected a way of life. John Hall Wheelock succinctly summed it up this way: "The function of an editor . . . is to serve as a skilled objective outsider, a critical touchstone by recourse to which a writer is enabled to sense flaws in surface or structure, to grasp and solve the artistic or technical problems involved, and thus to realize completely his own work in his own way." (*Editor to Author*, 1950)

Among their other temperamental differences are the characteristic moods of the two men. Fitzgerald was a romantic, fluctuating between elation and depression. Perkins' rationality is visible in his balance and moderation. Neither a rightist nor a leftist, he occupied the middle ground when many literary figures, including Fitzgerald, veered toward the left. He often acted the part of conciliator, forgiving Wolfe his injustices, trying to patch up Fitzgerald's quarrels with Hemingway and Harold Ober, and answering would-be censors calmly but firmly. Perkins preferred Erasmus, "a temperate man," to the "impetuous and violent" Luther. And as Fitzgerald admired the Romantic Poets and Dostoyevski, Perkins admired eighteenth-century writers and Tolstoy.

Their temperamental differences are reflected in sharply divergent epistolary styles. Fitzgerald's letters – most of them handwritten – tend to be long, rather disjointed and rambling, while Perkins' typewritten letters are short or medium length, coherent and tight. Fitzgerald is usually personal and passionate, paying little attention to grammar, syntax, punctuation and spelling. Perkins, though far from indifferent, is guarded and reasonable, and he always writes precisely. The letters of Fitzgerald are often metaphoric and comic; those of Perkins, bare and witty. Fitzgerald is dynamic; Perkins, graceful.

What, then, accounts for their intimacy? Possibly similar heritages, these being far less disparate than they seem.

In *An Autobiography* (1965), Van Wyck Brooks says of his lifelong friend Maxwell Perkins: "I have known few other Americans in whom so much history was palpably and visibly embodied." This observation stems from Perkins' background. His great, great grandfather had signed the Declaration of Independence, and his namesake, the maternal grandfather, William Maxwell Evarts, had served as Attorney General under Andrew Johnson and Secretary of State under Rutherford B. Hayes prior to becoming a United States Senator. Because of him, who informed Henry Adams, "I pride myself on my success in doing not the things I like to do but the things I don't like to do," young Perkins met President Harrison and General Sherman. Of the maternal side, he wrote Fitzgerald: "The Evartses in general are rigorous for duty, the rights of property, the established church, the Republican Party, etc."

With respect to an American aristocracy colored by puritanism, Fitzgerald's background resembled Perkins'. But the ingredients were paternal and southern rather than maternal and northern. Edward Fitzgerald's great, great grandfather was the brother of Francis Scott Key, author of "The Star Spangled Banner," and his first cousin the son-in-law of Mrs. Suratt, executed for involvement in Lincoln's assassination. Through Edward Fitzgerald's mother, Cecilia Ashton Scott, her grandson descended from Maryland families that, according to Andrew Turnbull, "had figured prominently in the colonial legislatures and on the governors' councils." (*Scott Fitzgerald*, 1962) A remarkable document, "The Death of My Father," tells us that Edward acted as Scott's "only moral guide," that the father's instincts came from "the colonies and the revolution." Like Dick Diver, who inherited the manners and code of morality Fitzgerald associated with the pre–Civil War South, the son grew up believing in "honor, courtesy, and courage."

This similarity of background led to parallels in the two men's behavior. Their gentlemanly conduct throughout the correspondence derives at least partially from their "aristocratic" heritage. It pervades money matters. Whether because of extravagance or adversity, Fitzgerald was almost never free of debt. He felt guilty about borrowing, recommended Scribners charge interest, and paid back even small sums religiously. Perkins discouraged his guilt, arranged a system of advances, and loaned him one thousand dollars. Fitzgerald, who urged Perkins to publish many lesser known authors including Lardner and Hemingway, was also generous, loyal and considerate.

It is clear that both were moralists. Fitzgerald said as much when he confessed to having "a New England conscience – developed in Minnesota" and wanting "to preach at people in some acceptable form." It is clear too that despite antipathy toward censorship and "professional uplifters," the strain of puritanism running through their backgrounds made them a bit squeamish toward sex. Fitzgerald found one sentence in *Tender Is the Night* – "I never did go in for making love to dry loins" – "definitely offensive," and Perkins could not bring himself to pronounce the three objectionable words he had uncovered in *The Sun Also Rises*. His comment about "a New England conscience which makes it always seem incumbant on one to be busy" applies to both men.

"Double vision" is the term used to describe Fitzgerald's ability to participate in fiction and at the same time to stand aside and critically observe. This most important aspect of his divided nature – active-passive: Mc Quillans-Fitzgeralds – gave the man as well as the work maturity and power, for although Fitzgerald was emotional, seldom with reference to others or to himself did he allow involvement to distort judgment. Jay Gatsby, Dick Diver and a certain Scott Fitzgerald might play the exhibitionist, the master of ceremonies, but only to be censured by a second Scott Fitzgerald whose "New England conscience" drove him to desire "to preach . . . rather than to entertain." There was a drunken Fitzgerald – destructive, bigoted, vulgar, petty – as well as the sober one – creative, tolerant, reverent, generous. There was a Fitzgerald who envied the mobility and grace of the wealthy and yet despised their indolence and lack of ethics, and a Fitzgerald who sympathized with Marxism, yet prized too highly self-reliance and the individual to be converted. The Fitzgerald that idolized football and military heroes called writing "a back door way out of facing reality," while the Fitzgerald that felt destined to write did not particularly like sports or soldiering. One produced more mediocre fiction than any American of similar stature except, perhaps, Mark Twain, and one considered his serious works labors of love.

Fitzgerald once remarked that "the test of a first-rate intelligence is the ability to hold two opposed ideas in the mind at the same time, and still retain the ability to function," and this applies to Perkins even more than to himself, for Perkins, whose heritage was also divided – though much less acutely – remained a unified personality. Wheelock has said: "In Max, the Puritan and the Cavalier, the shrewd Yankee and the generous and disarming artist, were subtly and perpetually at war." Against the Puritan side represented by the Evartses stood the Cavalier side represented by the Perkinses. The latter had been East India magnates, some of them Loyalists during the Revolution. Max's paternal grandfather, Charles Callahan Perkins, the Bostonian, the art critic, the friend of Browning, Longfellow and Lowell, had studied painting and music abroad and later wrote *Tuscan Sculptors* and conducted concerts of the Handel and Haydn Society. His son, Edward – Max's mugwump, lawyer father – was more adept at reading to the children than at making money. His uncle had discovered William Rimmer; his widow's house in Newport contained numerous *objets d'art*; and his well-known grandson possessed considerable talent for drawing. Brooks, who has brilliantly analyzed the effects of Perkins' divided background, found it symbolized by two pictures behind Perkins' desk: one of an austere old New England schoolmaster and the other of a Saint-Gaudens monument.

The Cavalier side, though not predominant, erupted through a vein of romanticism which cut across the realism of rationality previously discussed. Throughout Perkins' early life, there were revealing factors. Cowley tells us that at St. Paul's School he was considered "a rebel" and at Harvard, "a gay dog." As a reporter on the *Times*, he succeeded after accompanying George Robertson in a dangerous effort to break an automobile speedway record. Later, while converting Scribners from a very conservative house to a more radical one, he became legendary for his eccentricities. Perkins, like Fitzgerald, whose boyishness he shared and whose Basil Duke Lee stories he praised, had a nostalgic attitude toward youth. The letters often refer to childhood and adolescence, and once when writing Marjorie Kinnan Rawlings about *The Yearling*, he insisted, "the best part of a man is a boy." Also like Fitzgerald, Perkins worshipped heroes. His sketch-book included the heads of Napoleon, Clemens and Shelley. Of Shelley this man with a taste for eighteenth-century authors and Tolstoy said: "Oh, I was a great Shelley fan, and I never fully got over it, though people think badly of him now." That he "never fully got over it" is apparent in his attachment to Lardner, Fitzgerald, Hemingway and Wolfe – all romantic figures – who, perhaps, depended on Perkins' steadiness more than Perkins needed their flare. Brooks tells us that he regarded Fitzgerald "almost as a son," and Wolfe and Fitzgerald tell us that they regarded him as a father. Fitzgerald wrote: "What a time you've had with your sons, Max – Ernest gone to Spain, me gone to Hollywood, Tom Wolfe reverting to an artistic hillbilly."

He and Fitzgerald complemented each other, Perkins playing Nick to Fitzgerald's Gatsby and Fitzgerald playing Luther to his Erasmus. This accounts in part for the depth of the friendship between two men so seemingly opposite.

They did not always agree, however. Perkins objected to "that passage about the Bible" in *The Beautiful and Damned*, stating: "Even when people are altogether wrong you cannot but respect those who speak with such passionate sincerity." After Fitzgerald's lengthy response which cited literary precedents, implied censorship, and argued character development, Perkins elucidated his position further. One could accept the "substance" of the passage while disliking its tone of "flippancy." Embarrassed, Fitzgerald made the necessary changes. Other instances of personal disagreement are scattered throughout the letters, though, most often, the bones of contention concern the younger man's impatience with Scribners' "ultra-conservatism." His attacks, ranging from the publicity department to the art department, included the firm's lack of exciting new foreign talent and its antagonism toward inexpensive editions. He was particularly annoyed when Scribners frustrated his desire to contribute something first-rate to a Modern Library collection of stories by distinguished writers, indirectly forcing him to submit "a new and much inferior story." In a subsequent letter that insisted Mr. Cerf be allowed to reprint *The Great*

Gatsby, Fitzgerald dismissed Perkins' explanation: "That 'they would almost all have been Scribner authors' was a most curious perversion of what should have been a matter of pride into an attitude of dog-in-the-manger."

Nevertheless, his relations with Scribners and Perkins were exceptionally cordial. After Charles Scribner II died, Fitzgerald remembered the man's "fairness" and "tolerance," and he consistently maintained a high opinion of the house, citing its "tremendous squareness, courtesy, generosity and open-mindedness" in 1925 and calling it America's "one great publisher" in 1936. That the respect was mutual is suggested by a confidential memorandum of 1934 to the sales department. Here Charles Scribner III, who regretted the circumstances which had interrupted the author's brilliant novel-writing career, said *Tender Is the Night* confirmed "as magnificent a talent as a novelist as has appeared in the last quarter century." Respect was mutual with regard to Perkins also. From beginning to end, he recognized Fitzgerald's ability. The two earliest novels were not merely entertaining but possessed "literary significance"; *The Last Tycoon* captured a "new world" and seemed "very remarkable." Perkins' favorite work, *The Great Gatsby*, represented "as perfect a thing as I ever had any share in publishing." He praised it often, though nowhere more enthusiastically than in the letter of November 20, 1924: the manuscript was "full of phrases which make a scene blaze with life"; the presentation and development of the characters was "unequalled"; the valley of ashes, the scene at Myrtle's apartment, the guest catalogue could "make a man famous." Then he discussed the book's "sense of eternity" and concluded: "You once told me you were not a *natural* writer – my God! You have plainly mastered the craft, of course; but you needed far more than craftsmanship for this." Fitzgerald, whose self-confidence Perkins unfailingly bolstered, replied he would rather have him like *Gatsby* than even Edmund Wilson. Yet his emotional debt consisted of a great deal besides enthusiasm and belief. On one hand, Perkins never reproached Fitzgerald or tried to inculcate moral lessons; on the other, only he and Gerald Murphy – unlike Hemingway, John Peale Bishop and Ober – remained constant friends during those dark years between 1935 and 1940. Mentioning the tribute in Wolfe's *Of Time and the River*, the best known among many dedications to Perkins, Fitzgerald said "Tom" could not "exaggerate the debt that he owes you – and that stands for all of us who have been privileged to be your authors." "Debt" implied professional as well as personal obligation.

Both men suffered deeply over a particular friend – Perkins over Wolfe, Fitzgerald over Hemingway – which explains why so much material on them appears in their letters. But before turning to these two relationships, we should first note the literary epoch the correspondence illuminates. It covers the Twenties and Thirties from several angles, treating domestic and foreign authors, popular and serious writing, large and small reputations. Perkins' September 10, 1924, letter, which surveys the literary scene at the time, illustrates this. He writes that *American Mercury* "provokes a large part of the conversation"; *So Big* by Edna Ferber "is the most popular book, and one of the best"; *The Tattooed Countess* "by that bucolic sophisticate, Van Vechten," is a "clever, but cheap and thin" volume with a wide appeal; *A Passage to India* by E. M. Forster has set "the somewhat conservative and substantial book readers" chatting; *These Charming People* by Michael Arlen "is very popular among people you would be likely to see here" and some individuals have even heard of *The Green Hat.*

The Perkins–Wolfe relationship began when Perkins first encountered Wolfe's work through a literary agent who sent Scribners the manuscript of a novel which had been rejected elsewhere. During October, 1928, he wrote the author in Austria to express admiration for his book qualified only by trepidation over its unwieldy form. Later, eleven hundred pages were reduced to about eight hundred and *O Lost* became *Look Homeward, Angel.* But Perkins' most extensive editing job came between December, 1933, when Wolfe delivered *Of Time and the River,* and January, 1935, when the novel emerged in page proofs. "We have got a good system now. We work every evening from 8:30 (or as near as Tom can come to it) until 10:30 or 11:00." He also told Hemingway in this letter of 1934 that the major difficulty concerned organization and that Wolfe shrank "from the sacrifices, which are really cruel often." Despite the novel's success and its laudatory dedication, Wolfe soon turned on his editor. He accused Perkins of controlling him and, oddly enough, saw the matter in political terms, the editor being an independent Democrat who had voted against the New Deal and himself, a recent convert to radicalism. According to Cowley, "The principal reason for the separation – it was never a quarrel – seems to be that Wolfe's pride was touched." He had to prove he could write his own books, so eventually transferred to Harpers. Their affection continued. Wolfe's very last letter confirms this – "I shall always think of you and feel about you the way it was that 4th of July day 3 yrs. ago" – as does his will, which made Perkins executor of the estate. Perkins cherished the letter and fulfilled the trust. Fitzgerald, whom he had urged to contact Wolfe during his illness and Wolfe's mother after his death, summed up Perkins' "position in the Wolfe matter" as "an exceedingly ironic one."

Fitzgerald's position with Hemingway contained an element of irony too. In 1924, he suggested that Perkins seek out "a young man named Ernest Hemmingway, who . . . has a brilliant future." And in the following months, Fitzgerald maneuvered Hemingway from Boni and Liveright to Scribners. He admired him as a man and artist more than any other contemporary. Like Perkins, Hemingway embodied an alter ego. Perkins' realism counterbalanced his romanticism, and Hemingway's aggressiveness and integrity, his passivity and glibness. But the friendship seems to have been one-sided even at the outset. For Fitzgerald, who tracked Hemingway down just after the publication of *The Great Gatsby*, their meeting represented "the brightest thing in our trip to Europe." To Hemingway, who described it condescendingly in *A Moveable Feast* (1964), it was merely "strange." Hemingway scorned Fitzgerald as a man: he talked too much, could not hold his liquor, missed appointments, maltreated inferiors, wrote trash for money, imagined himself ill, married a crazy woman; as an artist, though, he ultimately produced "two very good books" and "some good short stories." Fitzgerald apparently acted badly, interrupting and competing with Hemingway's work. Hemingway, however, never extended the kind of understanding Fitzgerald did during his own bad times. Instead, Hemingway became furious over the Callaghan affair. He made negative comments about *Tender Is the Night* and ridiculed *The Crack-Up* articles. Most damaging of all, he slipped a disparaging personal allusion into "The Snows of Kilimanjaro." Yet Fitzgerald's letters always queried Hemingway's activities and opinions. He wrote Perkins on April 15, 1935: "I always think of my friendship with him as being one of the high spots of life."

Scattered assertions about the art of Hemingway and Wolfe help us to see the development of Fitzgerald's talent embedded throughout this correspondence. Reviewing *In Our Time* for *The Bookman* during 1926, he said that the stories make you "aware of something temperamentally new" – the author's ability to give characters an emotion "without the aid of a comment or a pointing finger." We do not require much exposition because the dialogue tells everything. Of structure, he observed, "There is no tail, no sudden change of pace at the end to throw into relief what has gone before," and of style, "there is not a bit to spare." Hemingway, who served as Fitzgerald's "artistic conscience," commanded his praise thereafter. In 1926 Fitzgerald liked *The Sun Also Rises* for its fiesta, fishing trip and minor characters; in 1939 he called *A Farewell to Arms* one of the "great English classics"; in 1940 *For Whom the Bell Tolls* was "a fine novel" and *To Have and Have Not* included passages which matched Dostoyevski's "undeflected intensity." Glenway Wescott has contended that Fitzgerald's inordinate esteem for Hemingway's work convinced him that Hemingway should do the really serious writing. This overstates the case, yet Fitzgerald did recognize how dangerous such enthusiasm was. During 1934 he told Hemingway about borrowing the concept of lingering after-effects and struggling against using his rhythms and remarks in *Tender Is the Night*, a book Hemingway came to like more and more.

Fitzgerald had mixed views concerning Wolfe's fiction. In 1930 he granted him more culture and vitality, if less poetry and craft, than Hemingway; in 1934 he said all three resembled each other through attempting "to recapture the exact feel of a moment"; later he cited Wolfe's assets – suggestiveness, delicacy, lyricism, observation – and his achievements – several stories and various aspects of the novels. But despite an early reaction to *Look Homeward, Angel* which supported his expansiveness, Wolfe's disregard of form and economy influenced Fitzgerald's fundamentally negative attitude. The fellow poured himself out, marshaled material awkwardly, and so represented only a half-grown artist. Replying to the advice that he become a more conscious craftsman, Wolfe argued that many great writers had succeeded by inclusion. This did not lessen Fitzgerald's antagonism toward sprawling fiction. Its style was repetitious and cluttered; the content, hackneyed and egocentric. In his copy of *Of Time and the River,* he jotted: "All this has been about as good as Dodsworth for chapter after Chapter," and "Trite, trite, trite, trite, page after page after page."

By the time the earliest of these assertions were made about the two novelists, Fitzgerald had already found a direction. He had progressed from the "novel of saturation" *(This Side of Paradise)* through a transitional novel *(The Beautiful and Damned)* to complete his first "novel of selection" *(The Great Gatsby).* From *Gatsby* he deleted enough for another volume, and from *Tender Is the Night* – composed between 1925 and 1934 and changed even after publication – three-quarters of the four hundred thousand words written. Fitzgerald, who respected the single word and the single line, fought against "fatal facility." And he sought ways to convey personal subject matter objectively; hence, the theory of "composite" characterization practiced in the books following *The Beautiful and Damned* and the technique of the observer-narrator employed in *Gatsby* and *The Last Tycoon.* His insistence on "shaping" and "pruning" and his tendency to render experience dramatically are reflected in his sympathy toward Hemingway's work and his antipathy for Wolfe's.

Because the Fitzgerald-Perkins correspondence covers Fitzgerald's entire professional career, it is valuable for charting Fitzgerald's artistic development. From beginning to end, he discusses his work in detail, giving us important information on the germination, content and technique of the stories and novels. For instance, at the beginning he reveals how *The Romantic Egotist* metamorphosed through *The Education of a Personage* into *This Side of Paradise* and what he was attempting with *The Beautiful and Damned,* just as later he makes several interesting remarks about *The Last Tycoon.* But the fullest, most illuminating disclosures concern his two masterpieces, *The Great Gatsby* and *Tender Is the Night.*

From an early reference to the first, we learn that the tale was originally located in "the middle west and New York of 1885"; that it was to contain fewer "superlative beauties" and a smaller time period than the preceding novels; and that there was to be "a catholic element." This "catholic element" substantially disappeared when Fitzgerald eliminated the prologue – "Absolution" – which "interfered with the neatness of the plan." Almost all references attest to his perfectionist attitude toward the book, though none more eloquently than where he confesses to being drained of "personal experience" and so "thrown directly on purely creative work . . . the sustained imagination of a sincere and yet radiant world." However, even after Perkins helped him make *Gatsby* the "artistic achievement" he desired, Fitzgerald felt dissatisfied over the hotel scene and the last chapter.

Tender Is the Night was equally ambitious: "something really NEW in form, idea, structure." A psychological novel tucked between dramatic novels, it gave Fitzgerald endless trouble. The notion of "an intellectual murder on the Leopold-Loeb idea" supported by another early comment about his plot resembling *An American Tragedy* got him off to a false start. The book's organization, as these letters demonstrate, proved to be exceedingly difficult. One dated February 5, 1934, is typical. Perkins must include the scene of arrest in Cannes, for without it both "unity" and Dick's character would suffer. Another letter dated a little earlier is also typical. Here Fitzgerald fears he has again produced a novelist's novel that will require two perusals. But even if plot readers fail to untangle the story, "there are times when you have to get every edge of your finger-nails on paper." Four years later – after a mixed critical reception and disappointing sales – he told Perkins, "Its great fault is that the *true* beginning – the young psychiatrist in Switzerland – is tucked away in the middle of the book," thus paving the way for Cowley's controversial edition.

Fitzgerald wasted some time during the Twenties on his play, *The Vegetable*, and during the Thirties on an abortive medieval novel, *Philippe, Count of Darkness*. Yet such dead ends did not interrupt his artistic development as much as turning out movie scenarios for Hollywood and potboilers for magazines. Serious work demanded more effort and paid less money than hack work, though he never rationalized the latter into anything else and he never allowed it to influence his literary taste or values. Consequently, the correspondence shows an author who appreciated fine writers and demanded high standards. The long diatribe in a 1925 letter to Perkins illustrates the point. Using Thomas Boyd's new book as an example, he attacks "American peasant" fiction, which seeks to remain static in a dynamic world, for presenting stereotyped characters and subject matter. The writers of such fiction think Sherwood Anderson is a man of ideas handicapped by inarticulateness, whereas he actually had few ideas and a style "about as simple as an engine room full of dynamoes."

Critical of himself and others, Fitzgerald desired, even encouraged, sincere and detailed criticism from people whom he respected, and when he felt the advice constructive, he accepted it. The concluding paragraph of one letter mentions Edmund Wilson's extensive March, 1922, article, which focused on *This Side of Paradise* and *The Beautiful and Damned*. Wilson had certainly penned "no blurb," yet Fitzgerald appreciated the piece – "jeers and all" – because this was the first time "an intelligent and sophisticated man" had treated him *"at length."*

If Fitzgerald could take criticism, Perkins could give it, though with special reservations. As we know, he believed an editor should remain obscure, offering expertise only to guide an author toward self-realization. The editor must never impose his own thwarted creativity on the author by arbitrarily amending style or structure. Instead, he should detect the author's intentions and help him fulfill them. This kind of assistance becomes particularly beneficial when the author hits a snag and rewriting proves futile. Once Perkins *did* enter the picture, he rarely provided the ordinary editorial services – correcting, adding, deleting, substituting, transposing. Rather, his task was to suggest how the author might develop a book's underlying pattern, for example, Zelda Fitzgerald's "A Couple of Nuts." On October 21, 1931, he discussed it, starting with praise for her "colorful, almost poetic" prose. But the metaphors, while "good in themselves," emphasized "the thing that she likens a thing to" and not "the thing she means to illuminate." Had there been less of a story – "the career of those poor nuts" – it would have been less detrimental to bury it under her language.

Perkins' reputation is based upon more than his critical-editorial skills. He was also an acute judge of both conventional and innovative fiction, believing that publishers should concern themselves primarily with talent. Thus, he played the key role in discovering and launching several very dissimilar writers: Scott Fitzgerald, Ernest Hemingway, Ring Lardner, Thomas Wolfe, J. P. Marquand, Erskine Caldwell, Marjorie Rawlings and James Jones, to name a few. Brooks says Perkins "inclined away from the old and the traditional and towards the experimental, the native and the new." This inclination led to a literary revolution at Scribners. Between 1846 when it was founded and 1914 when Perkins became an editor, the firm had been, according to Cowley, "the most genteel and the most tradition encrusted of all the publishing houses" to outlive the Victorian era. Scribners rated the British novel above the American novel and published many notable British novelists. If the firm did publish an American, he would certainly not be a depraved novelist like Theodore Dreiser, but a distinctly undepraved one like Edith Wharton. Yet things were beginning to change as early as 1917, and the revolution was *fait accompli* by 1920 when *This Side of Paradise* appeared.

The interaction between writer and editor represents the most vital aspect of this correspondence, since it goes beyond the autobiographical and demonstrates how a creative editor can affect serious writing. These letters are ideal for this purpose. Fitzgerald, who required less help than Wolfe yet more than Hemingway, received advice largely through the mail. And not only that. He had but a single publisher and editor, and his connection with them spanned two decades. Perkins' hand is everywhere, one illustration being *The Vegetable*, which Martin Esslin has called "an early example of the Theatre of the Absurd" and which opened and closed in Atlantic City on November 20, 1923.

The previous December Perkins had informed Fitzgerald that he had written down "some comments" about the play. According to these, "the underlying motive," though perceptible, had not been made sufficiently clear. This motive – a sentimental view of democracy – must be rendered through the protagonist's story. It is a good theme, as are "the means" for developing it, but Act Two introduces a pair of unassimilated and consequently confusing "subordinate motives." Fitzgerald might "satirize" as much as he could and be as "fantastic" as he wanted if, instead of becoming "lost in the maze," he carefully followed "the green line" of his principal motive. The "wild second act" must have "a kind of wild logic." However, "doubled edged satire" had been used erratically there, sometimes giving way to ineffective dream-like sequences with no further meaning. Perkins, who admired *The Vegetable's* "motive," "characters" and "invention," summed up by saying "each part of the second act should do three things – add to the quality of a fantastic dream, satirize Jerry and his family as representing a large class of Americans, and satirize the government or army or whatever institution is at the moment in use."

Nowhere in the correspondence are Perkins' special skills more apparent or important than in his criticism of *The Great Gatsby*. The letter of November 20, 1924, raving about the book also contained many shrewd suggestions. After agreeing with Fitzgerald that there was "a certain slight sagging in chapters six and seven," Perkins offered "two actual criticisms." Both treated the hero's characterization, the first focusing on his vagueness – for Gatsby seemed an older man; the second on how he acquired his money. In the first instance, Fitzgerald ought to describe him physically and provide some special bodily traits as distinctive as the expression "old sport." To take care of the second problem, it would not be necessary or even advisable to impart definitely what Gatsby did, but rather "interpolate some phrases, and possibly incidents, little touches of various kinds" hinting "that he was in some active way mysteriously engaged." Perkins added one further point. When Gatsby presents his biography directly to Nick, the novel's narrative mode of unfolding the story through the flow of events is violated. This could be remedied by letting the truth of the hero's claims emerge a little at a time.

Fitzgerald termed Perkins' insights "excellent and most helpful" in one letter and in another tackled the problem of characterization: *"I myself didn't know what Gatsby looked like or was engaged in* & you felt it. If I'd known & kept it from you you'd have been *too impressed with my knowledge to protest."* By the same token, he seemed older because the individual upon whom he was based was "half-unconsciously" older. But now Fitzgerald, having studied the "Fuller–McGee" case, understood him better than his own daughter. During February, 1925, he listed all the major revisions: Gatsby had been given life; the wealth had been accounted for; Chapters Six and Seven and the first party scene had been improved; the lengthy narrative of Chapter Eight had been divided. And during July, he wrote, "Max, it amuses me when praise comes in on the 'structure' of the book – because it was you who fixed up the structure, not me."

This remark, among many others, serves to indicate that the professional relationship between the two men was as considerate and constructive as their remarkable friendship.

599 Summit Ave.
St. Paul, Minnesota
July 26th, 1919[1]

Dear Mr. Perkins:

After four months attempt to write commercial copy by day and painful half-hearted imitations of popular literature by night I decided that it was one thing or another. So I gave up getting married and went home.

Yesterday I finished the first draft of a novel called

THE EDUCATION OF A PERSONAGE

It is in no sense a revision of the ill-fated *Romantic Egotist** but it contains some of the former material improved and worked over and bears a strong family resemblance besides.

But while the other was a tedius, disconnected casserole this is definate attempt at a big novel and I really believe I have hit it, as immediately I stopped disciplining the muse she trotted obediently around and became an erratic mistress if not a steady wife.

Now what I want to ask you is this – if I send you the book by August 20th and you decide you could risk its publication (I am blatantly confident that you will) would it be brought out in October, say, or just what would decide its date of publication?

This is an odd question I realize especially since you havn't even seen the book but you have been so kind in the past about my stuff that I venture to intrude once more upon your patience.

Sincerely

*The title of the first book-length manuscript which Fitzgerald had submitted to Scribners in 1918.

17

July 28, 1919

Dear Mr. Fitzgerald:
Your letter about "The Education of a Personage" (which strikes us as an excellent title) arouses a great curiosity to see the manuscript. But there is one thing certain: no publisher could publish this book in October without greatly injuring its chances; for the canvasing of the trade for the fall season began several months ago, and the book sellers have invested their money in fall books, and would now order grudgingly, and in much lesser quantities than they would at the beginning of a season. Your book for its own advantage ought to be published after January 1st, all the more because you will be a new author and should have every advantage of carefully prepared publicity. The book should be talked up ahead of its appearance to the trade: they should see sheets in advance, etc. This is the plain truth of the matter. The book should be published in February or March, and the selling of it should begin before Christmas.

But we hope you will let us see this manuscript. Ever since the first reading of your first manuscript we have felt that you would succeed. Did Mr. Bridges* write you how much he liked your last story? And how near to taking it he came?

Sincerely,

599 Summit Ave.
St. Paul, Minn.
August 16th, 1919

Dear Mr. Perkins:
I appreciated both your letters† and I'm sure you wont be dissapointed in the book when you get it. It is a well-considered, finished *whole* this time and I think its a more *crowded* (in the best sense) piece of work than has been published in this country for some years.

It is finished, except for one last revision or rather correction and the typewriting, so I think you'll get it before September 1st. As to sample chapters – it seems hardly worth while to send them to you now. The title has been changed to

This Side of Paradise

from those lines of Rupert Brookes

*Robert Bridges, poet and essayist, then editor of *Scribner's Magazine*.
†Perkins had written Fitzgerald again, on August 13th, urging him to send along chapters of the novel as they were completed.

18

. . . Well, this side of paradise
There's little comfort in the wise.

About two chapters are from my old book, completely changed and rewritten, the rest is new material.

On the next page I've written the chapter names.

BOOK I

The Romantic Egotist

Chapter I   Amory, son of Beatrice

"   II   Spires and Gargoyles

"   III   The Egotist considers

Interlude

March 1917 – February 1919

BOOK II

The Education of a Personage

Chapter I   The Debutante

"   II   Experiments in Convalescense

"   III   Young Irony

"   IV   The Supercillious Sacrifice

"   V   The Egotist becomes a Personage

Book One contains about	35,000 words		
The Interlude	"	"	4,000 words
Book Two	"	"	47,000 words
Total	"	"	86,000 words

about publication – I asked you the chances of an early publication (in case you take it) for two reasons: first – because I want to get started both in a literary and financial way; second – because it is to some extent a timely book and it seems to me that the public are wild for decent reading matter – "Dangerous Days"* and "Ramsey Milholland"† – My God!

Thanking you again for past favors – I am

Sincerely

*By Mary Roberts Rinehart.
†By Booth Tarkington.

599 Summit Ave.
St. Paul, Minn.
Sept. 4th 1919.

Dear Mr. Perkins:

I sent the book today under a separate cover. I want to discuss a few things in connection with it.

You'll notice that it contains much material from the *Romantic Egotist*.

(1) Chapter II Bk. I of the present book contains material from "Spires & Gargoyles, Ha-Ha Hortense, Babes in the Wood & Crecendo" – rewritten in third person, cut down and re-edited

(2) Chapter III Bk I contains material from "Second descent of the Egotist and the Devil." rewritten ect.*

(3) Chapter IV Bk I contains material from "The Two Mystics, Clara & the End of Many Things"

(4) Chapter III Bk II is a revision of Eleanor in 3d person – with that fur incident left out.

Chap I Bk I, & Chaps I, II, IV, & V of Bk II are entirely new.

You'll see that of the old material there is all new use, outside the revision in the 3d person. For instance the Princeton characters of the R.E.† – Tom, Tump, Lorry, Lumpy, Fred, Dick, Jim, Burne, Judy, Mcintyre and Jesse have become in this book – Fred, Dick, Alec, Tom, Kerry & Burne. Isabelle & Rosalind of the R.E. have become just Isabelle while the new Rosalind is a different person.

Beatrice is a new character – Dr. Dudly becomes Monsignor Darcy; is much better done – in fact every character is in better perspective.

The preface I leave to your discretion – perhaps its a little too clever-clever; likewise you may object to the literary personalities in Chap II & Bk II and to the length of the socialistic discussion in the last chapter. The book contains a little over ninety thousand words. I certainly think the hero gets somewhere.

I await anxiously your verdict.

Sincerely

P.S. Thorton Hancock is Henry Adams – I didn't do him thoroughly of course – but I knew him when I was a boy.

*Fitzgerald frequently misspelled etc. to read ect.
† *The Romantic Egotist.*

Sept. 16, 1919

Dear Mr. Fitzgerald:

I am very glad, personally, to be able to write to you that we are all for publishing your book, "This Side of Paradise". Viewing it as the same book that was here before, which in a sense it is, though translated into somewhat different terms and extended further, I think that you have improved it enormously. As the first manuscript did, it abounds in energy and life and it seems to me to be in much better proportion. I was afraid that, when we declined the first manuscript, you might be done with us conservatives. I am glad you are not. The book is so different that it is hard to prophesy how it will sell but we are all for taking a chance and supporting it with vigor. As for terms, we shall be glad to pay a royalty of 10% on the first five thousand copies and of 15% thereafter, – which by the way, means more than it use to now that retail prices upon which the percentage is calculated, have so much advanced.

Hoping to hear from you, we are,

Sincerely yours,

P.S. Our expectation would be to publish your book in the early Spring. Now, if you are ready to have us do this, and have the time, we should be glad to have you get together any publicity matter you could for us, including a photograph. You have been in the advertising game long enough to know the sort of thing.

599 Summit Ave.
St. Paul, Minn
Sept 18th, 1919

Dear Mr. Perkins:

Of course I was delighted to get your letter and I've been in a sort of trance all day; not that I doubted you'd take it but at last I have something to show people. It has enough advertisement in St. Paul already to sell several thousand copies & I think Princeton will buy it (I've been a periodical, local Great-Expect[at]ions for some time in both places.)

Terms ect I leave to you but one thing I can't relinquish without at least a slight struggle. Would it be utterly impossible for you to publish the book Xmas – or say by February? I have so many things dependent on its success – including of course a girl – not that I expect it to make me a fortune but it will have a psychological effect on me and all my surroundings and besides open up new fields. I'm in that stage where every month counts frantically and seems a cudgel in a fight for happiness against time. Will you let me know more exactly how that difference in time of publication influences the sale & what you mean by "early Spring"?

Excuse this ghastly handwriting but I'm a bit nervous today. I'm beginning (last month) a very ambitious novel called "The Demon Lover" which will probably take a year also I'm writing short stories. I find that what I enjoy writing is always my best – Every young author ought to read Samuel Butler's Note Books.

I'm writing quite a marvellous after-the-war story. Does Mr. Bridges think that they're a little passé or do you think he'd like to see it?

I'll fix up data for advertising and have a photo taken next week with the most gigantic enjoyment (I'm trying H.G. Well's use of vast garagantuan [sp.]* words)

Well thank you for a very happy day and numerous other favors and let me know if I've any possible chance for earlier publication and give my thanks or whatever is in order to Mr. Scribner or whoever else was on the deciding committee.

Probably be East next month or Nov.

Sincerely

(over for P.S.)†

P.S. Who picks out the cover? I'd like something that could be a set – look cheerful and important like a Shaw Book. I notice Shaw, Galesworthy & Barrie do that. But Wells doesn't – I wonder why. No need of illustrations is there? I knew a fellow at College who'd have been a wonder for books like mine – a mixture of Aubrey Beardsly, Hogarth & James Montgomery Flagg. But he got killed in the war.[2]

Excuse this immoderately long and rambling letter but I think you'll have to allow me several days for recuperation.

Yrs.

Sept. 27th, 1919
599 Summit Ave. St. Paul.

Dear Mr. Perkins:

I am returning herewith your copy of the contract.

Now in regard to a little matter – "Babes in the Woods" was published in Smart Set in August. I have written them for their release of it. Also a preliminary form of part of the chapter "The Debutante" just the boudoir scene will be published in Smart Set on Oct 15th. I sent it to them

---

*These brackets are Fitzgerald's.
†The postscript to this letter appears on the other side of the page, in the original.

before I began the novel and afterwards they seemed to want to use it very much. I will get their release in writing on both things & send it to you.

I notice the contract is headed St. Louis, Missouri. I've changed it to St. Paul, Minnesota on my copy. I am relieved that you feel as I do in regard to illustrations. I'm against 'em. Will I have a whack at the proof? – I have a few very minor changes – or I could make 'em in Nov. when I come east.

Lets see – Oh yes – I'll send you photo & data within a month. I don't suppose there's any particular hurry.

. . . . .

Sincerely

599 Summit Ave.
St. Paul, Minn.
[ca. November 15, 1919 ?]

Dear Mr. Perkins:

Thanks a lot for your letter. I feel I've certainly been lucky to find a publisher who seems so interested generally in his authors. Lord knows this literary game has been discouraging enough at times.

. . . . .

My book plans have changed or rather enlarged. I'm going to obey my own mandate and write every book as if it were the last word I'd have on earth. I think Wells does that. So I think that the ms. I send you about next April or May will be rather a lively bolt!

As Ever

You see I'm trying to make myself out as a poet and play-write, as well as a novelist and short story writer! Innocuous humor!

[December 1919]

Dear Mr. Fitzgerald:

I do not know whether I wrote you that the publicity material you sent has come together with the picture, which will do very well indeed; as "The Four Fists" will appear before the novel, we have put this in the hands of the magazine to use in part by way of announcement. "The Four Fists" is certainly a very fine story told in an entirely independent way. It seems to me most promising. So too do the other stories, although the magazine did not find them exactly adapted to our needs. You certainly will have no difficulty in placing them at all and they seem to me to indicate that you are pretty definitely lodged as a writer of short stories. The great beauty of them is that they are all alive. Ninety percent of the stories that appear are derived from life through the rarifying medium of literature. Yours are direct from life it seems to me. This is true also of the language and style: it is that of the day. It is free of the conventions of the past which most writers love along with them to their great inconvenience. I hope when you have occasion to write again you will tell me where your stories are appearing. I want to try to keep track of them.

Sincerely yours,

Jan. 6, 1920

Dear Mr. Fitzgerald:

We have your book in hand and shall soon begin to send you proof. Hill has done a picture for the wrap, and it is very successful we think, particularly the girl in it. He also spoke very highly of the book which he had read through although that was not nominated in the bond: he need only have read enough to get at its general character but it interested him very much and he finished it. He was very curious to know about you and I told him of your short stories. I put forward your views about the binding, etc. but we felt, after consultation, that there would be great risk in getting the book out in that way. It would look too essay like, too esoteric. We want it to look popular. I will send you a cover as soon as we have one ready.

Mr. Bridges tells me you wrote him a rather pessimistic letter to the effect that you had had a slump in inspiration; but that did not worry me.

Sincerely yours,

[*599 Summit Avenue*]
[*St. Paul, Minn.*]
[*ca. January 10, 1920*]

Dear Mr. Perkins:

I was delighted to hear from you – and tickled to death that W.E. Hill liked my book & has done the cover. I admire him more than any artist in the country. I can hardly wait to see it.

I came home in a thoroughly nervous alcoholic state & revised two tales that went the complete rounds of magazines last April.* I did 'em in four days & sent 'em to Reynolds† in hopes he could get enough for 'em so that

---

*One of these was certainly "Myra Meets His Family," originally composed in April, 1919, under the title "Lilah Meets His Family" and published in the *Post* on March 20th. The other was probably "Head and Shoulders," which the *Post* published on February 21st.

†Paul R. Reynolds, then Fitzgerald's literary agent.

I could go south because I'm afraid I'm about to develop tuberculosis. Last Monday he sent me a check for a thousand from the Post for 'em so I'm leaving for New Orleans tomorrow night. I'll write you my adress when I have one – meanwhile anything sent here will be forwarded.

Now for several questions. When would a novel have to be finished to have it published serially & then brought out by you for the fall season? Do you think a book on the type of my first one would have any chance of being accepted for serial publication by any magazine? I want to start it but I don't want to get broke in the middle & start in and have to write short stories again – because I don't enjoy it & just do it for money. There's nothing in collections of short stories is there? About how many copies of John O'May* were sold?

Everything goes serenely except that I feel written out on this short stuff. I've had two vaudeville offers for my current play in *Smart Set*† & I've just sent $1000 worth of movies to the *metro* people. I have two stories for Mr. Bridges both stuck in the middle & two *Post* stories cut off in their first paragraphs.

My *Drunkards Holiday* and *Dairy of a Literary Failure* are also defunct.

The more I think of that advertisement I wrote for my book the more I dislike it. Please dont use it unless you have it already set up in which case I'll make a few small changes in proof & it'll have to go.

I'm deadly curious to see if Hill's picture looks like the real "Rosalind".** I suppose he did either the boudoir scene or the mellow parting. May be in New York in March if I can get rid of this damn cough. By the way I liked Maxwell Burt's *Cup of Tea*†† so well that I wrote him a note about it & got a very pleasant one in return. He's a sort of Richard Harding Davis only literary instead of journalistic – but he's the only real romantiscist there is – we have the daughters of Henry James – Gerrould,* Glaspell† & the other female phychological hair-splitters & the Yiddish descendents of O Henry – Fanny & Edna** and that's all – except Burt, so I like him.

As Ever

---

*A collection of short stories by Maxwell Struthers Burt.

†"Porcelain and Pink."

**Rosalind, in *This Side of Paradise*, was modelled on Zelda Sayre Fitzgerald.

††A short story published in Burt's collection, *John O'May*.

*Novelist and critic Katharine Fullerton Gerould.

†Novelist Susan Glaspell, founder with her husband, George Cram Cook, of the Provincetown Playhouse, where the plays of Eugene O'Neill were first presented.

**Fannie Hurst and Edna Ferber.

Dear Mr. Fitzgerald:

Your New Orleans address has just come and I am sending you quite a large batch of the galleys of "This Side of Paradise". I will be able to send you a wrap in two or three days, as well. The rest of the proof will follow rapidly. In your question about serialization, I do not know whether you were thinking of the matter in general or entirely of our magazine. We hope you will give us a chance to consider any novel you write from this angle; but we may as well say in advance that as we can only serialize one novel a year and there are generally one, two or three under way which are destined for our pages, we often have to let a good thing go when we do not want to because we should otherwise have to postpone it much longer than the author would think wise. If we could not serialize your novel for any reason, we should want to help you to place it elsewhere, partly because it would be advantageous to the book to have it serialized in any magazine but those of the very largest circulation. The question of time is a hard one because it all depends on what a magazine already has under way. They usually cannot begin serialization until several months after acceptance and if a long novel they would require about six to eight months more to complete serialization. According to this you would have to finish a novel very soon indeed to make book publication in the Fall possible. We could publish as late as November first – although that would be later than we would like. This would mean that the serialization must end in the November number and would have to begin in the April number. It would therefore only be by making exactly the right connections all around, so to speak, that the thing could be managed. But it is almost useless to speculate on the question when so few facts are known. The best thing would be just to finish the novel as quickly as possible and then take up the question of serialization.

As to short stories, it is generally true that collections of them do not constitute selling books; but there are exceptions such as Davis, Kipling, and Henry as you know. The truth is, it has seemed to me that your stories were likely to constitute an exception, after a good many of them had been printed and your name was widely known. It seems to me that they have the popular note which would be likely to make them sell in book form. I wish you did care more about writing them because of this, and also because they have great value in making you a reputation and because they are quite worthwhile in themselves. Still we should not like to interfere with your novels.

Sincerely yours,

2900 Prytania Street, New Orleans, La.
Jan 21st 1920.

Dear Mr. Perkins:

I am returning herewith the first batch of proofs, corrected. There is one change I would like to have you make if you can possibly see your way clear to doing it. It is in regard to the type used in those sub-headings throughout the chapters, such as "A kiss for Amory" and "Preparatory to the great adventure" – you know what I mean.

Now I have a very strong instinct about having those in a different sort of type. It may seem a small point but I got the idea originally from the Shaw prefaces & the exact sort of type *does* make a difference. Those sub-headings are intended as *commentaries,* sort of *whimsical commentarties* rather more than they are intended as titles and the correct type would be that sort used in the first two words of the book. The words "Amory Blaine" that begin chapter one are in exactly the sort of type I mean. I dont know what you call it but it has capitals slightly bigger than the ones in the present sub-headings and the first letter of the important words is slightly bigger.

I should have explained that to you before – you see I think that this sort of type I mean gives the sort of effect of a marginalia – really doesn't break it up as much as these small, severe headings you're using now.

Of course this is my fault but I feel very strongly about [it] so if it can be done without inconvenience I wish you'd have it fixed up.

As Ever

P.S. It looks damn good. Thanks for your letter. O Henry said this was a story town – but its too consciously that – just as a Hugh Walpole character is too consciously a character.

2900 Prytania St.
New Orleans
February 3d [*1920*]

Dear Mr. Perkins:

I certainly touched the depths of depression tonight. The action on that book *Madeline,* has knocked hell out of my new novel *"Darling Heart"* which turned completely on the seduction of the girl in the second chapter. I was afraid all along because of *Susan Lennox,** and the agitation against Drieser but this is the final blow. I don't know what I'll do now – what in

*By David Graham Phillips.

hell is the use of trying to write decent fiction if a bunch of old women refuse to let anyone hear the truth!

I've fallen lately under the influence of an author who's quite changed my point of view. He's a chesnut to you, no doubt, but I've just discovered him – Frank Norris.[3] I think *McTeage* & *Vandover* are both excellent. I told you last November that I'd read *Salt* by his brother Charles and was quite enthusiastic about it. Odd! There are things in "Paradise" that might have been written by Norris – those drunken scenes for instance – in fact all the realism. I wish I'd stuck to it throughout! Another of my discoveries is H.L. Menken who is certainly a factor in present day literature. In fact I'm not so cocksure about things as I was last summer – this fellow Conrad seems to be pretty good after all.

I've decided I'd rather not use Nathan's* name at all in connection with my book and in fact that whole forward strikes me as being rather weak. Couldn't one of your advertising men write it?

I'm glad you're fixing it up about those sub-titles.† I'm anxiously awaiting the cover.

Those stories I sold the *Post* will start to appear Feb. 21st. I have *Dalyrimple* & *Bendiction* in the current *Smart Set* & I had a one act play in the January number which got several vaudeville offers. Read it if you can. It was called *Porcelain & Pink* and its excellent. *Smart Set, Scribners* & *Post* are the only three magazines.

I'm going to break up the start of my novel & sell it as three little character stories to *Smart Set*. I'll only get $40 apiece but no one else would take them, I don't think – and besides I want to have Menken & Nathan hot on my side when my book comes out. As soon as I've done that I'm going to do two or three stories for Mr. Bridges. If I give up the idea of *"Darling Heart"* which I've practically decided to do, at least as a serial and plan not to start my fall novel until June & finish it in August, my idea will be to do 3 stories a month, one for *Smart Set*, one for *Scribners*, and one for the *Post*. The latter are now paying me $600.00 which is a frightful inducement since I'm almost sure I'll get married as soon as my book is out.

Have you any idea of the date yet? And when my short stories will begin to appear?

Faithfully Yours

P.S. Please forward any mail that may come there for me. I expect to be in New York about the 24th – leave here the 20th.

---

*Critic George Jean Nathan.

†Perkins had written, on January 28th, that as soon as the proof sheets were returned, he would have the section heads changed.

The Allerton House
143 E. 39th St.
[*ca. February 21, 1920*]

Dear Mr. Perkins –
Excuse the pencil – I'm just enclosing you the typing of Zelda's diary. This is *verbatim* but is only about half. You'll recognize much of the dialogue. Please don't show it to anyone else.

Both last week & this noon at lunch I tried to say this but both times couldn't get started because you personally have always been so awfully good to me – but Mr. Perkins I really am very upset about my book not coming out next month. I explained to you the reasons financial, sentimental & domestic but more than any of these its for the psychological effect on me. Seeing my story today in the Sat. Eve. Post* raised my spirits greatly – I think there's some nessesity for an author to see his work occasionally outside & be critisized and I won't feel safe until the darn thing is out.

So if it can possibly be done in March I do wish you'd move it up. Moved into the Allerton this aft. I don't like it here.

Yours Sincerely the most bothersome
man this side of Paradise

Cottage Club
[*Princeton, N.J.*]
[*ca. March 10, 1920*]

Dear Mr. Perkins:
Can't work here so have just about decided to quit work and become an ash-man. Still working on that Smart Set novellette.

Everyone in college – I mean *literally everyone* in college seems to have read *Head & Shoulders* so I wish you'd have the following ad inserted in "The Daily Princetonian" the first two days after my book appears

---

THE FIRST NOVEL OF
F. Scott Fitzgerald '17
THIS SIDE OF PARADISE
A story about a Princeton man
Chas. Scribners Sons $1.75 Princeton Univ Store

See you about the 17th

*"Head and Shoulders."

29

March 26, 1920

Dear Mr. Fitzgerald:

Your book is out today. The pyramid which we have made of it in one of our windows is striking; and I have myself seen two copies sold in the store. I think we shall have some considerable reviews very soon in the papers as we have talked to a good many of the literary editors hereabouts and they will be prompt in looking into the copy we have sent. Now we shall see what comes of it, but at any rate you have had and have the enthusiastic support of our entire staff.

Sincerely yours,

The Commodore Hotel, New York City,
April 29, 1920.

Dear Mr. Perkins:

I am sending herewith eleven stories, with my own selection of the seven best for publication in book form. As you will see from the suggested table of contents, I am also sending six poems, three of which drew quite a bit of notice in the *Second Book of Princeton Verse*. The other three have never been published. All the stories have been published or will be before June 1st. They average about 8000 words.

Beside the title *Flappers & Philosophers*, here are several others in the order of my choice: (2) We are Seven. (3) Table D 'hote. (4) A La Carte. (5) Journeys and Journey's End. (6) Bittersweet. (7) Short Cake

If you think the book would go better without the poems, with more stories, with different stories, in a different arrangement or under a different title it will be O.K. with me.

Sincerely,

P.S. I find I have no copy of "The Four Fists" (June, Scribners)

June 29, 1920

Dear Mr. Fitzgerald:

I am sending you a copy of "The Ordeal of Mark Twain" by Van Wyck Brooks, because while reading it, views which you had expressed frequently came to my mind. He is a brilliant chap and very attractive and if you do care for the book I would like to have you meet him at lunch some day.

I hope Westport* is becoming more interesting.

As ever,

*Early in May, the Fitzgeralds had rented a house in Westport, Connecticut.

Westport, Conn.
July 7th 1920

Dear Mr. Perkins:

In regard to this English edition of *Paradise*⁴ I want to ask you a favor. It seems to me that if the book appears there in a land of much more intense scholarship with *approximately 100* mispellings and misprints it would hurt it.

. . . . .

As I told you over the phone I'm delighted over the English edition. My novel⁵ ought to be finished about Sept. 15th & I will send you a copy. The Metropolitan will probably begin to serialize it right off after that so if you care to I imagine it will be eligible for book publication in the spring.

I can't tell you how I liked "The Ordeal of Mark Twain." Its one of the most inspirational books I've read and has seemed to put the breath of life back in me. Just finished the best story I've done yet & my novel is going to be my life masterpiece.

Is there any new dope on *Paradise* – further editions I mean? Menken is giving it a very favorable review in the next Smart Set. If I finish my novel by Sept 15th I plan to go abroad with the serial money about October 15th & also with the money that will have accrued from Paradise by that time. Including seven thousand for the serial & at least three thousand more from the book (?) I ought to be able to stay over six months. I think it would give me a better perspective on the U.S. & broaden my outlook.

. . . . .

Sincerely

˙*Oct. 13, 1920*

Dear Fitzgerald:

I enclose a review of "Flappers and Philosophers"* which you will probably not get from your clipping bureau. It is curious how much diversity of opinion there is as to which stories are the best.

I am also sending you a copy of Galsworthy's "The Country House" and one of the sequel to it, "In Chancery". We are to begin a third book in the series in the January Scribner's. Galsworthy sustains his theme throughout these three large volumes and carries the same people through all of them. I think it is a really astonishing accomplishment in fiction. I think you will be interested in these if you have time to read them.

Sincerely yours,

---

*Published late in September.

38 W 59th St.
New York City
[ca. November 7, 1920]

Dear Mr. Perkins:

It'll be O.K. I've forgotten the date, though. Will you drop me a line telling me?*

About another matter. This Side of Paradise came out March 24th. Statement due Sept 24th – money due Jan 24th. Now I've already had about $3000 – I'm not sure exactly. Anyway though the date is 2½ months off I'm going to request $1500. more. This would be still way within the amount for at the seventh printing my share had reached about $7500.

If you think this plan is unfeasable please don't ask Scribners for me but I hate to knock off the novel again & my family seem to need a furcoat ect.

Leslie told me about his review.† I was glad to see it. I love his prose style. Hovey of the Met.** says he could begin the novel in February & thus you could publish in Oct.

Faithfully and only too consistently

in your debt

Nov 10th, 1920
38 W. 59th St.

Dear Mr. Perkins:

I thank you very much for the $1500.00. I thought as there have been 41,000 printed the sales would be more than 33,796 but I suppose there are about five thousand in stock and two thousand given away or sold at cost.[6]

The novel goes beautifully. Done 15,000 words in last three days which is very fast writing even for me who write very fast. My record is still 12,000 words "The Camel's Back" begun eight o'clock one morning and finished at seven at night & then copied between seven and half past four & mailed at 5 in the morning. That's the story the O. Henry Memorial people are using in their second collection.

I'm awfully mixed on this Art society thing. I remember they wrote me asking me to come on Thurs the 18th (I think) & I accepted. But I have a note in my note-book about the 11th & your letter says the seventeenth. I'd just as soon go twice if necessary but I sure am mixed up.

Sincerely

---

*Fitzgerald was to make a speech at the National Arts Club.
†Shane Leslie reviewed *This Side of Paradise* in the Fall, 1920, issue of the *Dublin Review*.
**Carl Hovey, editor of *Metropolitan Magazine*.

December 2nd 1920
38 W. 59th St.

Dear Mr. Perkins:

With the settlement still over a month away I'm begging for another thousand! This will still leave me a balance of twenty-six hundred.

I've taken two weeks out to write a scenario for Dorothy Gish on order – for which I hope to get a lot of money. So it sets my novel back until Jan. 1st

Can this nth advance be arranged?

Faithfully

Dec. 6, 1920

Dear Fitzgerald:

We gladly send you the check for a thousand dollars herewith. I hope that Dorothy Gish scenario turns out satisfactorily.

By the way, I am going to Boston at the end of this week and it occurred to me that I might do well to call on Biggs,* the author of that book which you have told us about. I suppose I could find him in Cambridge, it might interest him to talk over the possibilities. It would certainly interest me to see him but still, it might be better to leave the matter entirely in your hands and you will be the best judge. If you think it would be a good idea, will you let me know before Thursday on which day I go.

As ever,

[*ca. December 8, 1920*]
38 West 59th Street
New York City

Dear Mr. Perkins:

Less than a month now & you'll be quit of the financial embarrasments of the w.h. F. Scott. Because there's only about $1400 left I think – and if I could have $1000 of it I think I could pay for my Xmas presents.

My novel approaches completion. I hope you're going to like Bigg's book.

As Ever (ah! too monotonously
as ever)

---

*John Biggs, a friend whom Fitzgerald had met at Princeton, where they were undergraduates together.

Dec. 27, 1920

Dear Fitzgerald:
Here is the check for one thousand. But I hope we shall soon owe you a lot more money and I suppose "Flappers and Philosophers" must have earned quite a bit.

Biggs brought his book in and we shall read it right away. I do not think I ever saw any writing that was more vivid. The letter to Mr. Scribner from Shane Leslie speaks of his review of "Paradise" in the Dublin Review and then asks what the Catholic papers said about it over here. Have you received any reviews from these papers that are interesting, particularly on account of Monseigneur Fay of course. I do not think I have seen anything in particular from Catholic sources. Mr. Scribner wants to tell Leslie what the Catholic reaction was if it has been distinctive in any respect.

Yours as ever,

38 W 59th St.
New York City
Dec 31st, 1920

Dear Mr. Perkins:
The bank this afternoon refused to lend me anything on the security of stock I hold – and I have been pacing the floor for an hour trying to decide what to do. Here, with the novel within two weeks of completion, am I with six hundred dollars worth of bills and owing Reynolds $650 for an advance on a story that I'm utterly unable to write. I've made half a dozen starts yesterday and today and I'll go mad if I have to do another debutante which is what they want.

I hoped that at last being square with Scribner's I could remain so. But I'm at my wit's end. Isn't there some way you could regard this as an advance on the new novel rather than on the Xmas sale which won't be due me till July? And at the same interest that it costs Scribner's to borrow? Or could you make it a month's loan from Scribner & Co. with my next ten books as security? I need $*1600.00*

Anxiously

Feb. 1, 1921

Dear Fitzgerald:
Here is the check. We shall simply charge it against your account. But, while I have not reckoned up what your books have earned, I know it is

34

more than this, I think very considerably. You ought to have told me about this at lunch yesterday.

Yours as ever,

38 W. 59th St.
New York City
Feb 13th, 1921

Dear Mr. Perkins:

Bunny Wilson* is reading Part II. Part III is still being worked over. I paid Reynolds back his $650 so I wouldn't have to write a short story so with the income tax impending I'm again short of money. Is there as much as another thousand cleared on Flappers and Philosophers?

The Inevitable Beggar

Feb. 17, 1921

Dear Fitzgerald:

Herewith I enclose your royalty reports since the last rendering on "This Side of Paradise" and since publication on "Flappers and Philosophers" which was a little less than five months ago. You see that there is still to your credit here the amount of $2602 so that you need not hesitate to call on us as you need more.

I am delighted to know that I shall be able to read the second third of the novel over Sunday.

Yours very truly,

6 Pleasant Ave
Montgomery, Ala
March 30th, 1921

Dear Mr. Perkins –

Will you please deposit $1000. of the remaining $1400. to my account at the Chatham and Phenix Bank, 33d St at 5th Ave?

I brought the completed novel south with me but when I got the last chapter from the typists I sat down & began to do that chapter over. I've changed the ending. Its too obvious to have him go crazy.

About the wrap – please don't let Hill start the wrap until I see him. I'm afraid he'll make it too "flapperish", too light as he did with the last one.

*Edmund Wilson.

And I don't want to give buyers the wrong impression. Will be in New York by the 6th

Sincerely

April 20, 1921

Dear Fitzgerald:

I just happened to have so many things on my hands at the moment you called up yesterday that I am a little indefinite as to what we arranged. There is one very important thing though, and that is that we should know at the earliest moment possible about serialization. It is hard for me to believe that the Metropolitan will easily forego the publication, but if they do, and the instant we know it, we must put the book into the fall list and get together with Hill and so on. So I am only writing to impress the importance of our knowing at the first possible moment.

As ever,

P.S. We have made a cover, uniform with that of Paradise.

April 21st 1921

Dear Mr. Perkins:

Part I goes to Metropolitan today with my letter, Part II tomorrow, Part III Monday. I am asking them to let me know at the *latest* by a week from Sat. which is the *last day of April.* I feel sure they will not serialize it but I think *Cosmopolitan* would. However I am saying definately to Reynolds that if Metropolitan doesn't take it. It must be done in 4 monthly parts if at all so that it will be free to publish by October. I am requesting Hovey not to take it.

I am glad about the cover.

I have to get some steamer tickets* I've reserved tomorrow & I wonder if you could advance six hundred. This of course would be repaid in one week in case of any change in publishing plans as I could not expect any advance from you and the Metropolitan too.

I am greatly improving the book. I'll bring it in Monday.

Yours

*The Fitzgeralds were preparing to sail for Europe.

May 2, 1921

Dear Fitzgerald:
You left your copy of the contract* here and I enclose it with this letter as you ought to have it. I take this opportunity, in order that the thing may be set down in writing, that we are only not agreeing to any advance on the understanding that you are free to call on us to any reasonable extent against your general account with us. That is, we shall always be ready to advance, not only amounts equivalent to what your books have already earned, although the payments may not then be due, but amounts which may be considered reasonable estimates of what it may be anticipated that they will earn. In other words, the only reason why we are not making you a very handsome advance is that the figure is perhaps a little difficult to fix upon, but chiefly because we thought that in view of our previous association, an arrangement by which you were free to draw against your account here and reasonably in excess of it, would be more convenient and satisfactory.

I enclose also a letter to Galsworthy whom I hope you will see, and a letter to Mr. Kingsley† who may be able to help you one way or another.

I hope it will be a great trip both for you and your wife.

As ever,

Royal Danielli, Venice
May 26th [1921]

Dear Mr. Perkins:
After a wonderful time in England and a rotten time in France, we're in Venice & enjoying ourselves hugely. Galesworthy had us to dinner. St. John Irvine** was also there & needless to say a good time was had by Scott & Zelda. My book†† comes out in England today.

The most beautiful spot in the world is Oxford, without a doubt.

Will you send one of those new pictures of me – the one writing (I gave you two of each, I think, to the Metropolitan?

Now, as usual, I'm going to ask for gold – because the rest of the Metropolitan money doesn't come until July, I mean.

I'd like to get it this way if its not too much trouble.

$200 to the Chatham & Phenix Bank, 33d St to my account

*For the publication of *The Beautiful and Damned*.
†Charles Kingsley, Scribners London representative.
**Irish playwright, critic and novelist.
†† *This Side of Paradise*.

$800 deposited by wire to my credit at the American Express at Rome to be handed over to me upon proper identification.

We'll call this the advance[.] I won't ask for more until November. Can it be done?

I'm writing a movie & intend to start a new book in July. I met Kingsley & went to tea where he lives in the old Richmond Palace. I liked him mighty well.

I'll write later

Yours always

June 13, 1921

Dear Fitzgerald:

I was mighty glad to get yours of the 26th with its evidences that you and Mrs. Fitzgerald are enjoying yourselves. If at any time you should feel inclined to write about the things that are happening, do it because nothing would interest me more than to know of them. Moreover, I should make the information into discreet but effective publicity. I have sent out a couple of notes about your trip already.

The wire of eight hundred dollars ($800) went this morning to Rome and a check for two hundred dollars ($200) will go this afternoon or tomorrow to the Chatham and Phoenix.

Yours as ever,

P.S. Delighted that you are soon to begin a new book. Everybody I see asks about "The Beautiful and Damned" and about what you are doing in general.

6 Pleasant Ave.
Montgomery, Ala
July 30th 1921

Dear Mr. Perkins:

I have been intending to write you the following letter for some months and I've been deterred for many causes – chief among which were the facts that any letter from me on this subject would sound like impertinent & unsollicited critisism and secondly because I have been the recipient of so many favors and courtesies from Scribners that it was scarcely my place to cavil at what I considered ultra-conservatism in their marketing and editorial policies. But in most business nowadays a box is set aside for employees suggestions and so perhaps even from outside you won't resent it if I speak whats on my mind.

What prompted this letter was the clipping on page D.* which I took from the Tribune. I happen [to] know that two weeks ago *Mooncalf* had not reached 50,000 copies. And I know also that it has not had nearly the vogue of my book in the libraries as is apparent from *The Bookman's* monthly score. Yet my novel so far as I have seen got not *one* newspaper add, not one *Times* or *Tribune* add or Chicago add since *six months* after publication. And Knopf has forcibly kept *Mooncalf* in the public eye for *twice that long*. What notoriety my book has preserved as well as what notoriety it got in the beginning, it got almost unaided. It's adds were small and undistinguished and confined almost entirely to college magazines and to *Scribners*. The only add from among my nine or ten suggestions that was used (except the "novel about flappers written for philosophers") was ruined by Black's "Make it a Fitzgerald Christmas." The adds gotten up in the office were small and so scattered as to have no follow up or reiterative punch. Don't gather from this that I have the idea that my book was slighted: on the contrary I think Whitney Darrow† & Rodgers & everyone who had anything to do with it there gave it much more personal attention than any book they were handling. Nevertheless the following facts remain

(1) Mooncalf, on its issue, was advertised in *Montgomery, Ala. This Side of Paradise,* tho it sold fifty or more copies here on Zelda's reputation was *not once* advertised. *Mooncalf* was advertised *two months* in St. Paul. *This Side of Paradise* appeared in the papers *3 times* in adds. It sold itself largely on personal home town unsollicited notices about me. This was also true to a great extent in Chicago. From the advertising section of the Chi daily news which I have on file together with the numbers of the Chi. Tribune during the weeks when my book was heading the list, I discover about eleven adds. It ran 18 wks as best seller in Chi. During that time it should have been advertised in 2 papers *at least* every other week. From my slight experience in advertising I know that much about campaignes. *Mooncalf* (not to mention *Lulu Bett* [and] *The Age of Innocence*** neither of which had 1/10th the initial publicity of my book & both of which are still selling. ect) has been adver[t]ised almost every week for 8 mos in Chicago papers and usually in both. Knopf runs almost daily adds for books that *he believes in* that may not sell 10,000 copies (like Zell†† for instance) in the *Tribune*. The greatest selling point my book had, Mencken's statement quoted on

---

*Reference is to a Knopf advertisement of *Mooncalf,* a recent novel by Floyd Dell, in which it was called "the most brilliantly successful first novel of many years."

†In charge of sales and promotion at Scribners.

**Novels by Zona Gale and Edith Wharton, respectively.

††Novel by Henry G. Aikman, the pen name of Harold Hunter Armstrong.

the wrapper (together with an entirely neutral statement from Phelps)*
was allowed to be forgotten with *one* exception, *one* add. Knopf would be
using it still, and keeping the book talked about by means of it. Sinclair
Lewis's remark in the Tribune "In Scott Fitzgerald we have an author who
will be the equal of any young European" was *absolutely* unused.†

August 3, 1921

Dear Fitzgerald:

I just got your letter about the advertising, on the edge of a vacation and
I am terribly hurried in getting things into shape so I can leave Friday
night; so I am writing you very hurriedly. But I do hope you will take me
in complete sincerity when I say that you must freely express any points
of dissatisfaction.

As for the next book, I can promise you that your suggestions will not
only be gladly considered but will generally be followed: I know how good
the ones you made on "Paradise" were. I can say too that we will map out
our campaign a month or more in advance, so as to show all the dates,
places, and advertisements, up to a certain date, to be agreed upon; and the
more you help us in connection with the make-up of these advertisements,
the better.

I think we did more advertising, very probably, than you were aware
of, but it was not as effective or as plainly visible as it should have been.
But we have now a man with excellent experience whom we believe will
do the work with skill and vigor. It is true that the book should have been
advertised more largely also in Montgomery and in St. Paul, but I do not
want to go into detail now. I only want to ask you always to criticize freely
– I am afraid you disliked writing this letter – and to convince you that, in
the case of "The Beautiful and Damned" we will work the scheme out with
you so that you will know all its details and will feel satisfied both with
the copy and with the campaign.

. . . . .

Yours as ever,

P.S. . . . . .

*Critic William Lyon Phelps.
†The letter breaks off here, unsigned.

Dellwood, White Bear Lake
Minn, Aug 25th 1921

Dear Mr. Perkins –

Excuse the pencil but I'm feeling rather tired and discouraged with life tonight and I havn't the energy to use ink – ink the ineffable destroyer of thought, that fades an emotion into that slatternly thing, a written down mental excretion. What ill-spelled rot!

About the novel – which after my letters I should think you'd be so bored with you'd wish it had never existed: I'd like very much if it came out in England simultaneously with America. You have the rights to it have you not? If you do not intend to place it would you be willing to turn them over to me on the same 10% basis as *Paradise.* So I could place it either with Collins or thru Reynolds?

Hope you're enjoying New Hampshire – you probably are. I'm having a hell of a time because I've loafed for 5 months & I want to get to work. Loafing puts me in this particularly obnoxious and abominable gloom. My 3d novel, if I ever write another, will I am sure be black as death with gloom. I should like to sit down with ½ dozen chosen companions and drink myself to death but I am sick alike of life, liquor and literature. If it wasn't for Zelda I think I'd dissapear out of sight for three years. Ship as a sailor or something & get hard – I'm sick of the flabby semi-intellectual softness in which I flounder with my generation.

Dellwood, White Bear Lake, Minn
[*ca. October 1, 1921*]

Dear Mr. Perkins –

I appreciate your courtesy and thoughtfulness in telegraphing me.[7] Zelda recieved the letter and is awaiting the book* with interest. In setting up the book are they including that table "By F Scott Fitzgerald" with my multitudinous & voluminous numbered beneath.

I have not seen *one single review* for 2 months but here are my prognostications for the fall. I have only read the 1st of these books.

(1.) *Brass* by Charles Norris. – Worthy, honest thorough but fundamentally undistinguished

(2) *Three Soldiers* by John Dos Passos – the book of the autumn

(3) *Eric Dorn* by Ben Hetch [Hecht] – probably the second best book of the autumn

* *To Let* by John Galsworthy.

(4) *The Beginning of Wisdom* by Stephen Vincent Benet. Beautifully written but too disjointed & paternless. Critics will accuse him of my influence but unjustly as his book was written almost simultaenously with mine

(5) *The Briary Bush.* Another rotten novel by Floyd Dell, which, because it is without a touch of grace or beauty or wit will be hailed as a masterpiece by all the ex-policemen who are now critics.

Will you send me that Brentano sketch* when it appears?

Sincerely,

Oct. 7, 1921

Dear Fitzgerald:

The page proofs of "The Beautiful and Damned" are beginning to come up. I shall send them on to you but you will not need to read them very carefully unless you wish to. Just look them over.

Of the books you speak of in your letter which shall have a marked success this season, I have only read "Three Soldiers." I think it descriptively a very remarkable book. Few books written about war have presented it as vividly in its physical aspect, – perhaps only "War and Peace"; and the characters too, have reality. I think as a complete presentation of the effect of the war on typical individuals, it is very incomplete, – I judge not so much from what people say as from what, it seems to me, is bound to be the case. These three men must have been exceptions rather than types. But there will be great controversy about the book and I think it will have a great sale. I read some of "The Beginning of Wisdom" in the Bookman and was disappointed. That part was about college and I did not think it so well written, – rather sprawly and immature, it seemed to me. But I don't doubt the book itself is an interesting one. Even the portion I saw shows that it has vitality, – that it is close to life. I am not so much interested in "The Briary Bush" because a survey of "Moon Calf" which I got at pretty late, did not make me think highly of Floyd Dell's future.

I sent you the Brentano sketch and I very much hope you will get around to doing an article for Bridges on those lines. It would be a most refreshing article.

Hoping all goes well with Zelda, I am,

Yours as ever,

"Three Cities," Brentano's Book Chat, September-October, 1921.

Oct. 10, 1921

Dear Fitzgerald:

I am sending you the first of the page proofs. You asked me about what dormitory Anthony should live in and I said Claverly without thinking of the implication of the context.* A boy with a good income would be likely to land in Claverly but that would be socially where he should land and you want him to be somewhat out of the center as one ignorant of the social system. I therefore suggest changing it to Beck Hall which a generation ago was fashionable but is so no longer and is rather out of the way. It would be just the sort of a place that a man of this kind would be likely to room in if he had no knowledge of the social system.

Sincerely yours,

Oct 14th 1921
New adress ⟶ The Commodore Hotel
Western Ave. St. Paul

Dear Mr. Perkins:

Thanks for the tip about Beck Hall. I shall change it. I am so glad you like *Three Soldiers*. I was rather curious to know if you would. *The Beginning of Wisdom* was something of a dissapointment to me.

Three matters I want to speak of

(1.) There was no table of "works" in the front of the proof you sent me. I want one.

(2) Are you going to have Hill draw the jacket? with a light blue back instead of orange.

(3) You have already advanced me about $1400. on the book. I am going to ask you for another thousand as Zelda expects the chee-ild in a fortnight and its going to cost. If that is O.K. will you put [it] in the Chatham & Phenix bank for me right away.

I see you have no date of publication on the book. Now the serial's last installment comes out Feb 14th. Do you intend to publish in Feb. or say on the 1st of March.[8]

The Brentano sketch came & I thank you.

As Ever

---

*Anthony Patch, the protagonist of *The Beautiful and Damned*, like Perkins, attended Harvard University.

43

Oct 20th 1921
The Commodore Hotel

Dear Mr. Perkins –

Thank you very much for the money.

Several things: (1st) I hope you'll have the card plate like the one I sent you. It looks as if I have a lot of works. (2nd) John Black wrote *Who's Who* to ask them to put me in. About November I recieved blanks from them & filled them out. I noticed that I wasn't in the book published last Spring. Now I don't care specially whether I'm in or not – nevertheless I'd like to know this. Do you have to pay for insertion of your name? I've heard recently that you did and I know I didn't pay anything. Didn't know you had to. Will you ask someone in the office there who's in it whether you do or not?[9]

My novel looks awfully good to me. Its almost a different book from the one you read in sections – I've made so many changes at various times. I hope to *God* that Hill draws a good looking girl – also that if there's a man he'll keep his tie outside his collar.

Sincerely

New Address   *626 Goodrich Ave*
Permanent!   *St. Paul, Minn.*
[*ca. December 1, 1921*]

Dear Mr. Perkins –

I've always hated & been ashamed of that damn story *The Four Fists*. Not that it is any cheaper than *The Off Shore Pirate* because it isn't but simply because its a mere plant, a moral tale & *utterly* lacks vitality.

Here's the point – I'd like Collins to substitute for it in his version* *The Camel's Back* which appeared in this years O. Henry memorial collection. How about it. Suppose I send it to him & let him decide. Also I hope to God his copy of *Flappers* had that ghastly error of mine corrected, the "let it lay" in *The Ice Palace*. Had I better write them? Practically every critic in America has spoken of it. Thank Heaven my new book is at least letter perfect.

I have just recieved $1500.00 from the Sat. Eve. Post for *one* short story,† my highest price so far. I think I may be able to use my European impressions a little later but at present except for that acidulous (and rather silly) explosion in *The Book-chat* I havn't many ideas on the subject. However I'll try again.

---

*The English edition of *Flappers and Philosophers*.
†"The Popular Girl," published in the issues of February 11th and 18th, 1922.

Bigg's story* is fine. Knopf is going to take Bishop's & Wilson's books,† simply, they believe, so he can have them on his lists. A glance at *The Briary Bush* convinces me that its one of the worst novels ever written by a civilized man.

Sincerely

P.S. Do you think I improved the chapter I hacked at so?

Dec. 6, 1921

Dear Fitzgerald:
I think almost every change you have made in "The Beautiful and Damned" has been a good one except that passage about the Bible.** I made a comment on the proof on that point, and I cannot add much to it. I think I know exactly what you mean to express, but I don't think it will go. Even when people are altogether wrong, you cannot but respect those who speak with such passionate sincerity. You may think Carlyle is all rubbish, for instance but you cannot but admire him, or at least feel strong – about him. What Maurey says is quite consistent with his character but this will seem to have been your point of view and I don't think it would be that.

As to the Collins matter, I think it would be just as well if you wrote them. For one thing, I think it would help you to be in personal touch with them. I rather think that they won't want to give up "The Four Fists" themselves. Collins' address is 48 Pall Mall, London, S. W., England.

As for the article on Europe, I think it is only a trifle, and it would be much better if you should give your time to something bigger, toward beginning a new novel. I heard from somebody, I think Nathan, that you were writing a play. Did anyone receive more than $1500 for a single short story? I think that is wonderful. I hope it will appear about the time or shortly before "The Beautiful and Damned" appears.

Thanks for the advertising suggestions. We shall be able to use them, all except the joke one which we do not object to as such, but which we do not think would be as effective as the other sort. Hill has done an excellent picture for the wrap of which I shall send you the first reproduction we have.

Yours as ever,

---

*"Corkran of the Clamstretch," *Scribner's Magazine*, December, 1921.

†Possibly *The Undertaker's Garland* by John Peale Bishop and Edmund Wilson, published by Knopf in 1922.

**The passage in *The Beautiful and Damned* where Maury Noble calls the Bible the work of ancient skeptics, whose primary goal was their own literary immortality.

626 Goodrich Ave.
St. Paul, Minn
[ca. December 10, 1921]

Dear Mr. Perkins –

Have just recieved your letter in re Bible anecdote in novel and I'm rather upset about it. You say:

"Even when people are wrong you cannot but respect those who speak with such passionate sincerity about it."

Now in that remark lies, I think, the root of your objection – except to substitute "be intimidated by" for "respect." I don't suppose any but the most religious minded people in the world believe that such interludes as The Song of Solomon, the story of Ruth have or ever had even in the minds of the original chroniclers the faintest religious significance. The Roman church insists that in the song of Solomon the bride is the church & the lover is Christ but it is almost universally doubted if any such thing was even faintly intended.

Now I feel sure that most people will know that my sketch refers to the old testament, and to Jehovah, the cruel hebrew God again[s]t whom such writers as even Mark Twain not to mention Anatole France & a host of others have delivered violent pyrotechnics from time to time.

As to the personal side of it don't you think all changes in the minds of people are brought about by the assertion of a thing – startling perhaps at first but later often becoming, with the changes of the years, bromidic. You have read Shaw's preface to Androcles and the Lion – that made no great stir – in fact to the more sophisticated of the critics it was a bit bromidic. His preface, moreover, is couched with very little reverence even tho it treats of Christ who is much less open to discussion than merely that beautiful epic of the bible. If you object to my phrasing I could substitute "deity" for "godalmighty" & get a better word than bawdy – in fact make it more dignified – but I would hate to cut it out as its very clever in its way & Mencken – who saw it – and Zelda were very entheusiastic about it. It's the sort of thing you find continually in Anatole France's Revolt of the Angels – as well as in Jurgen & in Mark Twain's Mysterious Stranger. The idea, refusing homage to the Bible & it's God, runs thru many of Mark Twain's essays & all through Paine's biography.*

In fact Van Wyke Brooks in The Ordeal† critisizes Clemens for allowing many of his statements to be toned down at the request of Wm. Dean Howells or Mrs. Clemens. If it was an incident which I felt had no particular literary merit I should defer to your judgement without question but

* Mark Twain by Albert Bigelow Paine.
† The Ordeal of Mark Twain by Van Wyck Brooks.

that passage belongs beautifully to that scene and is exactly what was needed to make it more than a beautiful setting for ideas that fail to appear. You say:

"Even when people are altogether wrong, you cannot but respect those who speak with such passionate sincerity."

I can imagine that remark having been made to Gallileo and Mencken, Samuel Butler & Anatole France, Voltaire and Bernard Shaw, George Moore and even, if you will pardon me, in this form once upon a time.

"You don't like these scribes and pharisees. You call them whitened sepulcheres but even when people are altogether wrong – ect"

I havn't seen the proof with your notation and have only read your letter. But I do feel that my judgement is right in this case. I do not expect in any event that I am to have the same person for person public this time that *Paradise* had. My one hope is to be endorsed by the intellectually élite & thus be *forced* on to people as Conrad has. (Of course I'm assuming that my work grows in sincerity and proficiency from year to year as it has so far). If I cut this out it would only [be] because I would be afraid and I havn't done that yet & dread the day when I'll have to.

Please write me frankly as I have you – and tell me if you are speaking for yourself, for the Scribner Co. or for the public. I am rather upset about the whole thing. Will wait until I hear from you

As Ever

*See next page**
P.S. Besides, as to the position of the thing in the story. It is nessesary to show the growth of Maury's pessimism and to do this I have invented a fable in which the *hoi poloi* do more than refuse to believe their wise men – but they twist the very wisdom of the wise into a justification of their own maudlin and self-satisfactory creeds. This would discourage anyone.

Dec. 12, 1921

Dear Fitzgerald:
Don't ever *defer* to my judgment. You won't on any vital point, I know, and I should be ashamed, if it were possible to have made you; for a writer of any account must speak solely for himself. I should hate to play (assuming V.W.B.'s position to be sound) the W. D. Howells to your Mark Twain.†

---

*The postscript was written on a separate sheet.
†In *The Ordeal of Mark Twain*, the influence of Howells on Twain is depicted as largely a restrictive and injurious one.

It is not to the *substance* of this passage that I object. Everyone of any account, anyone who could conceivably read this book, under forty, agrees with the substance of it. If they did not there would be less objection to it in one way – it would then startle them as a revelation of a new point of view which, by giving a more solid kind of value, would lessen the objection on account of flippancy (I hate the word. I hate to be put in the position of using such words as "respect" and "flippancy" which have so often enraged me, but there is some meaning in them). The old testament ought not to be treated in a way which suggests a failure to realize its tremendous significance in the recent history of man, as if it could simply be puffed away with a breath of contempt, it is so trivial. That is the effect of the passage at present. It is partly so because Maury is talking and is talking in character; – and that is the way men do talk too, so far as ability enables them, even when they fully appreciate every side of the matter. It is here that the question of the public comes in. They will not make allowance for the fact that a character is talking extemporaneously. They will think F. S. F. is writing deliberately. Tolstoi did that even, and to Shakespeare. Now, you are, through Maury, expressing your views, of course; but you would do so differently if you were deliberately stating them as your views. You speak of Gallileo: he and Bruno showed themselves to have a genuine sense of the religious significance of the theories they broke down. They were not in a state of mind to treat the erroneous beliefs of men with a light contempt. France does not so treat Christ in that story of Pilate in his old age. And a "Whited Sepulchre" is an expression of a high contempt, although applied to an object which had no such quality of significance as the Bible.

My point is that you impair the effectiveness of the passage – of the very purpose you use it for – by giving it that quality of contempt and I wish you would try so to revise it as not to antagonize even the very people who agree with the substance of it. You would go a long way toward this if you cut out "God Almighty" and put "Deity". In fact if you will change it on the line indicated by that change you will have excised the element to which I object.

I do agree that it belongs in Maury's speech; that it does bring it to a focus. But you could so revise it that it would do this without at the same time doing the thing to which we object.

I hope this gets over to you. If I saw you for ten minutes I know you would understand and would agree with me.

As ever,

626 Goodrich Ave
[St. Paul, Minn.]
[ca. December 16, 1921]

Dear Mr. Perkins –
Your second letter came and I want to apologize to you for mine. I might have known you did not mean what in haste I imagined you did. The thing *was* flippant – I mean it was the sort of worst of Geo. Jean Nathan. I have changed it now – changed "godalmighty" to deity, cut out "bawdy" & changed several other words so I think it is all right.

Why, really, my letter was so silly with all those absurd citations of "Twain", Anatole France, Howells ect was because I was in a panic because I was afraid I might have to cut it out and as you say it does round out the scene.

I hope you'll accept my apology.

Is the girl *beautiful* in the W. E. Hill picture? Are you going to have a light blue background on the jacket as I suggested – I mean like you had for your Lulu Ragdale book two years ago? And did you catch that last correction I sent you before it was too late?

I have put a new ending on the book – that is on the last paragraph, instead of the repitition of the Paradise scene of which I was never particularly fond. I think that now the finish will leave the "taste" of the whole book in the reader's mouth as it didn't before – if you know what I mean.

I can't tell you how sorry I am about that silly letter. I took that "Oh Christ" out as you suggested. As you say "Oh, God" won't fill the gap but "oh my God" does it pretty well.[10]

With my changing of the extreme last & fixing up the symposium I am almost, but not quite, satisfied with the book. I prophecy that it will go about 60,000 copies the first year – that is, assuming that Paradise went about 40,000 the first year. Thank God I'm thru with it.

As ever

Dec. 27, 1921

Dear Fitzgerald:
We are depositing the five hundred dollars your letter* asked for in the Chatham & Phenix today. I am having a statement made up on your account so that you will know just how things are. We did not delay the check to do this.

I telegraphed you this morning, "I agree with Zelda", after considerable hesitation. I did not hesitate though on the question of which ending

*Written about December 24th.

49

was intrinsically the best. I think she is dead right about that. Anthony's final reflection is exactly the right note to end upon. My hesitation was purely on the popular side – whether from that viewpoint a pointing of the moral was not desirable. But finally I did not think the advantage was such as to overcome the artistic effect of the other end of it. Shall I therefore, cut out the last half page?[11]

As ever,

Dec. 31, 1921

Dear Fitzgerald:
The letter from Reynolds which you sent and which I return is rather pathetic, but so far as it concerns your writing, I think it represents a temporary condition. The time ought to come when whatever you write will go through and where its irony and satire will be understood. They will know what you stand for in writing and they do not really know yet. It is in recognition of this that I want very much to have this book so announced in our lists and so on, that it will be regarded as "important" as well as the other things.

There is especially in this country, a rootless class of society into which Gloria and Anthony drifted, – a large class and one which has an important effect on society in general. It is certainly worth presenting in a novel. I know that you did not deliberately undertake to do this but I think "The Beautiful and Damned" has in effect, done this; and that this makes it a valuable as well as brilliant commentary upon American society. Perhaps you have never even formulated the idea that it does do this thing, but don't you think it is true? The book is not written according to the usual conventions of the novel, and its greatest interest is not that of the usual novel. Its satire will not of itself be understood by the great simple minded public without a little help. For instance, in talking to one man about the book, I received the comment that Anthony was unscathed; that he came through with his millions, and thinking well of himself. This man completely missed the extraordinarily effective irony of the last few paragraphs.

As ever,

626 Goodrich Ave. St. Paul,
Jan 9th, 1921 [1922]

Dear Mr. Perkins – I see what you mean about the book and I am in entire accord with you. When the *Metropolitan* advertised it as "a novel of the Revolt of American Youth" I was wild.[12]

50

As to the "rootless" idea in your pentultimate letter – I think it would be ideal if you can get across the rootless idea without in any way giving the impression that it is a novel of Bohemian life, which of course it isn't. Do you remember how the subtitle "A novel about Flappers written for Philosophers[''] was bruited about – perhaps something like that could be done with "A novel of the Rootless" – or would that be punned upon as a novel of the fruitless or given meanings still more grotesque & Rabelaisian.

And the flapper idea – God knows I am indebted to it but I agree with you that its time to let it go. There is only one type of advertisement for which I (& the general public too, I believe) have a profound aversion – one that contains the phrase "Surely the book of the Spring". However Scribners never sins in this respect.

I see by the memo that I have had a $3,143.00 advance – (more really because its been ahead. I have been working for two months on a play & will be at it three weeks more. Could I have $500.00 more? Shades of John Fox!* But this absolutely, positively the last. If O.K. will you deposit for me in the Chatham & Phenix, 33d?†

Sincerely

626 *Goodrich Ave.*
St. Paul, Minn.
[*ca. January 18, 1922*]

Dear Mr. Perkins:
Thank you for the deposit. I am in a mood of terrific depression which nothing will lift except the enormous success of my book. I wish I didn't have to be here when it appears as the philistine pressure is terrific and I shall probably be gazed at stonily by many robust dowagers. We expect to come east March 15th – which is the date set for the baby's weaning. I never knew how much I cared for New York. My play[13] is a gem but I can't do the last act. What do you think of *Sideshow* or *A Sideshow* as the title for my book of short stories next fall?

Idea: If you are advertising *Flappers* on the wrap-edge of my new book why not do it this way.

"Contains the famous 'Head & Shoulders' story." There was a caption in the Times rotogravure section last week which included the phrase "Head & Shoulders" in quotes. It really was much read & the movie

*A best-selling Scribners author. Fitzgerald signed this letter "F. John Scott Fox Fitzgerald Jr."
†On January 11th, Perkins wrote that he had deposited the $500.

advertised it – I think a reference like I suggest on the wrap is better than the conventional "contains eight of Mr. F.'s best short stories." Is March 1st the definate date?[14]

. . . . .

As Ever

[*626 Goodrich Avenue*]
[*St. Paul, Minn.*]
[*ca. January 31, 1922*]

Dear Mr. Perkins –

The books came* & I'm delighted with the blurb on the back which I suspect you wrote yourself. I think it strikes exactly the right note, gives a moral key to the stupider critics on which to go, and justifies the book to many who will think it is immoral! Thank you.

I like the way it is got up – it surprised me to find that it is half again as long as Paradise.

I wired you last night about the color of the jacket which has come out, in my copies at least, a sickly yellow. It was a deep reddish orange, you remember, in the jacket you sent me before.

The more I think of the picture on the jacket the more I fail to understand his drawing that man. The girl is excellent of course – it looks somewhat like Zelda but the man, I suspect, is a sort of debauched edition of me. At any rate the man is utterly unprepossessing and I do not understand an artist of Hill's talent and carefullness going quite contrary to a detailed description of the hero in the book.

Note these divergences –

1. Anthony is "just under six feet" – Here he looks about Gloria's height with ugly short legs
2. " " dark haired – this bartender on the cover is light haired
3. Anthony's general impression is described on page 9. – in not a single trait does this person on the jacket conform to that impression. He looks like a sawed-off young tough in his first dinner-coat.

Everybody I've talked to agrees with me and I'm a little sore. When a book has but one picture to give the impression the illustrater ought to be careful. The Metropolitan illustrations were bad enough God knows but at least the poor botch of an illustrater tried to give Anthony the physique and atmosphere assigned to him.

As you can see I'm an ill-natured crabber. I ought not to be. The girl

*Advance copies of *The Beautiful and Damned*.

is excellent & I suppose Hill thought it would please me if the picture looked like Zelda & me. But I'd rather have the man on the *Paradise* jacket even with his tie tucked neatly under his collar in the Amherst fashion. Hill has done about 9 figures for my covers altogether and I suppose 8 good out of 9 is a good average.

Excuse this letter – its just to get rid of an inhibition of anger so I can get back to my play this morning. Wilson's article about me in the March 1st *Vanity Fair** is suberb. It's no blurb – not by a darn sight – but its the first time I've been done *at length* but [by] an intelligent & sophisticated man and I appreciate it – jeers and all.

As Ever

626 Goodrich Ave.
St. Paul, Minn.
Feb 6th 1922

Dear Mr. Perkins –
I was delighted with your letter, the quotation from Syd Howard & the encouraging news generally.† In the same mail came a wonderful letter from Howard himself, even more entheusiastic. I am glad – for after so committing himself on the wrap it would be ghastly if he thot the bk. was rotten. My deadly fear now is not the critics but the public. Will they buy – will you & the bookstores be stuck with forty thousand copies on your hands? Have you overestimated my public & will this sell up to within seven thousand of what *Paradise* has done in two years? My God! Suppose I fell flat! I feel that in your blurbs so far you have struck exactly the right note, a moral note almost, with no rah-rah-ing about "The Revolt of American Youth" as Hovey couldn't keep from doing. Either your advertising man is as keen as hell or you have been engineering all this yourself – in which case I congratulate you on what I consider an astute tack.

But I have a guilty feeling that its all much ado about nothing, and will have until it starts to go – if it does. If it doesn't – may the saints intercede for me to the Christian God who comforteth the afflicted.

The Selling Point thing seems to me excellent. It makes me swell with pomposity.

. . . . .

---

*Fitzgerald apparently is referring to Wilson's unsigned essay in the March, 1922, issue of *The Bookman*.
†On February 3rd, Perkins had sent Fitzgerald a letter praising *The Beautiful and Damned* by playwright, critic and novelist Sidney Howard.

I see that Jackson Gregory* has also borrowed your name for his title page. I think its a crime the timidity Doran is showing over *Three Soldiers*. Never in my knowledge has a book had more free publicity than that (possibly excepting *Main Street*) and less paid advertising. Doran, too, is usually a voluminous advertiser.

The wrap grows better. I guess you are right about the review copies.[15]

I don't suppose there's any hurry but next fall when my new book comes out, the table of works which is in the B.&D. should go in all four of my books.

Also I've caught a few more errors in the B.&D. But I'll wait until the 40,000 sell before I send you a list of them. I'm sending a copy to Collins. I hope a copy went to Mencken & Nathan both as I havn't sent one to either of them.

About my new book. Here it is.

Title –	"In One Reel"
Contents –	*Fantasies*

These are in my "new" manner

{
The Diamond in the Sky (Smart Set?)
The Russet Witch (Met. Feb '21)
Tarquin of Cheapside (Smart Set Feb '21)
The Curious Case of Benjamin Button (Met?)
}

My Last Flappers

May Day (*Smart Set, June '20*)
The Camel's Back (*Post, April '20*)
The Jellybean (*Met. Sept. '20*)

Comedies

Mr Icky (Play) (*Smart Set, Jan '20*)
Porcelain & Pink (Play) (*Smart Set, Mar '20*)
Jemima (*Vanity Fair, Jan 21*)

And So Forth

The Crusts of Love (*Chi Tribune, Nov '20*)
Two for a Cent (*Met.?*)

This includes all my stuff to date except two stories I left purposely out of Flappers (Myra Meets Her Family, [Post] and A Smile for Sylva [Smart Set) and this $1,500 story I just sold the Post (appears this week) which is too cheap to print.†

*American novelist, writer of Western and detective stories.
†"The Popular Girl."

The others are all excellent, much better than *Flappers*, except *The Camel's Back* which was in the O Henry Memorial collection & is funny tho cheap.

May Day & *The Diamond in the Sky** are novellettes. *Smart Set* will publish the latter soon. *Two for a Cent* & *Curious Case of Benjamin Button* will appear in the Metropolitan this summer. I am going over the lot of them this Spring & will send them on. They are, almost all of them, tremendously original and I think will go better than *Flappers* because all the fantasies are something new & the critics will fall for them. What do [you] think of the new title. I agree with you *Sideshow* is no good.[16]

Remember me to Mrs. Perkins.

As Ever

626 Goodrich Ave, St. Paul, Minn
[ca. February 10, 1922]

Dear Mr. Perkins:

Knapp† came through here yesterday. I took him to lunch & we had a long bicker. He sold 1050 copies in St. Paul & hopes to do the same in Minneapolis. If the sale was in that ratio all over the country the original 40,000 would be gone the day of publication. I realize of course that it *won't* be in that ratio. I have finished the *Mind in the Making*** and agree with you about it. But I think the man has read his Wells "not wisely but too Wells" – to make a rotten epipun (also a new word).

As you've probably noticed my story leads off the current *Post* which delights me. I wish it were a better story. It has fine illustrations. I do not expect ever to reprint it.

The Kilmarnock Books here have ordered 250 copies of my book & may order more. They are spending $216.00 on an advertising moving picture to be shown in all St. Paul theatres, which will have a picture of me, of the store with the windows full of the B.&D., a close up of the book & the title in big letters. It will be quite a thing. They would appreciate any advertising data your Mr. Myers could send them. T. A. Boyd†† who is only 22 is owner of the shop. It is his wife who wrote *The Love Legend* concerning which I wired you.[17] He also runs the book page in *The St. Paul Daily News*, which he has made the best book page west of the Hudson.

---

*Published as "The Diamond as Big as the Ritz."

†A Scribners salesman, assigned to the Midwest.

**By James Harvey Robinson.

††Novelist and critic Thomas A. Boyd, most famous for his *Through the Wheat*, published by Scribners in 1923.

Altogether, according to my scrapbook my name has appeared on it over forty times since I came to St. Paul. (These two sentences look funny together! Ha-Ha!) He has advertised me in a hundred ways & will do so much more – special announcements of my book, and a big two column review to appear when the book comes out. Do you think you could manage to have an add or two for the book appear in his page on consecutive Sundays?

As to the advertising. It seems to me that after the first blurb in *The New Repub[l]ic* & periodicals of that class it would be best to concentrate on the newspapers – say the *N.Y. World* on the page with Broun & F.P.A. or the *Chi Tribune* on Hanson's* page or even the N. Y. Tribune, tho I believe the book buyers of the latter (followers of Broun & F.P.A.) have switched to the *World.* What I mean is that the readers of the literary periodicals know me pretty well by this time and any extended campaigne in *The Bookman* ect would be carrying coals to Newcastle – anyways I *think* it would. What do you think.

The Forsyte Saga is quite an achievement in the way its gotten up. The more I think of that *selling points* you wrote for the B.&D. the more I think it ought to be included in the book itself. Its a wonder! Knapp thinks so too & everyone I've shown it to.

Someone told me the other day that they thot the *Metropolitan* would fail – someone who's pretty close to gossip down there. But Reynolds doesn't think so & keeps shovelling my stories at them. They have one now they accepted in September they havn't paid a cent for & Reynolds has just sent them another. I have two weeks more work on my play – which is a perfect sure-fire marvel – and I am at my wits end how to carry on until I finish it. With fear and trembling I approach you for $500.00 – which would, if you could give it to me, make a total of about $4,500 above the sales to date of *Paradise* & *Flappers.* I am aware that this constitutes a large advance, but with the book at $2.00 it is only an advance on a sale of 13,000 copies – and as you have printed up about 40,000 it is really not much of a risk with publication less than two weeks off.

Will you wire me only if you can *not* deposit $500.00 in the Chatham & Phenix Bank, 33d St.

(How many times have I written that sentence!)

Yours Ever

---

*Heywood Broun, Franklin P. Adams and Harry Hansen, respectively, all of whom were columnists and book reviewers.

626 *Goodrich Ave.*
St. Paul, Minn.
[*ca. March 5, 1922*]

Dear Mr. Perkins –
This is to thank you for the money.[18] I was in a tight place – had actually cashed a bad check & didn't know it. However the Metropolitan has begun to pay a little & I think I'm out of the woods.

When I wrote you about *The Mind in the Making* I'd only read two chapters. I have finished it & entirely changed my views on its importance. I think its a thoroughly excellent book. It states the entire case for modernity's lingering hope of progress. It is a depressing book, I think, as are Well's & Shaw's late things and all those of that brave company who started out in the nineties so full of hope and joy in life and faith in science and reason. Thomas Hardy survives them all. I think when I read Upton Sinclaires *The Brass Check* I made my final descision about America – that freedom has produced the greatest tyrrany under the sun. I'm still a socialist but sometimes I dread that things will grow worse and worse the more the people nominally rule. The strong are too strong for us and the weak too weak. I shall not right another novel for a year but when I do it will not be a realistic one. At least I don't think it will.

The more I think of the B & D's chances the more I think that your blurb will save it if anything can.[19]

Nathan writes me: "A very substantial performance. There is a wealth of sound stuff in it. You are maturing rapidly. It pleases me to have so good a piece of work dedicated in part to me.[20] You have done a first rate job."

I don't want to use this though as he's funny about that sort of thing.

I've read my book over and I've decided that I like it fine. I think it is as good as *Three Soldiers* – which is high praise from me.

The Knopf man was here awhile ago & I had quite a talk with him in Boyd's bookstore. It seemed to me that he was personally dishonest & utterly disloyal to his company – that is he was trying to sell one of his sample books and he said that "Knopf was as honest as any publisher" with a wink! I doubt if Knopf gives his authors a full 15% on those $2.50 books – of course he shouldn't as they cost more. I had an interesting time with Hergeshiemer* – he came through & came to dinner. However what I started to say was how favorably Knapp compared with the Knopf man.

Please don't get the impression that I was fooled by the size of the St. Paul orders. I knew they were chiefly "on sale". I think I'm going to have a great non-fiction book ready for you about next January. And if my play is a big success will you bring it out in book form – or do you think its best

*Novelist Joseph Hergesheimer.

to wait until I have three of them, as O'Niell has done following Shaw & Barrie & Galesworthy.

I'm glad you liked "In One Reel". Wait till you see the stories. You havn't seen half of them. Read "Chrome Yellow".* Best to Roger.† Knapp seemed devoted to you, which was our chief bond of union.

Yours Ever

April 17, 1922

Dear Fitzgerald:

"The Beautiful and Damned" is going on at about the same pace it held when you were here. It has sold about 33,000 copies actually. I doubt if we can hope that it will be an overwhelming success now, but when you speak of me as being disappointed,[21] you're wrong. I think the book has consolidated your position, so to speak, – has convinced people that as Sidney Howard says, "This Side of Paradise" was very far indeed from being all. Of course I wanted it to sell a hundred thousand or more and I hoped that the extraordinary exhilaration of your style from paragraph to paragraph might make it do so in spite of the fact that it was a tragedy and necessarily unpleasant because of its nature, so that its principal elements were not of such a kind as in themselves to recommend it to the very great mass of readers who read purely for entertainment and nothing else. Now, at least this book is going to have a pretty large sale. The trade are going to get rid of it easily. It has made a stir among the discriminating and has therefore been all to the good except from the most purely commercial viewpoint. I know that that is an important viewpoint to you as well as to us; but for our part we are backing you for a long race and are more than ever convinced that you will win it.

. . . . .

As ever,

May 11th, [1922] 626 goodrich

Dear Mr. Perkins:

After careful consideration by The Fitzgerald menage, two book sellers & several friends I am strongly in favor of keeping the "Jazz Age" title.[22] Here's my line of reasoning

(1.) If it were a novel I should say the salesmen were undoubtedly right – the word flapper or jazz would be passé & kill a big sale.

---

*A novel by Aldous Huxley.
†Probably Roger Burlingame, a Scribners editor.

(2.) Short stories do not sell and "Flappers" was an exception chiefly on account of my 1st novel & what was then the timeliness of the title.

(3.) I do not expect the new collection to have an advance sale of more than four or five thousand & the total will never reach more than nine or ten thousand (that is the first year or so.

(4) It will be bought by *my own personal public*, that is by the countless flappers and college kids who think I am a sort of oracle.

(5) The question of *Jazz* or *not Jazz* is a Sylla & Charbydis anyhow. If I use such a title as *Half Portions* ect or *Chance Encounters* no one will buy it anyhow – it will just be another book of short stories. It is better to have a title & a title-connection that is a has-been than one that is a never-will-be. The splash of the flapper movement was too big to have quite died down – the outer rings are still moving.

(6) If I could think of a wonderful selling title unconnected with Jazz I'd use it but I can't, so we better use a safe one that has a certain appeal. Short story collections are the hardest things on earth to name – to get a title which is at once arresting, inviting, applicable and inclusive and doesn't sound like a rehash of the titles of O. Henry, or isn't an aenemic Namby Pamby wishy-washy phrase.

(7.) In any case I think it will be wise to under-sell the booksellers – a few, I fear from your silence, are going to be stuck with The B. & D. and though *Flappers* seems to be still trickling along there are two book-stores in St Paul that have quite a few left –

(8) The only possible other title I can think of is *The Diamond as Big as the Ritz* – and other stories. I hate titles like *Sideshow* and *In One Reel* & *Happy End* They have begun to sound like viels [veils] and apologies for bringing out collections at all. Only good short story titles lately are *Limbo* & *Seven Men.** I might possibly call my book *Nine Humans and Fourteen Dummies* if you'd permit such a long title (in this case I'd have to figure out how many humans & how many dummies there are in the collection) – but if you feel awfully strongly against "Jazz Age", I insist that it be an arresting title if it spreads over half the front cover.

Please let me know at once what you think.

I'm sure in any case the stories will be reviewed a great deal, largely because of the *Table of Contents.*†

*By Aldous Huxley and Max Beerbohm, respectively.
†The Table of Contents was annotated with Fitzgerald's comments on each story.

Wire me if nessessary.

As Ever

. . . . .

The Yatch Club, White Bear Lakes, Minn.
[*ca.* June 20, 1922]

Dear Mr. Perkins:

The first four stories, those that will comprise the section "My Last Flappers" left here several days ago. The second four, "Fantasies" leave either this afternoon or tomorrow morning. And the last three "And So Forth" will leave here on the 24th (Sat.) & should reach you Tuesday without fail. I'm sorry I've been so slow on this – there's no particular excuse except liquor and of course that isn't any. But I vowed I'd finish a travel article & thank God its done at last.

Don't forget that I want another proof of the Table of Contents. There's been one addition to the first section and one substitution in the 3d. Its damn good now, far superior to *Flappers* & the title, jacket & other books ought to sell at least 10,000 copies and I hope 15,000. You can see from the ms. how I've changed the stories. I cut out my last Metropolitan story not because it wasn't technically excellent but simply because it lacked vitality. The only story about which I'm in doubt is *The Camel's Back*. But I've decided to use it – it has some excellent comedy & was in one O. Henry Collection – though of course that's against it. Here are some suggested blurbs.

1. Contains the famous "Porcelain and Pink Story" – the bath-tub classic – as well as "The Curious Case of Benjamin Button" and nine other tales. In this book Mr. F. has developed his gifts as a satiric humorist to a point rivalled by few if any living American writers. The lazy meanderings of a brilliant and powerful imagination.

2. TALES OF THE JAZZ AGE

   Satyre upon a Saxaphone by the most brilliant of the younger novelists. He sets down "My Last Flappers" and then proceeds in section two to fresher and more fantastic fields. You may like or dislike his work but it will never bore you.

3. TALES OF THE JAZZ AGE

   Have you met "Mr. Icky" and followed the ghastly carreer of "Benjamin Button"? A medly of Bath-tubs, diamond mountains, Fitzgerald Flappers and Jellybeans.
   Ten acts of lustrous farce – and one other.

That's probably pretty much bunk but I'm all for advertising it as a cheerful book and not as "eleven of Mr. Fitzgerald's best stories by the y.a. of T.S.O.P."

———————

Thank you immensely for the $1000.00. and also for the Phila. Ledger picture. Has the book gone over 40,000 yet? I'm delighted you like Boyd.* He hasn't a very original mind – that is: he's too young to be quite his own man intellectually but he's on the right track & if he can read much more of the 18th century – and the middle ages and ease up on the moderns he'll grow at an amazing rate. When I send on this last bunch of stories I may start my novel and I may not. Its locale will be the middle west and New York of 1885 I think. It will concern less superlative beauties than I run to usually & will be centered on a smaller period of time. It will have a catholic element. I'm not quite sure whether I'm ready to start it quite yet or not.[23] I'll write next week & tell you more definate plans.

As Ever

August 2, 1922

Dear Fitzgerald:
The proof girl – the girl you admired for hirsute reasons – the girl someone said looked like 'a lighted match' – whose mind is preoccupied with tennis racquets and bathing suits just now – sent those galleys back to the press instead of to you;[24] so they went into pages and you will so see them and are justified in making free with corrections.

But here is a matter: will you omit "Tarquin of Cheapside?" I never before read it and I think it would shock many people not because of the particular crime recorded, but because of the identity of the man accused of it.† The crime is a peculiarly repugnant one for it involves violence, generally requires unconsciousness, is associated with negroes. All this would make no difference, or little, if the story were artistically convincing: I don't think it is. The narrative is not adequate to the ending. The poem, with its philosophical beginning and all, does not suggest (I think) the psychology of an author in the situation you present. Anyhow, this is my view, – for your consideration, if you will give it.

As ever,

---

*Thomas A. Boyd.
†William Shakespeare, who is depicted as a rapist.

The Yatch Club
White Bear Lake
Minn
[ca. August 12, 1922]

Dear Mr. Perkins –

I've labored over these proofs for a week and feel as if I never want to see a short story again. . . . You ought to penalize the lighted-match-girl twenty yards.

Now as to *Tarquin of Cheapside.* It first appeared in the Nassau Literary Magazine at Princeton and Katherine Fullerton Gerrould reviewing the issue for the Daily Princetonian gave it high praise, called it "beautifully written" and tickled me with the first public praise my writing has ever had. When Mencken printed it in the Smart set it drew letters of praise from George O'Niell, the poet and Zoe Akins. Structurally it is almost perfect and next to *The Off-Shore Pirate* I like it better than any story I have ever written.

If you insist I will cut it out though very much against my better judgement and Zelda's. It was even starred by O'Brien* in his year book of the short story and mentioned by Blanche Colton Williams in the preface to the last O. Henry Memorial Collection. Please tell me what you think.

As to another matter. My play, *Gabriel's Trombone* is now in the hands of Arthur Hopkins. It is, I think, the best American comedy to date & undoubtedly the best thing I have ever written. Noting that Harpers are serializing "The Intimate Strangers", a play by Booth Tarkington I wonder if Scribners Magazine would be interested in serializing *Gabriel's Trombone* that is, of course, on condition that it is to be produced this fall. Will you let me know about this or shall I write Bridges.

Also, last but not least, I have not yet recieved a statement from you. I am awfully hard up. I imagine there's something over $1000.00 still in my favor. Anyways will you deposit a $1000.00 for me when you recieve this letter. If there's not that much due me will you charge off the rest as advance on *Tales of the Jazz Age?* After my play is produced I'll be rich forever and never have to bother you again.

Also let me know about the *Tarquin* matter & about *Gabriel's Trombone.*

As Ever

. . . . .

*Edward O'Brien, who annually published a collection of the year's best short fiction which had originally appeared in magazines and used a system of stars to rate other outstanding stories which he did not reprint.

August 15, 1922.

Dear Fitzgerald:

I enclose herewith royalty report due on August 1st, and as I wired yesterday, I have deposited the money in your bank.

I'm mightily interested to hear about the play. It would be most unusual if we should publish a play in Scribner's, but we have no rule against it and would like to consider the possibility. I'll tell you, – send it to me for I'm eager to read it, and let me take it up with Mr. Bridges. Perhaps you haven't a copy now but whenever you can give me one. We'll see what can be done.

As for "Tarquin", I have left it in. If it has not affected those you name in the way I feared it certainly should please the public. My objections anyway are in a sense extraneous to the story. They simply arise from the fact that people have a sort of reverence for Shakespeare, although of course they know that he was none too well behaved.

As ever,

[*ca. December 26, 1922*]

COMMENT ON "FROST"[25]

(To save space I've omitted most of the "I thinks," "It seems to mes," and "I may be wrong buts": they should, however, be understood)

I've read your play three times and I think more highly of its possibilities on the third reading than ever before; – but I am also more strongly convinced that these possibilities are far from being realized on account of the handling of the story in the second act. The reader feels, at the end, confused and unsatisfied: – the underlying motive of the play has not been sent home. And yet this motive, or idea, has been sufficiently perceived to prevent the play from being a sheer burlesque, like a comic opera. In the second act it seems to me that you yourself have almost thought it *was* that.

The underlying idea, a mighty good one, is expressed, or should be, in the story of Jerry Frost.

God meant Jerry to be a good egg and a postman; but having been created, in a democratic age, Free and Equal, he was persuaded that he ought to want to rise in the world and so had become a railroad clerk against his taste and capacity, and thought he ought to want to become President. He is therefore very unhappy, and so is his wife, who holds the same democratic doctrine.

Your story shows, or should, that this doctrine is sentimental bunk; and to do this is worthwhile because the doctrine is almost universal: Jerry and his wife are products of a theory of democracy which you reduce to the absurd. The idea is so good that if you hold to it and continuously develop it, your play, however successful simply as fun, will be deeply significant as well.

Moreover, the means you have selected to develop the idea are superb – the bootlegger, the super-jag his concoction induces, Jerry thereby becoming President, etc. (and dreams have a real validity nowadays on account of Freud). In fact all your machinery for expressing the idea is exactly in the tune of the time and inherently funny and satirical.

But when you come to the second act, which is the critical point in the play, and so in the expression of your idea, you seem to lose sense of your true motive. Partly, this is because you have three motives here, the main motive of Jerry's story and its meaning, and two subordinate motives – (1) of conveying through the fantastic visions and incidents which are the stuff of a dream caused by a 1923 prohibition brew, *the sense of a comic nightmare*, and (2) of satirizing the general phenomena of our national scene. You have, I think, simply got more or less lost in the maze of these three motives by a failure to follow the green line of the chief one – Jerry's actual story, or that stage of it which shows him that he *doesn't* want to be President. Satirize as much as you can, the government, the army, and everything else, and be as fantastic as you please, but keep one eye always on your chief motive. Throughout the entire wild second act there should still be a kind of *wild logic*.

Aside then from imparting in this act the sense of a dream, you are using the difficult weapon of double edged satire – you are satirizing the conception held by Jerry and his like of the High Offices of President, Secretary of the Treasury, etc., and you are at the same time satirizing those high offices themselves. You begin excellently by making all the appertenances of the Presidency, like the house, white; and the behavior of Jerry's wife and sister-in-law are all within the scope of your purpose. The conduct of Dada as Secretary of the Treasury seems as though it ought to be a fine piece of two edged satire cutting both against the popular idea of the business of that official and against the official himself as he usually is, but the psychology of it is not made quite comprehensible; and the best instance of double satire is seen when General Pushing appears with fifer and drummer and medals – that is just the right note. Why couldn't you do the same for bankers, and senators, etc.?

Maybe I can better express what I mean by examples. The selection of so obscure a man as Jerry for President is itself the stuff of satire in view of present political methods, and much could be made of it. The coffin episode as you use it results as things do in a dream from Jerry's talk with Fish etc. and so it helps to give the sense of a dream, and that is all it does.

But suppose coffins were being cornered by "The He-Americans Bloodred Preparedness League" as a preparedness measure, and that this was tied up with General Pushing's feeling that a war was needed: – that would be a hit at extravagant patriotism and militarism as well as having its present value as part of a dream. Suppose the deal over the Buzzard Isles resulted in the Impeachment of Jerry – what a chance that would give to treat the Senate as you have the general and the Army, and also to bring Jerry's affairs to a climax. You could have Jerry *convicted*, and then (as a hit at a senatorial filibuster) you could have his party place the Stutz-Mozart Ourangatang Band outside the Capitol (it would have appeared for the wedding of Fish), and every time the Justices of the Supreme Court began in chorus to pronounce the sentence, Stutz-Mozart would strike up the National Anthem in syncopated time and everyone would have to stand at attention. At present, the narrative of the second act lacks all logic; the significance of the approaching end of the world eludes me, – except as a dreamer's way of getting release from a desperate situation.

I've now used a great many words to make this single point: – each part of the second act should do three things – add to the quality of a fantastic dream, satirize Jerry and his family as representing a large class of Americans, and satirize the government or army or whatever institution is at the moment in use. And my only excuse for all this verbiage is, that so good in conception is your motive, so true your characters, so splendidly imaginative your invention, and so altogether above the mere literary the whole scheme, that no one could help but greatly desire to see it all equalled in execution. If it were a comparative trifle, like many a short story, it wouldn't much matter.[26]

[*January 1923*]

IDEAS FOR "FROST"*

Cover by John Held –
    Either

(1.) Cover something like the Jazz Age, with a different color background and little figures – Dada, Jerry, Doris, Charlotte, Fish, Snooks and Gen Pershing scattered over it

or (2) A Jazz picture of the proposed set for Scene I, Act II – with small figures of the principles in a characteristic scene on the lawn of the White House

*Although undated and unsigned, this page is written in Fitzgerald's handwriting.

Book bound, of course, like my others & made *thick*. It must be more than 40,000 words long and it seems to me could be made as thick as Gale's *Lulu Bett* which is only 30,000, rather than thin like the original thin edition of Ethan Fromme which is about the same length.

To be advertised, it seems to me rather as a book of humor, like the Parody outline of History or Seventeen than like a play – because of course it is written to be read.

I suggest that I write a preface to it – we can discuss this immediately

To be printed, it seems to me, rather as "Dulcy" was printed than as a Shaw play is printed. I mean with lots of space. I havn't seen a Barrie play recently but I suppose your own method is probably the best. At any rate the way the typist has prepared this with the capitalizing of all "He's" ect. is *all wrong* as you'll see.

A page to be inserted, reading

By F. Scott Fitzgerald

Novels
This Side of Paradise
The Beautiful & Damned

Stories
Flappers & Philosophers
Tales of the Jazz Age

And a Comedy
Frost

If its not too late I'd like the subtitle "or from President to postman" (note small p.) put on title page. At least it should be used in advertising.

On the next page is a suggested blurb to be used either on the back of the jacket if not too late or on a mimeographed loose notice put in the front of each book sent to a critic. If used on the back of the [jacket] it could be run together with the blurb you already have. I want to talk to you about this.

On second thoughts I have not mentioned Wilson or Nathan by name in the blurb. Their support will be more valuable later.

Incidently God help the poor typesetter!

6 Pleasant Ave.
Montgomery, Ala.
[ca. March 1923]

Dear Mr. Perkins:

I'm awfully curious to hear any new opinions on the book* so when Whitney Darrow or anyone else who hasn't read it, reads it, do let me know. I expect to be here about a week or 10 days longer. I'm working on the "treatment"† of *This Side of Paradise*. They've paid me $1000. and are to pay $9000. more on delivery of this so I'm anxious to get it down by the first.

I'll want two extra galley proofs of the play if its convenient, to send to the managers.

I have a few changes for Act III, bits of polyphonic prose that I'm going to insert. Its good weather here but I'm rather miserable and depressed about life in general. Being in this town where the emotions of my youth culminated in one emotion makes me feel old and tired. I doubt if, after all I'll ever write anything again worth putting in print.

As Ever

Great Neck.
[ca. November 5, 1923]

Dear Max:

I have got myself into a terrible mess. As you know for the past month I have been coming every day to the city to rehearsals** and then at night writing and making changes on the last act and even on the first two. Its in shape at last and everybody around the theatre who has seen it says its a great hit. I put aside the novel three weeks ago and wrote a short story but it was done under such pressure that it shows it and Hovey doesn't want it. I am so hard pressed now for time trying to write another for him that I'm not even going [to] the Harvard Princeton game Saturday. The show opens in Atlantic City a week from Monday.

I went up to the American Play Company yesterday and tried to get some money on the grounds that the show was in rehearsal. They sighed and moaned a little but said firmly that it was against their rules.

I'm at the end of my rope – as the immortal phrase goes. I owe the Scribner Company something over $3,500.00 even after deducting the

---

*Fitzgerald's play *The Vegetable*, which Scribners published in May of 1923.
†For the movies.
**Of his play *The Vegetable*.

reprint money from the Beautiful and Damned. I owed them more than that before the B. & D. was published but that was garanteed by the book being actually in your hands.

Could this be done. Could I assign the 1st royalty payments on the play to you to be paid until the full amount be cleared up? I meant to pay some of it if there was a margin anyhow on account of the delay in the novel. But this would at least garantee it.

What I need to extricate myself from the present hole is $650.00 which will carry me to the 15th when Hovey will have my next story. And the only grounds on which I can ask for this additional is for me to assign you those rights up to the figure outstanding and to include also the interest on the whole amount I owe you.

If I don't in some way get $650 in the bank by Wedensday morning I'll have to pawn the furniture. Under the assignment of the royalties to you the full amount would be paid back at between 500.00 and 1,100.00 a week before January 15th.

I don't even dare come up there personally but for God's sake try to fix it.

Yours in Horror

Jan. 25, 1924

Dear Scott:
We have now these stories by Ring Lardner:*

> The Facts
> A Caddy's Diary
> Some Like Them Cold
> Champion
> "Along Came Ruth"
> A Frame-Up
> Golden Honeymoon

That is, two stories about prize fighters, one about baseball, one about golf, and two not about sport at all. This would make quite a representative collection. There is a good deal of variety too in the nature of the stories. "Champion" is a grim story almost. "Some Like Them Cold," about a flirtation, while exceedingly funny, is at the same time piercing; – at least I found it so. It is much more than a funny story. "The Facts" is simply exceedingly amusing, but it is not told in the manner of the baseball

---

*Fitzgerald had recommended that Scribners and Perkins look at Ring Lardner's stories with the object of publishing them in a collected volume.

stories. "A Caddy's Diary" is more the same sort of story as "Some Like Them Cold" but is not poignant. Taken all together these stories show various sides of Ring Lardner's talent. They include two of the three Post stories I have been trying to get. And the only reason I haven't got the third is that the date he gave me was evidently incorrect for I got the number and found no story. These stories would line up very well with that preface he gave us.

I have read "The Big Town"* and liked it greatly and I have looked over "Symptoms of Being 35"* with great amusement. But "My Four Weeks in France"* was not so good. I wish you would come in and talk about this matter some time soon. I would like to take up with Mr. Scribner the matter of publishing a book of stories right off.

As ever,

Great Neck
[*Long Island*]
[*ca. April 10, 1924*][27]

Dear Max:
A few words more relative to our conversation this afternoon. While I have every hope & plan of finishing my novel in June you know how those things often come out. And even [if] it takes me 10 times that long I cannot let it go out unless it has the very best I'm capable of in it or even as I feel sometimes, something better than I'm capable of. Much of what I wrote last summer was good but it was so interrupted that it was ragged & in approaching it from a new angle I've had to discard a lot of it – in one case 18,000 words (part of which will appear in the Mercury as a short story).†
It is only in the last four months that I've realized how much I've – well, almost *deteriorated* in the three years since I finished the Beautiful and Damned. The last four months of course I've worked but in the two years – over two years – before that, I produced exactly *one* play, *half a dozen* short stories and three or four articles – an average of about *one hundred* words a day. If I'd spent this time reading or travelling or doing anything – even staying healthy – it'd be different but I spent it uselessly, niether in study nor in contemplation but only in drinking and raising hell generally. If I'd written the B & D at the rate of 100 words a day it would have taken me *4 years* so you can imagine the moral effect the whole chasm had on me.

What I'm trying to say is just that I'll have to ask you to have patience about the book and trust me that at last, or at least for the 1st time in years,

---

*These are additional pieces by Lardner.
†"Absolution," published in June 1924.

I'm doing the best I can. I've gotten in dozens of bad habits that I'm trying to get rid of.

1. Laziness.

2. Referring everything to Zelda – a terrible habit, nothing ought to be referred to anybody until its finished

3. Word consciousness – self doubt

ect. ect. ect. ect.

I feel I have an enormous power in me now, more than I've ever had in a way but it works so fitfully and with so many bogeys because I've *talked so much* and not lived enough within myself to develop the nessessary self reliance. Also I don't know anyone who has used up so much personal experience as I have at 27. Copperfield & Pendennis were written at past forty while This Side of Paradise was three books & the B. & D. was two. So in my new novel I'm thrown directly on purely creative work – not trashy imaginings as in my stories but the sustained imagination of a sincere and yet radiant world. So I tread slowly and carefully & at times in considerable distress. This book will be a consciously artistic achievement & must depend on that as the 1st books did not.

If I ever win the right to any liesure again I will assuredly not waste it as I wasted this past time. Please believe me when I say that now I'm doing the best I can.

Yours Ever

April 16, 1924

Dear Scott:

I delayed answering your letter because I wanted to answer it at length. I was delighted to get it. But I have been so pressed with all sorts of things that I have not had time to write as I meant and I am not doing so now. I do not want to delay sending some word on one or two points.

For instance, I understand exactly what you have to do and I know that all these superficial matters of exploitation and so on are not of the slightest consequence along side of the importance of your doing your very best work the way you want to do it; – that is, according to the demands of the situation. So far as we are concerned, you are to go ahead at just your own pace, and if you should finish the book when you think you will, you will have performed a very considerable feat even in the matter of time, it seems to me.

My view of the future is – particularly in the light of your letter – one of very great optimism and confidence.

The only thing is, that if we had a title which was likely, but by no means sure to be the title, we could prepare a cover and a wrap and hold them in readiness for use. In that way, we would gain several weeks if we should find that we were to have the book this fall. We would be that much to the good. Otherwise we should have done no harm. If we sold the book under a title which was later changed, no harm would have been done either. I always thought that "The Great Gatsby" was a suggestive and effective title, – with only the vaguest knowledge of the book, of course. But anyway, the last thing we want to do is to divert you to any degree, from your actual writing, and if you let matters rest just as they are now, we shall be perfectly satisfied. The book is the thing and all the rest is inconsiderable beside it.

Yours,

June 5, 1924

Dear Scott:

. . . . .

I am glad you are deep in Milton and Byron. Trevelyan wrote an exceed- ingly interesting book about both of them – perhaps you have read it. I came across it in college. He told about how Shelley not only had that physical peculiarity which prevented his heart from burning, but that other one of sinking to the very bottom of a pool when Trevelyan told him that all a man needed to swim was self-confidence. No ordinary human being would, of course, sink to a depth of more than three feet or so. There was also a most interesting book by James Hogg about Shelley. Oh, I was a great Shelley fan, and I never fully got over it, though people think badly of him now.

I read your story in the Mercury and it seemed to me very good indeed, and also different from what you had done before, – it showed a more steady and complete mastery, it seemed to me. Greater maturity might be the word. At any rate it gave me a more distinct sense of what you could do, – possibly because I have not read any of your other stories in the magazines except "How to Live on Thirty-six Thousand"* which of course was a trifle. This seemed to show a remarkable strength and re- source. I was greatly impressed by it.

Did you get the "War and Peace"? Don't feel any obligation to read it because it is better that you should follow your inclination, and time is valuable. The reason I mention it is that it did not get on the steamer† in

* "How tŏ Live on $36,000 a Year," an article published in the *Saturday Evening Post*, on April 5, 1924.
† The Fitzgeralds had sailed for Europe for the summer.

spite of the assurances of office boys, etc., that it would, and so I had to send it by mail.

The reason I went down to Ring Lardner's – but I am ashamed to tell you about it. I meant to have a serious talk with him, but we arrived late and the drinks were already prepared. We did no business that night. He was very amusing. The book* is out – you will have had your copy of it. The reviews have been excellent and so far as the reviewers are concerned, the title got across perfectly. I will pick out a bunch of clippings and send them after certain others like H.L.M.† have been heard from. So far there has not been much of a sale, but all the publicity we have got ought to accomplish something for us. . . .

. . . . .

Yours,

Villa Marie, Valescure
St. Raphael, France
June 18th, 1924

Dear Max:

Thanks for your nice long letter. I'm glad that Ring's had good reviews but I'm sorry both that he's off the wagon & that the books not selling. I had counted on a sale of 15 to 25 thousand right away for it.

Shelley was a God to me once. What a good man he is compared to that collosal egotist Browning! Havn't you read *Ariel* yet? For heaven's sake read it if you like Shelley. Its one of the best biographies I've ever read of anyone & its by a Frenchman. I think Harcourt publishes it. And who "thinks *badly*" of Shelley now?

We are idyllicly settled here & the novel is going fine – it ought to be done in a month – though I'm not sure as I'm contemplating another 16,000 words which would make it about the length of Paradise – not quite though even then.

I'm glad you liked *Absolution*. As you know it was to have been the prologue of the novel but it interfered with the neatness of the plan. Two Catholics have already protested by letter. Be sure & read "The Baby Party" in Hearsts & my article in the Woman's Home Companion.**

Tom Boyd wrote me that Bridges had been a dodo about some Y.M.C.A. man – I wrote him that he oughtn't to fuss with such a silly old man. I hope

How to Write Short Stories [*With Samples*] by Ring Lardner.
†American journalist, essayist and literary critic H. L. Mencken.
**"Wait Till You Have Children of Your Own."

he hasn't – you don't mention him in your letter. I enjoyed Arthur Trains story in the Post but he made three steals on the 1st page – one from Shaw (the Arabs remark about Christianity) one from Stendahl & one I've forgotten. It was most ingeniously worked out. I never could have handled such an intricate plot in a thousand years. War & Peace came – many thanks & for the inscription too. Don't forget the clippings. I will have to reduce my tax in Sept.

As Ever, Yours

P.S. If Struthers Burt* comes over give me his address.

Villa Marie
Valescure
St. Raphael, France
[ca. July 10, 1924]

Dear Max:
Is Ring dead? We've written him three times & not a word. How about his fall book. I had two suggestions. Either a collection called Mother Goose in Great Neck (or something nonsensical, to include his fairy tales in Hearsts, some of his maddest syndicate articles, his Forty-niners' Sketch, his Authors League Sketch ect.
   – or "My Life and Loves" (Privately printed for subscribers only – on sale at all bookstores). I believe I gave you a tentative list for that but he'd have to eke it out by printing some new syndacate articles that way. I thought his short story book was *great* – Alibi Ike, Some Like 'em Cold & My Rooney are as good almost as the Golden Honeymoon. Menckens review was great. Do send me others. Is it selling?
   Would you do me this favor? Call up Harvey Craw, 5th Ave – he's in the book and ask him if my house is rented. I'm rather curious to know & letters bring me no response. He is the Great Neck agent.
   I'm not going to mention my novel to you again until it is on your desk. All goes well. I wish your bookkeeper would send me the August statement even tho no copies of my book have been sold. How about Gertrude's Steins novel?† I began *War & Peace* last night. So write me a nice long letter.

As Ever

---

*A poet, essayist and novelist whose works were published by Scribners. Perkins had expressed the hope that Burt and Fitzgerald would meet.
   † *The Making of Americans*, then running serially in the *Transatlantic Review*.

August 8, 1924

Dear Scott:

I had yesterday a disillusioning afternoon at Great Neck, not in respect to Ring Lardner, who gains on you whenever you see him, but in respect to Durant's where he took me for lunch. I thought [about] that night a year ago that we ran down a steep place into a lake. There was no steep place and no lake. We sat on a balcony in front. It was dripping hot and Durant took his police dog down to the margin of that puddle of a lily pond, – the dog waded almost across it; – and I'd been calling it a lake all these months. But they've put up a fence to keep others from doing as we did.

About the renting of your house, which has been accomplished, you have heard from Ring Lardner, who says he will see you at Hyeres during September. He did not look well and he coughed. He ate almost nothing and smoked while he ate that. He ordered high-balls. I said I didn't want anything at all; but he stuck to one for himself and so later I took one. I saw no further use in denying myself. We had a number. But Ring told me that to-morrow he would drop both liquor and nicotine so as to do enough work to go safely abroad. He won't drop the strip: – the artist hasn't an idea in his head and counts upon Ring for his living; – is even building a house on the strength of the association. I'd gone through Ring's syndicate articles and found much good in them; and he told me of articles in Liberty and then there are the Hearst articles. I proposed a book selection from all these, – I to select and he to approve, or otherwise; and of this he thought well. But that's for 1925: we hope to carry over the stories through the fall and have planned advertising for mid-August. This Sunday there's to be an excellent ad in the Times. I'll send it over.

Then I proposed that *we* try to acquire the Doran and Bobbs Merrill books[28] ourselves, – if possible, by frank but tactful correspondence, and get prefaces for them and carry them on our lists for the trade and at the same time form a set of five volumes: – a magazine and subscription set such as you first proposed. He thought well of this.

Then I said, "Ring, if it were a matter of money we would be willing to help toward a novel, you know. But I judge the $5,000 or so we'd gladly put up wouldn't count." And of course he said it wasn't at all a question of money: – but I wanted him to know we were ready to back him anyway.

Great Neck is Great Neck even when the Fitzgeralds are elsewhere. He told me of a newcomer who'd made money in the drug business – not dope but the regular line. This gentleman had evidently taken to Ring. One morning he called early with another man and a girl and Ring was not dressed. But he hurried down, unshaven. He was introduced to the *girl only* and he said he was sorry to appear that way but didn't want to keep them waiting while he shaved.

At this the drug man signals the other, who goes to the car for a black bag and from it produces razors, strops, etc., etc., and publicly shaves Ring. *This* was the drug man's private barber; the girl was his private manicurist. But as he was lonely he had made them also his companions. Ring declares this is true!

We're living in a quiet cottage near New Canaan. You would hate it but I like it. The nearest we've come to a party was a "beefsteak supper" on the Heyward Broun or Ruth Hale estate,* – an abandoned farm of 100 acres, a ruin of thickets, grass-grown roads, broken walls and decaying orchards. About the only person I knew there, really, among a rather Semitic-looking crowd, was snakey little Johnny Weaver,† – and that didn't help much. But I had a swim in the lake with Heyward and a man whose name I've forgot. Ruth Hale led me instantly to the punch and filled me a cup because, she said, "I long to see an Evarts** drunk"; – and she added, "I loathe all Evartses": – she knew some, for her brother, who died – and I liked him much – married a cousin of mine; and during his long, terrible illness there was war between the families as to his care, and I don't know which acted the more crazily. But the Evartses in general are rigorous for duty, the rights of property, the established church, the Republican Party, etc. I suppose that's what sets her against them.

Your standing with the public was never better. I'm always hearing people tell the ideas of your new stories. The novel, if it comes soon, will come at a good time. How will Hovey's leaving Hearst affect serialization? But I'm afraid you'll have to serialize.

My regards to Zelda.

Yours,

> *Villa Marie, Valescure*
> *St. Raphael, France*
> *[ca. August 25, 1924]*

Dear Max:

1. The novel will be done next week. That doesn't mean however that it'll reach America before October 1st. as Zelda and I are contemplating a careful revision after a weeks complete rest.

2   The clippings have never arrived.

---

*Columnist-critic Heywood Broun and reviewer-critic Ruth Hale were married from 1917 to 1933.

†John V. A. Weaver, American critic, poet and playwright.

**Evarts was Perkins' mother's family name.

3. Seldes* has been with me and he thinks "For the Grimalkins" is a wonderful title for Rings book. Also I've got great ideas about "My Life and Loves" which I'll tell Ring when he comes over in September.

4   How many copies has his short stories sold?

5   Your bookkeeper never did send me my royalty report for Aug 1st.

6   For Christs sake don't give anyone that jacket you're saving for me. I've written it into the book.†

7   I think my novel is about the best American novel ever written. It is rough stuff in places, runs only to about 50,000 words & I hope you won't shy at it

8   Its been a fair summer. I've been unhappy but my work hasn't suffered from it. I am grown at last.

9. What books are being talked about. I don't mean bestsellers. Hergeshiemers novel in the Post** seems vile to me.

10. I hope you're reading Gertrude Steins novel in the *Transatlantic Review*.

11 Raymond Radiguets best book (he is the young man who wrote *"Le diable au Corps"* at sixteen [untranslatable]††) is a great hit here. He wrote it at 18. Its called *"Le Bal de Compte Orgel"* & though I'm only half through it I'd get an opinion on it if I were you. Its cosmopolitan rather than French and my instinct tells me that in a good translation it might make an enormous hit in America where everyone is yearning for Paris. Do look it up & get at least one opinion of it. The preface is by the da-dist Jean Cocteau but the book is not da-da at all.

12. Did you get hold of Rings other books?

13. We're liable to leave here by Oct 1st so after the 15th of Sept I wish you'd send everything care of Guarantee Trust Co. Paris

14 Please ask the bookstore, if you have time, to send me Havelock Ellis' "Dance of Life" & charge to my account.

*Gilbert Seldes, American journalist and critic.

†The dust jacket referred to showed two enormous eyes, supposedly those of Daisy Fay, brooding over New York City. This picture inspired the image of the eyes of Dr. T. J. Eckleburg in *The Great Gatsby*.

** *Balisand*.

††These brackets are Fitzgerald's.

15. I asked Struthers Burt to dinner but his baby was sick.

16 *Be sure* & and answer *every* question, Max.

I miss seeing you like the devil.

                                                    September 10, 1924
Dear Scott:
I would have written you sooner, but if you had ever had hay-fever you
would forgive me for waiting a couple of weeks until the "storm" of pollen
had somewhat abated. It was worse than usual because our landlady
thought she would make profit for her garden by the fact that there were
strangers on the premises, with a crop of buckwheat. I knew buckwheat
by reputation, but not by appearance, and so it was some time before I
found out what was the matter.
. . . . .

. . . . .
As to the questions you asked: – The Ring Lardner clippings must have
reached you some time ago.
    I read a great part of Seldes' book* and got a great deal of fun out of
it and considerable illumination. I got it to read the Ring Lardner especially and showed that part of it to Mr. Scribner.
    We have sold about 12,000 copies of "How to Write Short Stories". We
have printed 15,000.
    There is certainly not the slightest risk of our giving that jacket to
anyone in the world but you. I wish the manuscript of the book would
come, and I don't doubt it is something very like the best American novel.
I found other people that were greatly impressed by your story in the
Mercury – a very promising young writer in Philadelphia whom I went
over to see, spoke of it without any introduction of the subject from me;
– he said he had always looked upon you as a leader, had been at times a
little bewildered, and had in this story felt a kind of renewal and advance.
    As to the literature talked of, – "The American Mercury" is read by
everybody and provokes a large part of the conversation. "So Big" by Edna
Ferber is the most popular book, and one of the best. For some reason a
good many people are reading a cheap affair by that bucolic sophisticate,
Van Vechten, called "The tattooed Countess". It is clever, but cheap and
thin. The somewhat conservative and substantial book readers talk a great
deal about a book by E. M. Fo[r]ster called "The Passage to India", but I

*Probably *The Seven Lively Arts* (1924).

77

have only read about a third of it. "These Charming People"* is very popular among people you would be likely to see here, and word has come to those who have been on the other side, about another novel of his called, "The Green Hat".

I have got Raymond Radeguet's book and am having it read. I am sending you "The Dance of Life" but personally I was very much disappointed in it because it fulfilled for me none of the expectations aroused by the opening statement of what the author proposed to do. Read individually all the essays are effective, but as a whole it fell down, – or else I did in reading it. All I have been able to get is one number of the Transatlantic Review, which did have one chapter of Gertrude Stein, and that Mr. Scribner†

> *Villa Marie,*
> *Valescure*
> *St. Raphael, France*
> [*ca. October 10, 1924*]

Dear Max:
The royalty was better than I'd expected. This is to tell you about a young man named Ernest Hemmingway, who lives in Paris, (an American) writes for the transatlantic Review & has a brilliant future. Ezra Pount published a a collection of his short pieces in Paris, at some place like the Egotist Press.** I havn't it hear now but its remarkable & I'd look him up right away. He's the real thing.

My novel goes to you with a long letter within five days. Ring arrives in a week. This is just a hurried scrawl as I'm working like a dog. I thought Stalling's book†† was disappointingly rotten. It takes a genius to whine appealingly. Have tried to see Struthers Burt but he's been on the move. More later.

P.S. *Important.* What chance has a smart young frenchman with an intimate knowledge of French literature in the bookselling business in New York. Is a clerk paid much and is there any opening for one specializing in French literature? Do tell me as there's a young friend of mine here just out of the army who is anxious to know.

> *Sincerely*

---

*A novel by Michael Arlen.
†The letter breaks off here, unsigned.
**Probably *In Our Time*, published by William Bird of Paris in the Spring of 1924. Ezra Pound helped Hemingway get the book published.
†† *Plumes* by Laurence Stallings.

DEAR SCOTT / DEAR MAX

Dear Scott:

As a correspondent you are tantalizing: each letter makes me almost expect the manuscript of the novel before the next week and so that I count upon reading it then. Take your time; – but when it does come I hope it will be at the end of a week so that I won't be continually interrupted in reading it. Today I could do nothing on account of callers: Ellsworth Huntington, geographer and anthropologist for whom we have just published a book* – he promised us an article I suggested for Scribner's; then Ernest Boyd, most amusing, who said he was somewhat apprehensive of your 'reaction' to his chapter on you in a book Doran is issuing† – we are to publish "Studies in Nine Literatures" for him in the spring; then VanWyck Brooks, who is now investigating Emerson; then Burton Rascoe** whom I introduced to Mr. Brownell;†† – and they chatted amicably for some time. And there were others too.

I think I shall soon have got something by Ernest Hemmingway though probably from abroad. Thanks for the tip. I am reading the Gertrude Stein as it comes out, and it fascinates me. But I doubt if the reader who had no *literary* interest, or not much, would have patience with her method, effective as it does become. Its peculiarities are much more marked than in "The Three Lives". As for "Plumes", I greatly liked those few pages about the earlier Plumes. I thought them remarkable in swift presentation and characterization; but I couldn't go the rest. His play, "What Price Glory" is a wonder everyone says. I must manage to see it.

The Lardners are I suppose with you. I wrote Ring we had acquired all the books and when he comes back I'll discuss the composition of a set. I hope he has talked it over with you. I enclose a string of ads. we are consistently running. "The Golden Honeymoon" one is, of course, out of key, altogether; – but the chief idea is to catch the eye and hold it a minute. Everyone thinks we have advertised the book well, – perhaps because, liking it, they have noticed the ads.

I told you we'd bought a house in New Canaan. It has the face of a Greek temple and the body of a spacious Connecticut farm house. It's recovering from a devastating raid of plumbers, carpenters, painters, roofers. I thought at one time it never would. We had always meant to leave Plainfield – a damnable flat, damp, dull, cheap place. *This* is better in almost

---

* *The Character of Races as Influenced by Physical Environment, Natural Selection, and Historical Development.*

† *Portraits: Real and Imaginary* (1924).

**American journalist, reviewer and dramatic critic.

††William Crary Brownell, writer and critic and senior editor at Scribners.

every respect, – not worse in any. Eleanor Wylie* lives here; – but I have not yet seen that face that launched the souls of three men into eternity. Someone who had, said he could understand about the two husbands but he didn't see why the other man should have committed suicide. – But Louise† thinks her charming and she must certainly be interesting. To-night we dine at one Gregory Mason's about whom I only know from having declined two of his novels. I think he's chiefly a newspaper correspondent.

Mr. Scribner always asks about you. We all miss your calls – that's a fact. I'm sending a good book – Sidney Howard's first.**

Yours,

> *October 27th, 1924*
> *Villa Marie, Valescure*
> *St. Raphael, France*
> *(After Nov. 3d care of*
> *American Express Co., Rome Italy)*

Dear Max:
Under separate cover I'm sending you my third novel:

The Great Gatsby

(I think that at last I've done something really my own), but how good "my own" is remains to be seen.

I should suggest the following contract.

15% up to 50,000

20% after 50,000

  The book is only a little over fifty thousand words long but I believe, as you know, that Whitney Darrow has the wrong psychology about prices (and about what class constitute the bookbuying public now that the lowbrows go to the movies) and I'm anxious to charge two dollars for it and have it a *full size book*.

Of course I want the binding to be absolutely uniform with my other books – the stamping too – and the jacket we discussed before. This time I don't want any signed blurbs on the jacket – not Mencken's or Lewis' or Howard's or anyone's. I'm tired of being the author of *This Side of Paradise* and I want to start over.

About serialization. I am bound under contract to show it to Hearsts

*Elinor Wylie, American poetess and novelist.
†Mrs. Maxwell E. Perkins.
** *Three Flights Up*, a collection of short fiction, published by Scribners in 1924.

but I am asking a prohibitive price, Long* hates me and its not a very serialized book. If they should take it – they won't – it would put of[f] publication in the fall. Otherwise you can publish it in the spring. When Hearst turns it down I'm going to offer it to Liberty for $15,000 on condition that they'll publish it in ten weekly installments before April 15th. If they don't want it I shan't serialize. *I am absolutely positive Long won't want it.*

I have an alternative title:

Gold-hatted Gatsby

After you've read the book let me know what you think about the title. Naturally I won't get a nights sleep until I hear from you but do tell me the absolute truth, *your first impression of the book* & tell me anything that bothers you in it.

As Ever

I'd rather you wouldn't call Reynolds as he might try to act as my agent. Would you send me the N.Y. World with accounts of Harvard-Princeton and Yale-Princeton games?

Hotel Continental
St. Raphael, France
(Leaving Tuesday)
[*ca. November 7, 1924*]

Dear Max:

By now you've recieved the novel. There are things in it I'm not satisfied with in the middle of the book – Chapters 6 & 7. And I may write in a complete new scene in proof. I hope you got my telegram.[29]

I have now decided to stick to the title I put on the book.

Trimalchio in West Egg

The only other titles that seem to fit it are *Trimalchio* and *On the Road to West Egg*. I had two others *Gold-hatted Gatsby* and *The High-bouncing Lover* but they seemed too light.

We leave for Rome as soon as I finish the short story I'm working on.

As Ever

I was interested that you've moved to New Canaan. It sounds wonderful. Sometimes I'm awfully anxious to be home.

But I am confused at what you say about Gertrude Stien. I thought it

---

*Ray Long, editor of *Hearst's International*.

was one purpose of critics & publishers to educate the public up to original work. The first people who risked Conrad certainly didn't do it as a commercial venture. Did the evolution of startling work into accepted work cease twenty years ago?

. . . . .

. . . . .

Dear Scott:

I think the novel is a wonder. I'm taking it home to read again and shall then write my impressions in full; – but it has vitality to an extraordinary degree, and *glamour*, and a great deal of underlying thought of unusual quality. It has a kind of mystic atmosphere at times that you infused into parts of "Paradise" and have not since used. It is a marvelous fusion, into a unity of presentation, of the extraordinary incongruities of life today. And as for sheer writing, it's astonishing.

Now deal with this question: various gentlemen here don't like the title, – in fact none like it but me. To me, the strange incongruity of the words in it sound the note of the book. But the objectors are more practical men than I. Consider as quickly as you can the question of a change.

But if you do not change, you will have to leave that note off the wrap. Its presence would injure it too much; – and good as the wrap always seemed, it now seems a masterpiece for this book. So judge of the value of the title when it stands alone and write or cable your decision the instant you can.

With congratulations, I am,

Yours,

November 20, 1924

Dear Scott:

I think you have every kind of right to be proud of this book. It is an extraordinary book, suggestive of all sorts of thoughts and moods. You adopted exactly the right method of telling it, that of employing a narrator who is more of a spectator than an actor: this puts the reader upon a point of observation on a higher level than that on which the characters stand and at a distance that gives perspective. In no other way could your irony have been so immensely effective, nor the reader have been enabled so strongly to feel at times the strangeness of human circumstance in a vast heedless universe. In the eyes of Dr. Eckleberg various readers will see different significances; but their presence gives a superb touch to the whole thing: great unblinking eyes, expressionless, looking down upon the human scene. It's magnificent!

I could go on praising the book and speculating on its various elements, and meanings, but points of criticism are more important now. I think you are right in feeling a certain slight sagging in chapters six and seven, and I don't know how to suggest a remedy. I hardly doubt that you will find one and I am only writing to say that I think it does need something to hold up here to the pace set, and ensuing. I have only two actual criticisms: –

One is that among a set of characters marvelously palpable and vital – I would know Tom Buchanan if I met him on the street and would avoid him – Gatsby is somewhat vague. The reader's eyes can never quite focus upon him, his outlines are dim. Now everything about Gatsby is more or less a mystery i.e. more or less vague, and this may be somewhat of an artistic intention, but I think it is mistaken. Couldn't *he* be physically described as distinctly as the others, and couldn't you add one or two characteristics like the use of that phrase "old sport", – not verbal, but physical ones, perhaps. I think that for some reason or other a reader – this was true of Mr. Scribner and of Louise – gets an idea that Gatsby is a much older man than he is, although you have the writer say that he is little older than himself. But this would be avoided if on his first appearance he was seen as vividly as Daisy and Tom are, for instance; – and I do not think your scheme would be impaired if you made him so.

. The other point is also about Gatsby: his career must remain mysterious, of course. But in the end you make it pretty clear that his wealth came through his connection with Wolfsheim. You also suggest this much earlier. Now almost all readers numerically are going to be puzzled by his having all this wealth and are going to feel entitled to an explanation. To give a distinct and definite one would be, of course, utterly absurd. It did occur to me though, that you might here and there interpolate some phrases, and possibly incidents, little touches of various kinds, that would suggest that he was in some active way mysteriously engaged. You do have him called on the telephone, but couldn't he be seen once or twice consulting at his parties with people of some sort of mysterious significance, from the political, the gambling, the sporting world, or whatever it may be. I know I am floundering, but that fact may help you to see what I mean. The *total* lack of an explanation through so large a part of the story does seem to me a defect; – or not of an explanation, but of the suggestion of an explanation. I wish you were here so I could talk about it to you for then I know I could at least make you understand what I mean. What Gatsby did ought never to be definitely imparted, even if it could be. Whether he was an innocent tool in the hands of somebody else, or to what degree he was this, ought not to be explained. But if some sort of business activity of his were simply adumbrated, it would lend further probability to that part of the story.

There is one other point: in giving deliberately Gatsby's biography when he gives it to the narrator you do depart from the method of the narrative in some degree, for otherwise almost everything is told, and beautifully told, in the regular flow of it, – in the succession of events or in accompaniment with them. But you can't avoid the biography altogether. I thought you might find ways to let the truth of some of his claims like "Oxford" and his army career come out bit by bit in the course of actual narrative. I mention the point anyway for consideration in this interval before I send the proofs.

The general brilliant quality of the book makes me ashamed to make even these criticisms. The amount of meaning you get into a sentence, the dimensions and intensity of the impression you make a paragraph carry, are most extraordinary. The manuscript is full of phrases which make a scene blaze with life. If one enjoyed a rapid railroad journey I would compare the number and vividness of pictures your living words suggest, to the living scenes disclosed in that way. It seems in reading a much shorter book than it is, but it carries the mind through a series of experiences that one would think would require a book of three times its length.

The presentation of Tom, his place, Daisy and Jordan, and the unfolding of their characters is unequalled so far as I know. The description of the valley of ashes adjacent to the lovely country, the conversation and the action in Myrtle's apartment, the marvelous catalogue of those who came to Gatsby's house, – these are such things as make a man famous. And all these things, the whole pathetic episode, you have given a place in time and space, for with the help of T. J. Eckleberg and by an occasional glance at the sky, or the sea, or the city, you have imparted a sort of sense of eternity. You once told me you were not a *natural* writer – my God! You have plainly mastered the craft, of course; but you needed far more than craftsmanship for this.

As ever,

P.S. Why do you ask for a lower royalty on this than you had on the last book where it changed from 15% to 17½% after 20,000 and to 20% after 40,000? Did you do it in order to give us a better margin for advertising? We shall advertise very energetically anyhow and if you stick to the old terms you will sooner overcome the advance. Naturally we should like the ones you suggest better, but there is no reason you should get less on this than you did on the other.

DEAR SCOTT / DEAR MAX

Hotel des Princes
Piazza di Spagna
Rome, Italy
[ca. December 1, 1924]

Dear Max:
Your wire & your letters made me feel like a million dollars – I'm sorry
I could make no better response than a telegram whining for money. But
the long siege of the novel winded me a little & I've been slow on starting
the stories on which I must live.

I think all your criticisms are true

(a) About the title. I'll try my best but I don't know what I can do.
Maybe simply "Trimalchio" or "Gatsby." In the former case I don't see
why the note shouldn't go on the back.

(b) Chapters VI & VII I know how to fix

(c) Gatsby's business affairs I can fix. I get your point about them.

(d) His vagueness I can repair by *making more pointed* – this doesn't
sound good but wait and see. It'll make him clear

(e) But his long narrative in Chap VIII will be difficult to split up. Zelda
also thought I was a little out of key but it is good writing and I don't think
I could bear to sacrifice any of it

(f) I have 1000 minor corrections which I will make on the proof &
several more large ones which you didn't mention.

Your criticisms were excellent & most helpful & you picked out all my
favorite spots in the book to praise as high spots. Except you didn't mention my favorite of all – the chapter where Gatsby & Daisy meet.

Two more things. Zelda's been reading me the cowboy book* aloud to
spare my mind & I love it – tho I think he learned the American language
from Ring rather than from his own ear.

Another point – in Chap. II of my book when Tom & Myrt[l]e go into
the bedroom while Carraway reads Simon called Peter – is that raw? Let
me know. I think its pretty nessessary.

I made the royalty smaller because I wanted to make up for all the
money you've advanced these two years by letting it pay a sort of interest
on it. But I see by calculating I made it too small – a difference of 2000
dollars. Let us call it 15% up to 40,000 and 20% after that. That's a good
fair contract all around.

Cowboys North and South by Will James.

85

By now you have heard from a smart young french woman* who wants to translate the book. She's equeal to it intellectually & linguisticly I think – had read all my others – If you'll tell her how to go about it as to royalty demands ect.

Anyhow thanks & thanks & thanks for your letters. I'd rather have you & Bunny† like it than anyone I know. And I'd rather have you like it than Bunny. If its as good as you say, when I finish with the proof it'll be perfect.

Remember, by the way, to put by some cloth for the cover uniform with my other books.

As soon as I can think about the title I'll write or wire a decision. Thank Louise for me, for liking it. Best Regards to Mr. Scribner. Tell him Galsworthy is here in Rome.

As Ever,

Dec. 16, 1924

Dear Scott:

Your cable changing the title to "The Great Gatsby" has come and has been followed; and as I just now cabled, we have deposited the seven hundred and fifteen [fifty].**

. . . . .

. . . . .

Ring came in at last and told me about being with you and Zelda, and then I got for the purposes of his book†† the proofs of his articles about the trip which are to appear in Liberty; – and you and Zelda figure therein. "Mr. Fitzgerald," he says, "is a novelist, and Mrs. Fitzgerald is a novelty." And he tells how you got to Monte Carlo with nothing but a full dress coat. His articles are most excellent and I think we shall get a very good book out of all the material we have.

I wish you would see Struthers Burt. You would probably think he was extremely prejudiced in some respects, but he has a very interesting mind. He has a theory on almost every topic that comes up and whether valid or not, all his theories are intricate and interesting.

I hope you are thinking over "The Great Gatsby" in this interval and will add to it freely. The most important point I think, is that of how he comes by his wealth, – some sort of suggestion about it. He was supposed to be a bootlegger, wasn't he, at least in part, and I should think a little

*Irene de Morsier.
†Edmund Wilson.
**The request for $750 and the title change were contained in a cable dated December 15th.
†† *What of It?*, published in 1925.

86

touch here and there would give the reader the suspicion that this was so and that is all that is needed.

Zelda wrote me a splendid letter from Rome in return for "The White Monkey";* – that, by the way, has sold about 75,000 copies, although it came out very late. Tom's book† has only sold about 3,000 but I really did not think it could do much more in view of its nature. I do think it a very interesting book which, though crudely, shows a great deal of power. We are publishing his stories in the spring.

I lunched the other day with John Biggs and the girl he is engaged to, a very feminine, wide awake, Wilmington girl. They must be going to be married pretty soon because they have bought a house which they are repairing, – that is, if he has any money left. I haven't.

As ever,

Dec. 19, 1924

Dear Scott:

When Ring Lardner came in the other day I told him about your novel and he instantly balked at the title. "No one could pronounce it," he said; – so probably your change is wise on other than typographical counts. Certainly it is a *good* title. I've just put in hand the material for a book by Ring and the first of it is an account of his European trip. Ober,** from whom you will have heard, called up this morning to say Liberty had decided not to take "The Great Gatsby" though Rex Lardner wanted to, because it was really above their readers and they did not want to run two serials at once. So we shall go ahead full speed; – and will you read the proof rapidly?

Not long ago I had a call from John Peale Bishop,†† who must get himself a job. He said nothing of *his* novel, nor did I. He looked, to me, quite a bit older than before he went abroad, – more than two years older; – said he and *she* were living in a roof house, – a little four room ediface, which sounded most attractive to me; but he did not regard it so poetically. He told of seeing you in Paris at a late hour in the early summer. By the way, I've only just now got word that something by that Hemingway you told me of is in a case at the custom's house, – a case of books. Did you ever look at that Will James book – not that I want you to: I'd rather you'd *write* than read. – But I have an idea that he could write a fine story – a sort of

---

*By John Galsworthy.

† *Through the Wheat* by Thomas A. Boyd.

**Literary agent Harold Ober, an associate at this time of Paul Reynolds. Ober was gradually taking over from Reynolds the placing of Fitzgerald's work.

††American poet and novelist who had attended Princeton with Fitzgerald.

cowboy's Odyssey about a cattle drive or some such episode; – that with the barest tale to tell he would gain a continuity of interest that would greatly enhance the attraction of his writing. It would give him a show. I've proposed it to him. To be illustrated, of course, by him.

Here we are in our house since a week ago, and last night the new kitchen ceiling fell down. Now what the hell! And the men who put it up don't even seem surprised. They're perfectly willing to put up another though at twelve dollars a day per man. They're a great bunch, these members of what Ring Lardner might laughingly call the "laboring class". But the *house* suits us anyway.

Yours as ever,

Hotel des Princes
Piazza di Spagna
Rome, Italy
[ca. December 20, 1924]

Dear Max:

I'm a bit (not very – not dangerously) stewed tonight & I'll probably write you a long letter. We're living in a small, unfashionable but most comfortable hotel at $525.00 a month including tips, meals ect. Rome does *not* particularly interest me but its a big year here, and early in the spring we're going to Paris. There's no use telling you my plans because they're usually just about as unsuccessful as to work as a religious prognosticaters are as to the End of the World. I've got a new novel to write – title and all, that'll take about a year. Meanwhile, I don't want to start it until this is out & meanwhile I'll do short stories for money (I now get $2000.00 a story but I hate worse than hell to do them) and there's the never dying lure of another play.

Now! Thanks enormously for making up the $5000.00* I know I don't technically deserve it considering I've had $3000.00 or $4000.00 for as long as I can remember. But since you force it on me (inexecrable [or is it execrable] joke) I will accept it. I hope to Christ you get 10 times it back on Gatsby – and I think perhaps you will.

For:

I can now make it perfect but the proof (I will soon get the immemorial letter with the statement "We now have the book in hand and will soon begin to send you proof" [what is 'in hand' – I have a vague picture of everyone in the office holding the book in the light and and reading it]†)

---

*The $750 as per Fitzgerald's telegram of December 15th made a total of $5000 advanced him on the publication of *Gatsby*.

†These brackets are Fitzgerald's.

will be one of the most expensive affairs since Madame Bovary. *Please* charge it to my account. If its possible to send a second proof over here I'd love to have it. Count on 12 days each way – four days here on first proof & two on the second. I hope there are other good books in the spring because I think now the public interest in *books* per se rises when there seems to be a group of them as in 1920 (spring & fall), 1921 (fall), 1922 (spring). Ring's & Tom's* (first) books, Willa Cathers *Lost Lady* & in an inferior, cheap way Edna Ferber's are the only American fiction in over two years that had a really excellent press (say, since Babbit).

With the aid you've given me I can make "Gatsby" perfect. The chapter VII (the hotel scene) will never quite be up to mark – I've worried about it too long & I can't quite place Daisy's reaction. But I can improve it a lot. It isn't imaginative energy that's lacking – its because I'm automaticly prevented from thinking it out over again *because I must get all those characters to New York* in order to have the catastrophe on the road going back & I must have it pretty much that way. So there's no chance of bringing the freshness to it that a new free conception sometimes gives.

The rest is easy and I see my way so clear that I even see the mental quirks that queered it before. Strange to say my notion of Gatsby's vagueness was O.K. What you and Louise & Mr. Charles Scribner found wanting was that:

I myself didn't know what Gatsby looked like or was engaged in & you felt it. If I'd known & kept it from you you'd have been *too impressed with my knowledge to protest.* This is a complicated idea but I'm sure you'll understand. But I know now – and as a penalty for not having known first, in other words to make sure I'm going to tell more.

It seems of almost mystical significance to me that you thot he was older – the man I had in mind, half unconsciously, *was* older (a specific individual) and evidently, without so much as a definate word, I conveyed the fact. – or rather, I must qualify this Shaw-Desmond-trash by saying that I conveyed it without a word that I can at present and for the life of me, trace. (I think Shaw Desmond† was one of your bad bets – I was the other)

Anyhow after careful searching of the files (of a man's mind here) for the Fuller Magee case** & after having had Zelda draw pictures until her fingers ache I know Gatsby better than I know my own child. My first instinct after your letter was to let him go & have Tom Buchanan dominate

---

*Thomas A. Boyd.

†Irish poet, dramatist and novelist.

**Edward M. Fuller and William F. McGee, partners in a brokerage firm, had been convicted, after four trials, of pocketing their customers' order money. Arnold Rothstein, the famous gambler and model for Meyer Wolfsheim in *Gatsby*, was the man behind Fuller and McGee. Fuller was Fitzgerald's neighbor in Great Neck.

the book (I suppose he's the best character I've ever done – I think he and the brother in "Salt" & Hurstwood in "Sister Carrie" are the three best characters in American fiction in the last twenty years, perhaps and perhaps not) but Gatsby sticks in my heart. I had him for awhile then lost him & now I know I have him again. I'm sorry Myrtle is better than Daisy. Jordan of course was a great idea (perhaps you know its Edith Cummings)* but she fades out. Its Chap VII thats the trouble with Daisy & it may hurt the book's popularity that its *a man's book.*

Anyhow I think (for the first time since The Vegetable failed) that I'm a wonderful writer & its your always wonderful letters that help me to go on believing in myself.

Now some practical, very important questions. Please answer every one.

1. Montenegro has an order called *The Order of Danilo.* Is there any possible way you could find out for me there what it would look like – whether a courtesy decoration given to an American would bear an English inscription – or anything to give versimilitude to the medal which sounds horribly amateurish.

2. Please have *no blurbs of any kind on the jacket!!!* No Mencken or Lewis or Sid Howard or anything. I don't believe in them *one bit* any more.

3. Don't forget to change name of book in list of works

4. Please shift exclamation point from end of 3d line to end of 4th line in title page poem. *Please!* Important!

5. I thought that the whole episode (2 paragraphs) about their playing the Jazz History of the world at Gatsby's first party was rotten. Did you? Tell me frank *reaction – personal.* don't *think!* We can all think!

Got a sweet letter from Sid Howard – rather touching. I wrote him first. I thought *Transatlantic* was great stuff – a really gorgeous surprise. Up to that I never believed in him 'specially & I was sorry because he did in me. Now I'm tickled silly to find he has power, and his own power. It seemed tragic too to see *Mrs. Viectch* wasted in a novelette when, despite Anderson the short story is at its lowest ebb as an art form. (Despite Ruth Suckow, Gertrude Stien, Ring there is a horrible impermanence on it *because* the overwhelming number of short stories are impermanent.

Poor Tom Boyd! His cycle sounded so sad to me – perhaps it'll be wonderful but it sounds to me like sloughing in a field whose first freshness has gone.

---

*A famous woman golfer who once won the women's national championship. Fitzgerald had met her when she was a classmate at Westover School of Ginevra King, a girl he dated while he was at Princeton.

See that word?* The ambition of my life is to make that use of it correct. The temptation to use it as a neuter is one of the vile fevers in my still insecure prose.

Tell me about Ring! About Tom – is he poor? He seems to be counting on his short story book, frail cane! About Biggs – did he ever finish the novel? About Peggy Boyd. I think Louise might have sent us her book!

I thot the *White Monkey* was stinko. On second thoughts I didn't like *Cowboys, West & South* either. What about *Bal de Compte Orget?* and Ring's set? and his new book? & Gertrude Stien? and Hemmingway?

I still owe the store almost $700 on my Encyclopedia but I'll pay them on about Jan 10th – all in a lump as I expect my finances will then be on a firm footing. Will you ask them to send me Ernest Boyd's book? Unless it has about my drinking in it that would reach my family. However, I guess it'd worry me more if I hadn't seen it than if I had. If my book is a big success or a great failure (financial – no other sort can be imagined, I hope) I *don't* want to publish stories in the fall. If it goes between 25,000 and 50,000 I have an excellent collection for you. This is the longest letter I've written in three or four years. Please thank Mr. Scribner for me for his exceeding kindness.

Always yours

Hotel des Princes
Rome
[ca. January 15, 1925]

Dear Max:

Proof hasn't arrived yet. Have been in bed for a week with grippe but I'm ready to attack it violently. Here are two important things.

1. In [Is] the scene in Myrt[l]es appartment – in the place where *Tom & Myrtle dissapear for awhile* noticeably raw. Does it stick out enough so that the censor might get it. Its the only place in the book I'm in doubt about on that score. Please let me know right away.

2. Please have *no quotations from any critics whatsoever on the jacket* – simply your own blurb on the back and don't give away too much of the idea – especially don't connect Daisy & Gatsby (I need the quality of surprise there.) Please be *very general*.

These points are both very important. Do drop me a line about them. Wish I could see your new house. I havn't your faith in Will James – I feel its old material without too much feeling or too new a touch.

As Ever,

---

*Fitzgerald had circled "whose" in the previous sentence.

Jan. 20, 1925

Dear Scott:

I am terribly rushed for time so I am answering your letter as briefly and rapidly as I can, – but I will have a chance to write to tell you the news, etc. etc., soon.

First as to the jazz history of the world: – that did jar on me unfavorably. And yet in a way it pleased me as a tour de force, but one not completely successful. Upon the whole, I should probably have objected to it in the first place except that I felt you needed something there in the way of incident, something special. But if you have something else, I would take it out.

You are beginning to get me worried about the scene in Myrtle's apartment for you have spoken of it several times. It never occurred to me to think there was any objection to it. I am sure there is none. No censor could make an issue on that, – nor I think on anything else in the book.

I will be sure not to use any quotations and I will make it very general indeed, because I realize that not much ought to be said about the story. I have not thought what to say, but we might say something very brief which gave the impression that nothing need any longer be said.

I certainly hope the proofs have got to you and that you have been at work on them for some time. If not you had better cable. They were sent first-class mail. The first lot on December 27th and the second lot on December 30th.

Yours,

P.S. The mysterious hand referred to in the immemorial phrase is that of the typesetter.

Hotel des Princes,
Rome, Italy.
January 24th. = 1925

(But address the American Express
Co. because its damn cold here
and we may leave any day.

Dear Max:

This is a most important letter so I'm having it typed. Guard it as your life.

1) Under a separate cover I'm sending the first part of the proof. While I agreed with the general suggestions in your first letters I differ with you in others. I *want* Myrtle Wilson's breast ripped off – its exactly the thing,

I think, and I don't want to chop up the good scenes by too much tinkering. When Wolfsheim says "sid" for "said", it's deliberate. "Orgastic" is the adjective from "orgasm" and it expresses exactly the intended ecstasy. It's not a bit dirty. I'm much more worried about the disappearance of Tom and Myrtle on Galley 9 – I think it's all right but I'm not sure. If it isn't please wire and I'll send correction.[30]

2) Now about the page proof – under certain conditions never mind sending them (unless, of course, there's loads of time, which I suppose there isn't. I'm keen for late March or early April publication)

The conditions are two.

a) That someone reads it *very carefully twice* to see that every one of my inserts are put in correctly. There are so many of them that I'm in terror of a mistake.

b) That no changes *whatsoever* are made in it except in the case of a misprint so glaring as to be certain, and that only by you.

If there's some time left but not enough for the double mail send them to me and I'll simply wire O.K. which will save two weeks. However don't postpone for that. In any case send me the page proof as usual just to see.

3) Now, many thanks for the deposit. Two days after wiring you I had a cable from Reynolds that he'd sold two stories of mine for a total of $3,750. but before that I was in debt to him and after turning down the ten thousand dollars from College Humor* I was afraid to borrow more from him until he'd made a sale. I won't ask for any more from you until the book has earned it. My guess is that it will sell about 80,000 copies but I may be wrong. Please thank Mr. Charles Scribner for me. I bet he thinks he's caught another John Fox now for sure. Thank God for John Fox. It would have been awful to have had no predecessor

4) This is very important. Be sure not to give away *any* of my plot in the blurb. Don't give away that Gatsby *dies* or is a *parvenu* or a *crook* or anything. Its a part of the suspense of the book that all these things are in doubt until the end. You'll watch this won't you? And remember about having no quotations from critics on the jacket – *not even about my other books!*

. . . . .

Do answer every question and keep this letter until the proof comes. Let

---

*To serialize *The Great Gatsby*.

me know how you like the changes. I miss seeing you, Max, more than I can say.

As ever,

P. S. I'm returning the proof of the title page ect. It's O.K. but my heart tells me I should have named it *Trimalchio*. However against all the advice I suppose it would have been stupid and stubborn of me. *Trimalchio in West Egg* was only a compromise. *Gatsby* is too much like Babbit and *The Great Gatsby* is weak because there's no emphasis even ironically on his greatness or lack of it. However let it pass.

new address { *Hotel Tiberio*
Capri
[*ca. February 18, 1925*]

Dear Max:
After six weeks of uninterrupted work the proof is finished and the last of it goes to you this afternoon. On the whole its been very successful labor

(1.) I've brought Gatsby to life

(2.) I've accounted for his money

(3.) I've fixed up the two weak chap[t]ers (VI and VII)

(4.) I've improved his first party

(5.) I've broken up his long narrative in Chap. VIII

This morning I wired you to *hold up the galley of Chap 40*. The correction – and God! its important because in my other revision I made Gatsby look too mean – is enclosed herewith. Also some corrections for the page proof.

We're moving to Capri. We hate home. I'm behind financially and have to write three short stories. Then I try another play, and by June, I hope, begin my new novel.

Had long interesting letters from Ring and John Bishop. Do tell me if all corrections have been recieved. I'm worried.

I hope you're setting publication date at first possible moment.

Feb. 24, 1925

Dear Scott:
I congratulate you on resisting the $10,000. I don't see how you managed it. But it delighted us, for otherwise book publication would have been deferred until too late in the spring. . . . Those [changes] you have made

do wonders for Gatsby, – in making him visible and palpable. You're right about the danger of meddling with the high spots – instinct is the best guide there. I'll have the proofs read twice, once by Dunn and once by Roger,* and shall allow no change unless it is certain the printer has blundered. I know the whole book so well myself that I could hardly decide wrongly. But I won't decide anything if there is ground for doubt.

Ring Lardner came back last week from Nassau looking brown and well, with the page proof of his new book – "What of It". I'll send you a copy soon. That and "How to Write Short Stories," "Alibi Ike," "The Big Town," and "Gullible's Travels," with new prefaces, constitute the set. I simply could not get Ring to pay enough attention to it to reorganize the material as we might have done. I tried to work out a book to contain "Symptoms of Being 35" and some of the shorter things; but without the war material – which, good as it was, seems dreadfully old now – there was not enough. And the subscription agents wanted to retain the familiar titles for their canvassing. "How to Write Short Stories" has sold 16,500 copies and it continues steadily to sell: the new book and the old books in new forms and wrappers, in the trade, will give it new impetus. We'll have a wonderful Ring Lardner window when we get all these books out.

As for Hemingway: I finally got his "In our time" which accumulates a fearful effect through a series of brief episodes, presented with economy, strength and vitality. A remarkable, tight, complete expression of the *scene*, in our time, as it looks to Hemingway. I have written him that we wish he would write us about his plans and if possible send a ms.; but I must say I have little hope that he will get the letter, – so hard was it for me to get his book. Do you know his address?

Here, the great recent piece of literary gossip arose from a luncheon to Sherwood Anderson given by his publisher Ben Heubsch. All the critics and commentators were guests, including Stuart P. Sherman† and Mencken; – and Mencken refused to meet Sherman. Not point blank, but in such a way that all the room was *aware*; and the general tension was not reduced when, upon Anderson's refusal to speak, old Dutch Van Loon** arose and said perhaps a question he had long wanted to ask him might suggest a topic: – why did he let Ben Heubsch publish his books? – If it *was* a jest, and heaven knows how it was, there was too much truth in the implication. As for the other situation, Sherman has set upon Mencken with violence, in his articles, a number of times. But Mencken is not the

---

*Charles Dunn and Roger Burlingame, Scribners editors.

†American literary critic, then editor of the New York *Herald Tribune* Sunday *Books* section.

**Hendrik Willem Van Loon, Dutch-American historian, then Associate Editor of the Baltimore *Sun*.

man to resent that, even when, as once he did, I suppose to draw him out, Sherman charged him with cowardice. Apparently Mencken has detested Sherman on account of some anti-German-American articles he wrote during the war. I'm to see Sherman Wednesday and may hear more about it, – not that it matters.

There are here two couples we much enjoy seeing: the Benets* and the Colums. Molly Colum I think is a wonder, quick as a cat. And Padriac trails along an atmosphere of good nature and peaceful humor. Elinor Wylie is very much of a person, and Benet I like. – At all events, there was no one in Plainfield of this sort whatever. It was a bore there to go anywhere unless artificial stimulant was plentiful.

The other day I sent Tom Boyd a cheque of about $683 in royalties. "The Dark Cloud" is to be published by Fisher Unwin in England, which will help. We're publishing his stories under the title, "Points of Honor", – not with the hope of much of a sale of course; but they will help him, and while I hardly took seriously his idea of a trilogy, I *have* hopes of the book he is now doing by itself, not because I know much of it but because I believe in him once he gets control of himself. Some of the best find that the hardest. I think he is utterly honest, and has strong, deep feeling, which is the great thing. He does not work hard over his writing – once it is down on paper it seems to bore him; – but this he realizes. . . .

. . . . .

As ever,

Hotel Tiberio, Capri
[*ca. March 12, 1925*]

Dear Max:

Thanks many times for your nice letter. You answered all questions (except about the account). I wired you on a chance about the title[31] – I wanted to change back to *Gold-hatted Gatsby* but I don't suppose it would matter. That's the one flaw in the book – I feel *Trimalchio* might have been best after all.

Don't forget to send Ring's book. Hemmingway could be reached, I'm sure, through the Transatlantic review. I'm going to look him up when we get to Paris. I think its amusing about Sherman and Mencken – however Sherman's such a louse that it doesn't matter. He wouldn't have shaken Mencken's hand during the war – he's only been bullied into servility and all the Tribune appointments in the world wouldn't make him more than

---

*William Rose Benét, American poet, novelist and critic, was married to poetess Elinor Wylie from 1923 until her sudden and premature death in 1928.

10th rate. Poor Sherwood Anderson. What a mess his life is – almost like Driesers. Are you going to do "Le Bal de Compte Orgel" – I think you're losing a big opportunity if you dont. The success of *The Little French Girl* is a pointer of taste – and this is really French, and sensational and meritorious besides.

. . . . .

. . . . .

March 19, 1925

Dear Scott:

This is not a letter, but a sort of bulletin. All the corrections came safely, I am sure, and all have been rightly made. I had to make two little changes: there are no tides in Lake Superior, as Rex Lardner told me and I have verified the fact, and this made it necessary to attribute the danger of the yacht to wind. The other change was where in describing the dead Gatsby in the swimming pool, you speak of the "leg of transept". I ought to have caught this on the galleys. The transept is the cross formation in a church and surely you could not figuratively have referred to this. I think you must have been thinking of a transit, which is an engineer's instrument. It is really not like compasses, for it rests upon a tripod, but I think the use of the word transit would be psychologically correct in giving the impression of the circle being drawn. I think this must be what you meant, but anyway it could not have been transept. You will now have page proofs and you ought to deal with these two points and make them as you want them, and I will have them changed in the next printing. Otherwise we found only typographical errors of a perfectly obvious kind. I think the book is a wonder and Gatsby is now most appealing, effective and real, and yet altogether original. We publish on April 10th.[32]

I am awfully sorry that Zelda has been ill, and painfully. I hope it is all over now. Pain is regarded altogether too likely in this world. It is about the worst thing there is.

I am sending you a wonderful story by Ring Lardner in Liberty. We worked his "Young Immigrunts" and "Symptoms of Being 35" into the set.

As ever,

March 25, 1925

Dear Scott:

I'm sending the French lady* a set of page proof, – the set that Ring had

*Irene de Morsier, who was to translate *Gatsby* into French.

over the week end. He liked the book greatly – so he said yesterday when seated in my box stall before an artist who was sketching him – and is writing you about it. He said also that he expected to have enough stories for a fall book and if he does he will have a much greater success, I think, than with the first. He is now almost as healthy looking as on that night at your house in West Egg when he had not smoked or drunk for a long time.

Didn't I send you "The Apple of the Eye"?* I don't know why not: I was mightily impressed by it – by its Hardy like inevitability – I really don't know much about Hardy and don't think Tess had the quality, but I mean what he is supposed to stand for. With the help of Ernest Boyd I came in touch with the author and although many people loathe him – largely on account of a sort of lispy, preciosity – an Oxford accent – I was not unfavorably affected at all; – and I could have got his next book if I had found any support. I missed you greatly then. (This is strictly confidential.)

As for your own book, – it is a magical book. I have not read it through again, but all your corrections I read in the context. All *my* criticisms vanished before them. I am sure that all corrections came, and both Dunn and Roger read the final page proof and compared it with the corrected proof. Can't you send us a new picture of yourself? The royalty report I enclose, – regretfully; but Gatsby ought to do much for his creator.

We had a fine party two nights ago at the Colums, – the Benets, and an extraordinary Irishman named Michael Monahan, about fifty, with the kind of a head that an Irish lion would have, if there were one. *He* was tight, and while everyone else sat, he stumped about on short, solid legs, collecting, refilling, distributing glasses, and reciting Byron, and various Irish poets. Eleanor Wylie is very decorative, and a lively and interesting companion.

I hope Zelda is well.

As ever,

Hotel Tiberio, Capri
[March 31, 1925]

Dear Max:

As the day approaches my nervousness increases. Tomorrow is the 1st and your wire says the 10th. I'll be here until the 25th, probably later, so if the book prospers I'll expect some sort of cable before I leave for Paris. All

---

*A novel by Glenway Wescott. Fitzgerald had asked the Retail Department of Scribners to send him a copy.

letters that you write after 15th of April should be addressed to the Guaranty Trust Co. Paris, but if there's any dope in the first two or three days of publication I'd love a reassuring line here, even if the success doesn't justify a cable.

I enclose you a picture of a naked woman, which you may add to your celebrated pornographic collection from Sumatra, Transalvania and the Polynesian islands.

. . . . .

I think Tom Boyds book is excellent – the preface is faintly pretentious but the stories themselves are great. By the way I think my new collection will be called *"Dear Money"*. It ought to be awfully good and there will be no junk in it.

Yours in a Tremble

Will you have a copy of my book sent to Miss Willa Cather, care of Knopf.

April 10th

Dear Max:

The book comes out today and I am overcome with fears and forebodings. Supposing women didn't like the book because it has no important woman in it, and critics didn't like it because it dealt with the rich and contained no peasants borrowed out of *Tess* in it and set to work in Idaho? Suppose it didn't even wipe out my debt to you – why it will have to sell 20,000 copies even to do that! In fact all my confidence is gone – I wouldn't tell you this except for the fact that by the [time] this reaches you the worst will be known. I'm sick of the book myself – I wrote it over at least five times and I still feel that what should be the strong scene (in the Hotel) is hurried and ineffective. Also the last chapter, the burial, Gatsby's father ect is faulty. Its too bad because the first five chapters and parts of the 7th and 8th are the best things I've ever done.

"The best since Paradise". God! If you you knew how discouraging that was. That was what Ring said in his letter together with some very complementary remarks. In strictest confidence I'll admit that I was disappointed in *Haircut** – in fact I thought it was pretty lousy stuff – the crazy boy as the instrument of providence is many hundreds of years old. However please don't tell him I didn't like it.

Now as to the changes I don't think I'll make any more for the present. Ring suggested the correction of certain errata – if you made the changes all right – if not let them go. Except on Page 209 old dim La Salle Street

*A short story by Ring Lardner.

Station should be old dim Union Station and should be changed in the second edition. Transit will do fine though of course I really meant compass. The page proofs arrived and seemed to be O.K. though I don't know how the printer found his way through those 70,000 corrections. The cover (jacket) came too and is a delight. Zelda is mad about it (incidently she is quite well again.

. . . . .

. . . . .

Life in New Cannan sounds more interesting than life in Plainfield. I'm sure anyhow that at least two critics Benet & Mary Colum will have heard about the book. I'd like her to like it – Benet's opinion is of no value whatsoever.

And thanks mightily for the $750.00* which swells my debt to over $6000.00.

When should my book of short stories be in?

P. S.

I had, or rather saw, a letter from my uncle who had seen a preliminary announcement of the book. He said:

"It sounded as if it were very much like his others."

This is only a vague impression of course but I wondered if we could think of some way to advertise it so that people who are perhaps weary of assertive jazz and society novels might not dismiss it as just another book like his others. I confess that today the problem baffles me – all I can think of is to say in general to avoid such phrases as "a picture of New York life" or "modern society" – though as that is exactly what the book is its hard to avoid them. The trouble is so much superficial trash has sailed under those banners. Let me know what you think.

April 20, 1925

Dear Scott:

I wired you today rather discouragingly in the matter of the sales and I could send no qualifications in a cable. A great many of the trade have been very skeptical. I cannot make out just why. But one point is the small number of pages in the book, – an old stock objection which I thought we had got beyond. To attempt to explain to them that the way of writing which you have chosen and which is bound to come more and more into practice is one where a vast amount is said by implication, and that therefore the book is as full as it would have been if written to much greater

*Requested in a telegram on March 31st.

length by another method, is of course utterly futile. The small number of pages, however, did in the end lead a couple of big distributors to reduce their orders immensely at the very last minute. The sale is up to the public and that has not yet had time to reveal itself fully. On the other hand, we have had a very good review, a very conspicuous one, in the Times, and an excellent one also in the Tribune from Isabelle Patterson. William Rose Benet has announced preliminary to a review in the Saturday Review, that this is distinctly your best book. And the individuals whom I encounter like Gilbert Seldes (who will write also), Van Wyck Brooks, John Marquand, John Bishop, think this too. Marquand and Seldes were both quite wild about it. These people understand it fully, which even the Times and Tribune reviewers did not.

I will send you anything that has much significance by cable. I know fully how this period must try you: it must be very hard to endure, because it is hard enough for me to endure. I like the book so much myself and see so much in it that its recognition and success mean more to me than anything else in sight at the present time, – I mean in any department of interest, not only that of literature. But it does seem to me from the comments of many who yet feel its enchantment, that it is over the heads of more people than you would probably suppose.

In the course of this week when they have had time to accumulate, I will get together ads. and reviews and send them on. The situation has really not developed sufficiently yet to say anything decisive, but you can at least have the satisfaction of knowing that I shall watch it with the greatest anxiety imaginable in anyone but the author.

Yours,

Marseille, en route to Paris
[ca. April 24, 1925]

Dear Max:

Your telegram* depressed me. I hope I'll find better news in Paris and am wiring you from Lyons. There's nothing to say until I hear more. If the book fails commercially it will be from one of two reasons or both.

1st The title is only fair, rather bad than good.

2nd *And most important* – the book contains no important woman character and women controll the fiction market at present. I don't think the unhappy end matters particularly.

*Perkins' telegram, dated April 20th, had read, "Sales situation doubtful. Excellent reviews."

It will have to sell 20,000 copies to wipe out my debt to you. I think it will do that all right – but my hope was it would do 75,000. This week will tell.

Zelda is well, or almost but the expense of her illness and of bringing this wretched little car of ours back to France which has to be done, by law, has wiped out what small progress I'd made in getting straight financially.

In all events I have a book of good stories for the fall. Now I shall write some cheap ones until I've accumulated enough for my my next novel. When that is finished and published I'll wait and see. If it will support me with no more intervals of trash I'll go on as a novelist. If not I'm going to quit, come home, go to Hollywood and learn the movie business. I can't reduce our scale of living and I can't stand this financial insecurity. Anyhow there's no point in trying to be an artist if you can't do your best. I had my chance back in 1920 to start my life on a sensible scale and I lost it and so I'll have to pay the penalty. Then perhaps at 40 I can start writing again without this constant worry and interruption.

Yours in great depression

. . . . .

. . . . .

April 25, 1925

Dear Scott:

I sent you just now a rather meaningless cable.* The fact is that not enough time has passed to disclose much. I have been very keenly conscious of your inevitable anxiety – which I have myself largely shared I can tell you, on account of the early appearance of the enclosed review by Ruth Hale and the one from the World by a man of no importance[33] – and I would have sent you a word, and tried to think of what I could say in a cable. But in reality there was nothing decisive to say. I enclose a lot of other reviews and while most of the reviewers seem rather to fumble with the book, as if they did not fully understand it, they praise it very highly, and better still, they all show a kind of excitement which they caught from its vitality. Of course none of the best people have reviewed yet and I have no doubt at all of their enthusiasm so that in the matter of reviews the situation will keep improving; – for people who will be heard from are those who will really understand and grasp it, and so far nobody has done that.

As to the sales situation, we have met a curious opposition in the trade.

*It read, "Developments favorable. Reviews excellent. Must still wait." The telegram was dated April 24th.

– Of course based upon an opposition they assume to exist in the public. But a very encouraging indication comes from Womrath in whose stores the popular reaction is first felt: – he ordered at first, 100. The next week he ordered in 25s, daily. In the next two days he ordered 100s and yesterday he ordered 200. Whenever I see anything of real significance, I will send you a wire.

At any rate, one thing I think, we can be sure of: that when the tumult and shouting of the rabble of reviewers and gossipers dies, "The Great Gatsby" will stand out as a very extraordinary book. Perhaps it's not perfect! It is one thing to ride a sleepy cob of a talent to perfection and quite another to master a wild young thoroughbred of a talent. That's the way I see it.

Yours,

P.S. Molly Colum is to do a review for the New Republic and Benet for the Saturday Review.

Guaranty Trust Co.
Paris, May 1st [1925]

Dear Max:

There's no use for indignation against the long suffering public when even a critic who likes the book fails to be fundamentally held – that is Stallings who has written the only intelligent review so far* – but its been depressing to find how quick one is forgotten, especially unless you repeat yourself *ad nauseam*. Most of the reviewers floundered around in a piece of work that obviously they completely failed to understand and tried to give it reviews that committed them neither *pro* or *con* until some one of culture had spoken. Of course I've only seen the *Times* and the *Tribune* – and, thank God, Stallings, for I had begun to believe no one was even glancing at the book.

Now about money. With the $1000. for which I asked yesterday (and thank you for your answer)[34] I owe you about $1200, or if the book sells 12,000 about $4000.000. If there is a movie right I will pay you all I owe – if not, all I can offer you at present is an excellent collection of stories for the fall entitled "All the Sad Young Men" – none of the stories appeared in the *Post* – I think *Absolution* is the only one you've read. Thank you for all your advertising and all the advances and all your good will. When I get ahead again on trash I'll begin the new novel.

*Laurence Stallings' review appeared in the April 22nd issue of the New York *World*.

I'm glad Ring is getting such a press and hope he's selling. The boob critics have taken him up and always take a poke at the "intelligentia" who patronize him. But the "intelligentsia" – Seldes & Mencken discovered him (after the people) while the boob critics let *The Big Town* and *Gullibles Travels* come out in dead silence. Let me know the sale.

A profound bow to my successor Arlen* – when I read *The London Venture* I knew he was a comer and was going to tell you but I saw the next day that Doran had already published *Piracy*. That was just before I left New York.

Which reminds me – it seems terrible that all the best of the young Englishmen have been snapped up. I tried to get Louis Golding for you in Capri but he'd signed a rotten cash contract with Knopf a week before. Also they've just signed Brett Young who might have been had any time in the last two years and who'll be a big seller and now I see *The Constant Nymph*† is taken. Wouldn't it pay you to have some live young Londoner watch the new English books. I imagine Kingsley gets his information a month late out of the *London Times Supplement*. This sounds ill-natured but I am really sorry to see you loose so many new talents when they are appearing as fast now in England as they did here in 1920. Liverite** has got Hemminway! How about Radiguet?

We have taken an appartment here from May 12th to Jan. 12th, eight months, where I shall do my best. What a six months in Italy! Christ!

I'm hoping that by some miracle the book will go up to 23,000 and wipe off my debt to you. I haven't been out of debt now for three years and with the years it grows heavy on my ageing back. The happiest thought I have is of my new novel – it is something really NEW in form, idea, structure – the model for the age that Joyce and Stien are searching for, that Conrad didn't find.

Write me any news – I havn't had or written [a] line since publication except a pleasant but not thrilling note from the perennial youth, Johnny Weaver. I am bulging with plans for – however that's later. Was Rings skit which was in Mencken's *American Language* incorporated into *What of It?* If not it should have been – its one of his best shorter things. And doesn't it contain his famous world's series articles about Ellis Lardners coat? If not they'd be a nucleous for another book of nonsense. Also his day at home in imitation of F.P.A.'s diary.

My adress after the 12th is *14 Rue de Tilsitt*. If you have my *Three Lives* by Gertrude Stien don't let anybody steal it.

---

*Novelist Michael Arlen.
†By Margaret Kennedy.
**American publisher Horace Liveright.

Many thanks to Mr. Scribner and to all the others and to you for all you've done for me and for the book.

The jacket was a hit anyhow.

P.S. And Tom Boyd's Book?

May 9, 1925

Dear Scott:

I was delighted to get your letter of May first. Now I will have a much better week end. I had been fancying you in the depths of dispair – and although I myself did not believe it was time to be anywhere near that, I could not cable you any actual evidence to dispel it. The present sale is about 12,000 which means that the original distribution is about overcome, and now is the time which is significant. But at all events you are going to get appreciation. Stallings' review was marred for me chiefly by his unjustifiable comments on the other books. But the Post review you will see is good and I know young Shenton understood the book in full, – although he will appear in the Record which does not count for much. But we will probably be able to spread his opinion about. Hergesheimer's comments you will have received and he said he would do all he could. In fact, I think so far as recognition goes, the end will be as it should be, and your position will have greatly advanced, in the eyes of the discriminating public anyway.

I am so glad you are going to do the other novel, and that you do not again refer to Hollywood. As for your debt to us, if there is any left, for Heaven's sake don't let that wear on you. If we wanted to be utterly hard-boiled we could look upon it as a good investment. I know you do not like to be in debt, but I mean don't let the idea of it, so far as we are concerned, prey on your mind.

I think your title is excellent for the stories. Are you going to send them over, or will you tell me how I can collect them? Has Reynolds got them? If I can get any time over this week end, I will write you at length. I am sorry all the letters I have written – although I do not know that they would have been of any help – have failed to get to you. I suppose they will gradually come upon you in Paris.

It is too bad about Hemingway. I had an extremely nice letter from him. I fully appreciate what you say about the English. It is a hard matter to handle. But there is one thing – they are absolutely cold-blooded about changing publishers over here, and always have been. See how Wells has scented out the big advances from one house to another.

The pieces you speak of are *not* in Ring's book. It is composed largely

105

of what I could pick out from his syndicate articles with his approval. I
sent you a copy and it also will catch up with you. His book has sold
something over 5,000 copies and is apparently just getting under way. We
greatly hope to bring out a volume of his stories this fall. He has written
five and must write about nine. Tom Boyd's "Samuel Drummond" is a
splendid piece of work. I will describe it to you when I write.

There were two Post reviews of Gatsby and both had great merit, but
I meant chiefly the one by Herschel Brickell.

. . . . .

Yours,

> *14 Rue de Tillsit*
> *Paris*
> *(Permanent adress)*
> *[ca. May 22, 1925]*

Dear Max:

I suppose you've sent the book to Collins.* If not please do and let me know
right away. If he won't take it because of its flop we might try Capes.† I'm
miserable at owing you all that money – if I'd taken the serial money I
could at least have squared up with you.

I've had entheusiastic letters from Mencken and Wilson – the latter says
he's reviewing it for that *Chicago Tribune* syndicate he writes for. I think
all the reviews I've seen, except two, have been absolutely stupid and
lowsy. Some day they'll eat grass, by God! This thing, both the effort and
the result have hardened me and I think now that I'm much better than
any of the young Americans *without exception*.

Hemminway is a fine, charming fellow and he appreciated your letter
and the tone of it enormously. If Liveright doesn't please him he'll come
to you, and he has a future. He's 27.

Bishop sent me *The Apple of the Eye* and it seemed pretty much the old
stuff that D. H. Lawrence, Anderson, Suckow and Cather did long ago and
Hardy before them. I don't think such a peasantry exists in America
– Ring is much closer to the truth. I suspect tragedy in the American
countryside because all the people capable of it move to the big towns at
twenty. All the rest is pathos. However maybe its good; a lot of people
seem to think so.

I will send *All The Sad Young Men* about June 1st or 10th. Perhaps the

---

*William Collins had been the English publisher of Fitzgerald's first two novels and first
two short story collections.
†Jonathan Cape, English publisher.

deferred press on Gatsby will help it but I think now there's no use even sending it to that crowd Broun, F.P.A., Ruth Hale ect. Incidently my being over here & the consequent delay in the proofs and review copies undoubtedly hurt the effect of the books appearance. Thanks again for your kind letters and all you've done. Let me know about Collins.

Please let me know how many copies sold & whether the sale is now dead.

14 Rue de Tilsitt, Paris, France
[June 1, 1925]

Dear Max:

This is the second letter I've written you today – I tore my first up when the letter in longhand from New Cannan telling me about Liveright arrived. I'm wiring you today as to that rumor – but also it makes it nessessary to tell you something I didn't intend to tell you.[35]

Yesterday arrived a letter from T. R. Smith* asking for my next book – saying nothing against the Scribners but just asking for it: "if I happened to be dissatisfied they would be delighted" ect. ect. I answered at once saying that you were one of my closest friends and that my relations with Scribners had always been so cordial and pleasant that I wouldn't think of changeing publishers. That letter will reach him at about the time this reaches you. I have never had any other communication *of any sort* with Liveright or any other publisher except the *very definate and explicit letter* with which I answered their letter yesterday.

So much for that rumor. I am both angry at Tom who must have been in some way responsible for starting it and depressed at the fact that you could have believed it enough to mention it to me. Rumors start like this.

Smith: (*a born gossip*) "I hear Fitzgerald's book isn't selling. I think we can get him, as he's probably blaming it on Scribners.

The Next Man: It seems Fitzgerald is disatisfied with Scribners and Liveright is after him.

The Third Man: I hear Fitzgerald has gone over to Liverite

Now, Max, I have told you many times that you are my publisher, and permanently, as far as one can fling about the word in this too mutable world. If you like I will sign a contract with you immediately for my next

---

*An editor at Boni & Liveright, publishers.

107

three books. The idea of leaving you has never for *one single moment* entered my head.

First. Tho, as a younger man, I have not always been in sympathy with some of your publishing ideas, (which were evolved under the pre-movie, pre-high-literacy-rate conditions of twenty to forty years ago), the personality of you and of Mr. Scribner, the tremendous squareness, courtesy, generosity and open-mindedness I have always met there and, if I may say it, the special consideration you have all had for me and my work, much more than make up the difference.

Second You know my own idea on the advantages of one publisher who backs you and not your work. And my feeling about uniform books in the matter of house and binding.

Third The curious advantage to a rather radical writer in being published by what is now an ultra-conservative house.

Fourth (and least need of saying) Do you think I could treat with another publisher while I have a debt, which is both actual and a matter of honor, of over $3000.00?

If Mr. Scribner has heard this rumor please show him this letter. So much for Mr. Liveright & Co.

Your letters are catching up with me. Curtis in *Town & Country* & Van Vetchten in *The Nation* pleased me.* The personal letters: Cabell, Wilson, Van Wyke Brooks ect. have been the best of all. Among people over here Ernest Hemminway & Gertrude Stien are quite entheusiastic. Except for Rascoe it has been, critically only a clean sweep. . . .

Ring's book has been a terrible disappointment to everyone here. He didn't even bother to cut out the connecting tags at the end of his travel articles and each of the five plays contain the same joke about "his mother – afterwards his wife." I shouldn't press him about his new collection, if I were you, because if you just took the first nine stories he writes, they couldn't be up to the others *and you know how reviewers are quick to turn on anyone in whom they have believed and who now disappoints them.* Of course I've only read *Haircut* and I may be wrong. I do want him to believe in his work & not have any blows to take away his confidence. The reviews I have seen of *What of it?* were sorry imitations of Seldes stuff and all of them went out of their way to stab Seldes in the back. God, cheap reviewers are low swine – but one must live.

---

*Two reviews of *The Great Gatsby*.

As I write word has just come by cable that Brady has made an offer for the dramatic rights of *Gatsby*, with Owen Davis, king of proffessional play doctors, to do the dramatization. I am, needless to say, accepting, but please keep it confidential until the actual contract is signed.

As you know, despite my admiration for *Through the Wheat*, I haven't an enormous faith in Tom Boyd either as a personality or an artist – as I have, say, in E. E. Cummings and Hemminway. His ignorance, his presumptious intolerance and his careless grossness which he cultivates for vitality as a man might nurse along a dandelion with the hope that it would turn out to be an onion, have always annoyed me. Like Rascoe he has never been known to refuse an invitation from his social superiors – or to fail to pan them with all the venom of a James-Oliver-Curwood-He-Man when no invitations were forthcoming.

All this is preparatory to saying that his new book sounds utterly lowsy – Shiela Kaye-Smith has used the stuff about the farmer having girls instead of boys and being broken up about it. The characters you mention have every one, become stock-props in the last ten years – "Christy, the quaint old hired man" after a season in such stuff as Owen Davis' *Ice Bound* must be almost ready for the burlesque circuit.

History of the Simple Inarticulate Farmer and his Hired Man Christy

(Both guaranteed to be utterly full of the Feel of the Soil)

1st Period

1855 – English Peasant discovered by Geo. Elliot in *Mill on the Floss, Silas Marner* ect.

1888 – Given intellectual interpretation by Hardy in *Jude* and *Tess*

1890 – Found in France by Zola in *Germinal*

1900 – Crowds of Scandanavians, Hamsun, Bojer ect, tear him bodily from the Russian, and after a peep at Hardy, Hamlin Garland finds him in the middle west.

Most of that, however, was literature. It was something pulled by the individual out of life and only partly with the aid of models in other literatures.

2nd Period

1914 – Shiela Kaye-Smith frankly imitates Hardy, produces two good books & then begins to imitate herself.

1915 – Brett Young discovers him in the coal country

1916 – Robert Frost discovers him in New England

1917 – Sherwood Anderson discovers him in Ohio

1918 – Willa Cather turns him Swede

1920 – Eugene O'Niell puts him on the boards in *Different* & *Beyond* [*the*] *Horizon*

1922 – Ruth Suckow *gets* in before the door closes
These people were all good second raters (except Anderson) Each of them brought something to the business – but they exhausted the ground, the type was set. All was over.

3rd Period

The Cheapskates discover him – Bad critics and novelists ect.

1923 Homer Croy writes *West of the Water tower*

1924 Edna Ferber turns from her flip jewish saleswoman for a strong silent earthy carrot grower and – the Great Soul of Charley Towne thrills to her passionately. Real and Earthy Struggle

1924 *Ice Bound* by the author of *Nellie the Beautiful Cloak Model* wins Pulitzer Prize
The Able Mcgloughlins wins $10,000 prize & is forgotten the following wk.

1925 *The Apple of the Eye* pronounced a masterpiece

1926 –TOM, BOYD, WRITES, NOVEL, ABOUT, IN-ARTICULATE, FARMER WHO, IS, CLOSE, TO SOIL, AND, HIS, HIRED, MAN CHRISTY! "STRONG! VITAL! REAL!"

As a matter of fact the American peasant as "real" material scarcely exists. He is scarcely 10% of the population, isn't bound to the soil at all as the English & Russian peasants were – and, if [he] has any sensitivity whatsoever (except a most sentimental conception of himself, which our writers persistently shut their eyes to) he is in the towns before he's twenty. Either Lewis, Lardner and myself have been badly fooled, or else using him as typical American material is simply *a stubborn seeking for the static in a world that for almost a hundred years has simply not been static.* Isn't it a 4th rate imagination that can find only that old property farmer in all this amazing time and land? And anything that ten people a year can do well enough to pass muster has become so easy that it isn't worth the doing.

I can not disassociate a man from his work. – That this Wescott . . . and Tom Boyd and Burton Rascoe . . . are going to tell us mere superficial "craftsmen" like Hergeshiemer, Wharton, Tarkington and me about the Great Beautiful Appreciation they have of the Great Beautiful life of the Manure Widder – rather turns my stomach. The real people like Gertrude Stien (with whom I've talked) and Conrad (see his essay on James) have a respect for people whose materials may not touch theirs *at a single point.* But the fourth rate & highly derivative people like Tom are loud in their outcry against any subject matter that doesn't come out of the old, old bag which their betters have used and thrown away.

For example there is an impression among the thoughtless (including Tom) that Sherwood Anderson is a man of profound ideas who is "handi-capped by his inarticulateness". As a matter of fact Anderson is a man of practically no ideas – *but he is one of the very best and finest writers in the English language today.* God, he can write! Tom could never get such rythms in his life as there are on the pages of *Winesburg, Ohio* – . Simple! The words on the lips of critics makes me hilarious: Anderson's style is about as simple as an engine room full of dynamoes. But Tom flatters himself that he can sit down for five months and by dressing up a few heart throbs in overalls produce literature.

It amazes me, Max, to see you with your discernment and your fine intelligence, fall for that whole complicated fake. Your chief critical flaw is to confuse mere earnestness with artistic sincerity. On two of Ring's jackets have been statements that he never wrote a dishonest word (maybe it's one jacket). But Ring and many of the very greatest artists have written thousands of words in plays, poems and novels which weren't even faintly sincere or ernest and were yet *artisticly sincere.* The latter term is *not* a synonym for plodding ernestness. Zola did not say the last word about literature; nor the first.

I append all the data on my fall book, and in closing I apologize for seeming impassioned about Tom and his work when niether the man or what he writes has ever been personally inimical to me. He is simply the scapegoat for the mood Rascoe has put me in and, tho I mean every word of it, I probably wouldn't have wasted all this paper on a book that won't sell & will be dead in a month & an imitative school that will be dead by its own weight in a year or so, if the news about Liveright hadn't come on top of the Rascoe review and ruined my disposition. Good luck to *Drummond.* * I'm sure one or two critics will mistake it for profound stuff

Samuel Drummond, Thomas A. Boyd's new novel.

111

– maybe even Mencken who has a weakness in that direction. But I think you should look closer.

With best wishes as always, Max,

Your Friend

DATA ON NEW FITZGERALD BOOK.

Title

ALL THE SAD YOUNG MEN

(9 short stories)

Print list of previous books as before with addition of this title under "Stories". Binding uniform with others.

Jacket plain (,as you suggest,) with text instead of picture

Dedication: To Ring and Ellis Lardner

The Stories (now under revision) will reach you by July 15th. No proofs need be sent over here.

It will be fully up to the other collections and will contain only one of those *Post* stories that people were so snooty about. (You have read only one of the stories *("Absolution")* – all the others were so good that I had difficulty in selling them, except two.

They are, in approximate order to be used in book:

1. The Rich Boy (Just finished. Serious story and very
        good)   13,000 wds.

2. Absolution (From *Mercury*)   6,500   "

3. Winter Dreams (A sort of 1st draft of the Gatsby idea
        from *Metropolitan* 1923)   9,000   "

4. Rags Martin-Jones and the Pr-nce of Wales
        (Fantastic Jazz, so good that Lorimer & Long*
        refused it. From *McCalls*)   5,000   "

5. The Baby Party (From *Hearsts*. A fine story)   5,000   "

6. Dice, Brass Knuckles and Guitar (From *Hearsts*. Exu-
        berant Jazz in my early manner)   8,000   "

---

*George Horace Lorimer, editor of the *Saturday Evening Post*, and Ray Long, editor of *Hearst's International*.

7. The Sensible Thing (Story about Zelda & me.
    All true. From *Liberty*)   5,000   "

8. Hot & Cold Blood (good story, from *Hearsts*)   6,000   "

9. Gretchen's Forty Winks (From Post. Farrar, Chris-
    tian Gauss and Jesse Williams thought it my best.
    It isn't.)   7,000   "

Total – about   – – – – – – – – – – – – – 64,500

(And possibly one other short one)

This title is because seven stories deal with young men of my generation in rather unhappy moods. The ones to mention on the outside wrap are the 1st five or the 1st three stories.

Rather not use advertising appropriation in *Times* – people who read *Times* Book Review won't be interested in me. Recommend *Mercury*, the F. P. A. page of the *World, Literary Review* and Fanny Bucher* page of *Chicago Tribune*.

No blurbs in ad. as I think the blurb doesn't help any more. Suggestion.

> Charles Scribners Sons
>
> Announce a new book of short stories
>
> by
>
> F. Scott Fitzgerald

Advertising Notes

Suggested line for jacket: "Show transition from his early exuberant stories of youth which created a new type of American girl and the later and more serious mood which produced *The Great Gatsby* and marked him as one of the half dozen masters of English prose now writing in America. . . . What other writer has shown such unexpected developments, such versatility, changes of pace"

    ect – ect – ect – I think that, toned down as you see fit, is the general line. Don't say "Fitzgerald has done it!" & then in the next sentence that I am an artist. People who are interested in artists aren't interested in people who have "done it." Both are O.K. but don't belong in the same ad. This is an author's quibble. All authors have one quibble.

    However, you have always done well by me (Except for Black's memo-

---

*Fanny Butcher, the regular book reviewer of the Chicago *Tribune*.

rable execretion in the *Allumni Weekly*; do you remember "Make it a Fitz-gerald Christmas! ") and I leave it to you. If 100,000 copies are not sold I shall shift to Mitchell Kennerley.

By the way what has become of Black? I hear he has written a very original and profound novel. It is said to be about an inarticulate farmer and his struggles with the "soil" and his sexual waverings between his inarticulate wife and an inarticulate sheep. He finally chooses his old pioneering grandmother as the most inarticulate of all but finds her in bed with none other than our old friend THE HIRED MAN CHRISTY!

CHRISTY HAD DONE IT!

[In 1962 Fitzgerald's famous letter to Perkins was sold at auction at Chrystie's (not old man Christy's) for £7000.]*

June 13, 1925

Dear Scott:

That was a great letter, as good as a cocktail. But in this book of Tom's there isn't anything of the peasant at all, – but of the American farmer as he unquestionably did exist at the time of the Civil War, and I myself have seen remnants of his race in Vermont – played with somewhat degenerated sons of it as a boy. It seems true to me. – By the way when I use the word sincere in connection with a piece of writing I mean artistically sincere. You are as bad as Mencken in taking me up on that. I should think anyone would understand that word applied to literature meant *that*.

I infer that the manuscript is on the way – I certainly hope it is and I will write you all the details about it when it comes, – how we plan it and everything else. I shall also supervise everything in connection with it myself.

As to the rumor. – The one who gave it me was Molly Colum and I immediately denied it altogether, but she came back with such positiveness that I wanted you to deny it. I did barely entertain the idea of its truth but only on the theory that you have been so cast down and harrassed about money that you had accepted some very large offer. This passed through my mind as a possibility but even that would not have happened if everything else had not seemed to be going wrong at the time, – I mean in personal affairs as well, Louis, etc. I do not believe Tom Smith was at fault anyhow. It was someone else in the office that told Molly.

I hope I will be able to write you in the next few days as there are a log [lot] of points in your letter that I want to speak of. But there is one thing

*This postscript appears in Fitzgerald's handwriting.

– I would not ever ask you to sign any permanent contract for the simple reason that it might be right for you sometime to change publishers, and while this would be a tragedy to me, I should not be so small as to stand in the way on personal grounds.

Yours,

P.S. . . . . .
    The sale is about 14,000. It goes ahead steadily, that is all.

June 26, 1925

Dear Scott:

. . . . .
    I cabled that Gatsby had gone to 15,000, – it is still some 50 or 60 copies short unless it has caught up today, but of course it will very soon exceed 15,000. I enclose herewith Mencken's review in the Mercury. He has spoken admirably for the book and even more highly verbally than in print, but I really do not think that he fully understood some elements in it, for if he had he would not keep speaking of its deficiencies *as a story.*

. . . . .
    All this about T.B.* I had meant to discuss, but what would be the use? Time will tell the story. I quite agree with your doctrine that a man's level as a writer is set by his own level as an individual, – but it is mighty hard to gauge people's levels even in that respect. And some mighty fine men have done some dirty tricks. How about that affair of Shakespeare's recorded in "Tales of the Jazz Age"? I do not feel quite right as a son of the "Puritan stock" in arguing this side of the case, but then I am also the son of a long line of lawyers.

    Ring says you are coming home soon. I wish to thunder you would. . . .

    My warmest regards to Zelda. Tell her I exhibited that picture of her daughter in the altogether to all of mine. She was vastly admired.

Yours,

14 Rue de Tilsitt
Paris, France
[ca. July 8, 1925]

Dear Max:
This is another one of those letters with a thousand details in them, so I'll number the details & thus feel I'm getting them out of the way.

*Thomas A. Boyd.

(1.) Will you have an account (bi-yearly statement) sent me as soon as you can. I don't know how much I owe you but it must be between 3 and 4 thousand dollars. I want to see how much chance *All The Sad Young Men* has of making up this difference. Thanks many times for the 700.00. It will enable me to go ahead next month with *Our Type** which is getting shaped up both in paper and in my head. I'd rather not tell about it just yet.

(2) Is Gatsby to be published in England. I'm awfully anxious to have it published there. If Collins won't have it can't you try Jonathan Cape? Do let me know about this.

(3) Will you tell me the figures on Ring's books? Also on *Through the Wheat*. I re-read the latter the other day & think its marvellous. Together with the Enormous Room and, I think, Gatsby, its much the best thing that has come out of American fiction since the war. I exclude Anderson because since reading *Three Lives* and his silly autobiography my feeling about him has entirely changed. He is a short story writer only.

(4) I spent $48.00 having a sketch of me done by Ivan Opfer.† It was lousy and he says he'll try another. If its no good I'll send a photo. The stories for the book leave here day after tomorrow.

(5) I think the number of Americans in Europe has hurt the book market. *Gatsby* is the last principle book of mine that I want to publish in the spring. I believe that from now on fall will be much the best season.

(6) I'm sorry about that outburst at Tom. But I am among those who suffer from the preoccupation of literary America with the drab as subject matter. Seldes points this out in a great review of *Gatsby* for the *London Criterion*. Also he says "Fitzgerald has certainly the best chance at present of becoming our finest artist in fiction". Quite a bit from Gilbert who only likes Ring, Edith Wharton[,] Joyce and Charlie Chaplin. Please get Myer** to put it on the cover of the new book and delete the man who says I "deserve the huzza's of those who want to further a worthy American Literature." Perhaps I deserve their huzzas but I'd rather they'd express their appreciation in some less boisterous way.

(7.) I'm sending back the questionairre.††

---

*The title Fitzgerald was then using for his new novel in progress.

†Perkins, on June 26th, had requested a drawing of the author for the jacket of *All the Sad Young Men*.

**Wallace Meyer, advertising manager and later editor at Scribners.

††On June 26th, Perkins had sent Fitzgerald a list of questions that an interviewer had submitted.

(8) I suppose that by now Gatsby is over 18,000. I hope to God it reaches 20,000. It sounds so much better. Shane Leslie thought it was fine.

No news, Max. I was drinking hard in May but for the last month I've been working like a dog. I still think *Count Orget's Ball* by Radiguet would sell like wildfire. If I had the time I'd translate it myself.

July 9, 1925

Dear Scott:
I wired you Tuesday to say that "The Great Gatsby" was now 16,000. It is at all events selling persistently. In that telegram I said "deposited" which referred to the three hundred and fifty. I have just wired you about the seven hundred. If this puts you in a position to go straight ahead with a new novel, we are certainly mighty glad to send it. A new novel is what you ought to do as soon as you are able. I had heard from somebody who had seen somebody who had seen you in Paris, that you had written half of a new novel, but that I thought quite impossible; – but I know that you have thoroughly thought out this novel because you spoke of it even when you were in Capri. If you could give me some idea of what you are doing in it, just in the briefest way, I wish you would; – but merely as a matter of interest, and not at all if you think that talking about it in advance is dangerous. I know it does sometimes dull the edge for the writer to do this.
. . . . .

As ever,

14 Rue de Tilsitt.
Paris, France
[ca. July 10, 1925]

Dear Max:
(1.) I'm afraid in sending the book I forgot the dedication, which should read

TO RING AND ELLIS LARDNER

Will you see to this?

(2.) I've asked *The Red Book* to let you know the first possible date on "The Rich Boy"[36]

(3.) I'm terribly sorry about the whooping cough but I'll have to admit it did give me a laugh.

(4.) Max, it amuses me when praise comes in on the "structure" of the book – because it was you who fixed up the structure, not me. And don't think I'm not grateful for all that sane and helpful advice about it.

(5) The novel has begun. I'd rather tell you nothing about it quite yet. No news. We had a great time in Antibes and got very brown & healthy. In case you don't place it its the penninsula between Cannes & Nice on the Rivierra where Napoeleon landed on his return from Elba.

As Ever

July 14, 1925

Dear Scott:

I'll have this letter copied, for it's written on a hot, cindery day on a train to Philadelphia; – where I'm to see the editor of the Ladies Home Journal for a few minutes, and then rush back.

I'm delighted about the novel. Is the title "Our Type"? That's what the cable implied. Tell me all you want to about it, but no more. Two things have lately impressed me with the veracity of your vision: the beach we belong to over the Fourth of July, and the strange conglomeration of the human species – strange in variety of origin and shape – almost equal to your catalogue of names in "Gatsby"; and the Scopes trial: – the stadium, the in-rush of publicity seekers, the fantastic levity of almost all concerned – or rather who concern themselves – with the frequent pretense of high seriousness. Can anything be taken seriously today, here? What of the seriousness of the Gallileo, Savanarola, Luther affairs, if they had been filmed, radioed, front-paged the moment they "broke"? Scopes said, when arrested, he was bitterly unpopular in his town. Then days later the populace awoke to find the sun of national publicity had spot-lighted Dayton; – and realized Scopes had put them on the map. – Scopes unpopular no longer! Bryan says he will fundamentalize the Constitution and Edgar Lee Masters, whom I saw at the Colums on Sunday, says he speaks the truth; – that it's no more improbable than was prohibition. You know Struthers Burt said two years ago that we'd end in the U.S. with a religious civil war. And he meant it and I ridiculed it, and now it seems far less improbable: – he argued, the fundamentalists, etc. would fix upon us by political means, such regulatory legislation as would finally become utterly intolerable.

Scott, I won't argue with you; but what difference does it make that a story is similar in rough outline, to one that somebody else wrote? How many of the best stories of any day have not been told before? – You must have great skill in rapid reading. I'm as slow as an ox, and envious of that talent.

Molly Colum came over last night to read me the first four pages of a book on the principles of criticism. She calls it "Wide Eyes and Wings" which suggests her belief that criticism should be emotional; that literature should not be measured by fixed intellectual standards. I admired her mind already, but I was astonished: there were surely four fresh *ideas* set forth, and with absolute clarity. – And I've so often argued (like so many others) that woman was incapable of grasping abstractions. – But I'd gladly turn feminist with my multitude of girls.

Liveright has annexed Edgar Lee Masters and has sold to a new publisher his Modern Library. V.W.B.* was immensely pleased with your letter about the Henry James. He's writing now a life of Emerson, who has hitherto been only pietistically presented in biographies, and therefore misrepresented. VanWyck has illuminating ideas of him – an artist by instinct: how he revealed in his journals his way of interpreting figures of history by actual characters of the village of Concord: – he saw them as possessing the same component elements as for instance, Mohammed, Napoleon, etc. And how he hated the odor of sanctity which in his time clung to so many otherwise vital persons and things, even, he thought, impairing the value of the Bible, – de-vitalizing it. Now (in absolute confidence) I can get this book if V.W.B. can loose himself from Dutton who have not done rightly by him, but have a contract.

Well, here's Philadelphia, so –

As ever yours,

Antibes, Rivierra, Aug 28th [1925]
(Permanent Adress Paris as usual)
Leaving here next week.

Dear Max:

I. Here's the stuff. I've been working over it for a month – especially this version of *The Rich Boy*. The Red Book hasn't yet published it but I have asked them to hurry & they should by November. Will ask Reynolds to inform you exactly.

II. You will notice that one story I included in my dummy Table of Contents that I sent you in July has been withdrawn, and another better one substituted.†

III. How about Chatto & Windus on Gatsby. Didn't they like it? Why not Capes? O.K. about syndicating Gatsby of course.[37]

---

*Van Wyck Brooks.
†Fitzgerald substituted "The Adjuster" for "Dice, Brass Knuckles and Guitar."

IV. *Our Type* is about several things, one of which is an intellectual murder on the Leopold-Loeb idea. Incidently it is about Zelda & me & the hysteria of last May & June in Paris. (Confidential)

V. Thanks for the terms of the contract & for all the advances.[38]

VI. I will write you fully about everything from Paris.

VII. Let me know what you think of the 1st four stories.[*]

> 14 Rue de Tilsitt
> Paris, France
> [*ca.* September 10, 1925]

Dear Max:
Several things have come up.

(1.) I thought Tom's book[†] undistinguished in the extreme. It did not seem to me "modern" (in the best sense) but a conventional novel full of conventional types and situation – something not more than two or three dozen Americans can do. Its characters have no more reality than those in, say, *Drums*,[**] and it lacks the facinating subject matter of the latter. Nor has it any scene that compares with the march of the Revolutionary army in the last pages of *Drums*.

(2.) I was curious to know about Ring's & Tom's sales (in general terms)

(3) And most important. When your letter says Chatto and Windus can't bring out *Gatsby* until fall[††] does it mean the fall of 1926? That seems incredible but if it is true I certainly want to protest – in fact I'd rather it were offerred to Capes (Jonathan) or not published at all than brought out a year & half late. Many of the Englishmen whose opinion is most valuable have already read it. I see no reason why when Lewis & Hergeshiemer are published simultaeneously in England and America & reap the full harvest of the double publicity, my book must wait 18 months. . . . I hope the Chatto & Windus arrangement isn't definate – if it is I wish you'd get Mr. Kingsley to try and change it. Why not Jonathan Capes. I can't tell you how strongly I feel about having it come out this spring *at the latest*. Do please let me know immediately – I noticed it wasn't on their fall list & then I read your letter over with dismay.[39]

[*]The letter breaks off here, unsigned.
[†]*Samuel Drummond* by Thomas A. Boyd.
[**]A novel by James Boyd, published by Scribners in 1925.
[††]This information was included in a Perkins letter of September 4th.

Collins never believed in me (He always wanted me to write "a long *Offshore Pirate*") and I know my public in England is small – but I have had enough entheusiastic letters to know it exists.

(4) Reynolds tells me *The Red Book* can't publish *The Rich Boy* (2 parts) until their Jan. & Feb. issues. In that case why not bring All the Sad Y.M. out in February. It will assure it a big press – the book *after* a large critical success always gets loud yells from the small caliber men. Did you like *The Rich Boy*? And the others? The Rich Boy is the best.

(5) What sale Gatsby? 20,000 yet?

(6) Enclosed is something left out from MS.

(7) The novel is going to be great

As Ever Your Friend

Oct. 6, 1925

Dear Scott:
I had your letter about "Gatsby" in England. It is not in the fall that they are to publish, but in the spring. This is certainly a pity, but Collins had the right to the first chance at the book and he was slow in deciding. He said in his letter: "With regard to 'The Great Gatsby', this has perplexed us all here. In a way it is the best book Scott Fitzgerald has done, and yet I think it is the one hardest to sell over here. I do not think the British public would make head or tail of it, and I know it would not sell. It is an awkward length too. We do not at all like to part with Scott Fitzgerald, but we feel very strongly that to publish 'The Great Gatsby' would be to reduce the number of his readers rather than to increase them. The point is, that the atmosphere of the book is extraordinarily foreign to the English reader, and he simply would not believe in it, and therefore I am regretfully returning it to you."[40]

"Gatsby" was then put before Duckworth and they came to the same conclusion. It then went to Chatto & Windus who took it. I can easily understand your liking for Cape because I also like him and like his books; but he is not in fact as strong a publisher as Chatto & Windus, and Mr. Scribner thinks you are much better off at present in their hands. . . .

I have just begun to get the proofs of "All the Sad Young Men" and as soon as I have the first story complete I will write you about it and the other stories.

As ever yours,

Oct. 12, 1925

Dear Scott:
Here is the royalty report on "The Great Gatsby". The sale is still a little short of twenty thousand copies, but except for that last three hundred, your indebtedness would have been only about $2700 which would have been soon wiped out with the appearance of "The Said [Sad] Young Men". I believe you will soon be in a much better financial position. I think you are progressing splendidly, – the first three stories which I have read in "All the Sad Young Men" show this, even if "The Great Gatsby" had not. They have more breadth, these stories, particularly the first and third,* than those of earlier collections. In fact, it is remarkable that you have been able to make them so entertaining for the crowd, when they have so much significance.

Yours,

14 Rue de Tilsitt
[Paris, France]
[ca. October 20, 1925]

Dear Max:
Thanks for your letters of 6th, 7th, & 12th. I'm delighted that you like the 1st four stories. The reason I want to get proof on *The Rich Boy* is that the original of the hero wants something changed – something that would identify him.

I'm relieved that *Gatsby* is coming out this Spring in England. – your first letter implied the Fall of 1927! But I'm disappointed that its only reached 19,640 copies. I hoped that it had reached nearer 25,000.

I was interested in the figures on Tom Boyd & Ring[41] – needless to say I won't mention them, but I thought *Through the Wheat* had sold much more. Considering the success of "What Price Glory?" I don't understand it. And Points of Honor only 1545! I'm astonished, and appalled. I see the New Yorker and the Nation (or New Republic) mention *Samuel Drummond* favorably.

There is no news. The novel progresses slowly & carefully with much destroying & revision. If you hear anything about the *Gatsby* dramatization – cast, date, ect. do let me know.

I wired you yesterday for $100.00 which brings me up to $3171.66 again – depressing thought! Will I ever be square. The short stories probably won't sell 5,000

Somewhat Mournfully

*"The Rich Boy" and "The Baby Party."

P.S. Did the Gatsby syndication with Bell Syndicate fall through?

P.S. A year & ½ ago Knopf published a book (novel) by Ruth Suckow called *Country People*. So he didn't risk her short stories It didn't go. But Mencken & I & many others think her stories wonderful. They're in the Smart Set (years 1921, 1922, 1923) and the American Mercury (1924, 1925), just enough to make about an 80,000 word book. A great press assurred – she could be the American Katherine Mansfield. This fine book The Perrenial Bachelor by Miss Parrish* derives from her I think. (She's the best woman writer in American under 50)

Why not approach her? Knopf seems to be letting her ride. You could probably get the next novel if she isn't signed up & you tried the stories first. I think this is an A.1. tip.

Nov. 25, 1925

Dear Scott:
The proofs of "The Sad Young Men" have come back and have gone to the printer and so the way is clear for publication. And I believe that these stories will make a new and strong impression.

I meant to have got some accounts of Princeton's wonderful football achievements to send you, but you seem very well in touch nowadays, and have probably read, in particular, of the magnificent victory at Yale. I had the unhappiness of seeing the Harvard-Princeton game, and although I thought Harvard was defeated more because they did not then play football, it was evident that Princeton had a most unusual team, and I thought they would beat Yale. – But Harvard gave satisfaction two weeks later by holding Yale back from a score throughout a game played almost altogether under the shade of her own goal posts.

I know Ruth Suckow is a person of great possibilities, but as soon as you spoke of her I noticed that a new book by her was announced by Alfred Knopf, – and our relations with Alfred Knopf are of an especially friendly sort so that he is one of the last publishers against whom we would want to work; – although if the situation had been as you thought, we could have acted in all fairness on your suggestion.

I am pinning great hopes on Sidney Howard who is writing a big novel which should be publishable next fall. "Drums" cannot be stopped. It is selling more rapidly this fall than it did in the spring. – I think his next novel will be much better for he told me not exactly the plot, but the general sort of scheme of it, and it is full of interest, although the interest

* *The Perennial Bachelor* by Anne Parrish (1925).

123

is rather in the scene, background, etc., than in the characters. Sidney's play "Lucky Sam McCarver" which was not quite worked through to clarity, was taken off after about four weeks of houses that looked good, but were not sufficiently so. I am waiting with much curiosity to see what they do with "The Great Gatsby" in the production. As for the syndicate, I told them to go ahead and they apparently were preparing to do it with enthusiasm for the book itself.

It is an age since I have written you a letter, and there are a lot of personal things I wanted to tell you. Louise and I went up to Arthur Train's* on a house party the last two weeks in October and had an amusing time. Did you and Zelda get the copy of "The Knave of Hearts"?† I came near asking you to go and interview a young French woman whom we are importing as governess, but we decided in the end to take a chance on her being suitable.

Wouldn't it be fun to get up a sort of burlesque on those dictionaries of biography – famous men, representative men, etc., etc. – for representation in which simple people will pay ten dollars or so, by persuading you and Ring and Benchley and Ernest Boyd and Donald Ogden Stuart, and old George Ade, etc., etc., etc., each to do a number of fictional biographies which hit off various types of people? And then to illustrate, make and bind the book in imitation of these volumes. The writers could satirize or burlesque as they pleased so they could be nearly nonsensical. This idea just occurred to me when a man came in in the idea of getting us to manufacture one of these books for him. He showed me some of the biographies and they were the most astonishing pieces of bunk, written in all solemnity.

As ever yours,

Dec. 17, 1925

Dear Scott:

I'm sending you for Christmas, or thereabouts, a book I've had especially bound; – for it is among the most original, beautiful, and terrible books of our time, and I want to do it what little honour I can by putting it in that dress into which great books eventually get themselves. – And you ought to have it in that form.

I had lunch yesterday with John Biggs who left his book,** – which

---

*Arthur Train, an American novelist, short-story writer and criminologist, most famous as the creator of Ephraim Tutt, perhaps the most popular fictional lawyer. Scribners published many of his books.

†A novel by Louise Saunders (Perkins), published by Scribners in 1925.

**_Demigods_, a novel published by Scribners in 1926.

Dunn once said had become a classic in this office without ever having been written. He asked for you, but I could tell him little except about "The Sad Young Men" and how notable it appeared to me to be and what depth and diversity the stories had; – so that taking them with "Gatsby" no one could say what you might yet do.

I ought to have sent you accounts of the football games which made pleasant reading for a Princetonian, – and that of Princeton vs. Yale, for everyone but a Yale man. But I note that you somehow keep in touch with things, unassisted by me; and for me to have sent you the story of Harvard vs. Princeton would have been too humiliating. – Enough to have had to sit it out! I thought also of sending you the strange story of "Red" Grange and his magic sphere – which the creator of Gatsby would value – although it is not yet ended; and the remarkable letters of Mrs. Leonard K. Rhinelander. – I *thought* of doing all this, but I felt sure that these things did not escape your eye. Even the gossip you get as soon as I, except the local – i.e. New Canaan: – such as how Padriac Colum, returning from a lecture in Montreal with two quarts of whisky in bottles was forced by the conductor – though he'd evaded the inspector – to surrender those and ten dollars too; and how, having no evening tie, in a strange city he appealed to a hotel waiter and got one 'tailor-made' which, as the waiter explained, you affixed to the collar button, – and on the platform at an eloquent moment, it ignominiously fluttered to the floor; and of how the Benets have left us from motives explained by Elinor by labyrinthine reasoning, in the face of the obvious facts, that if she couldn't be in London or Paris, she had to be in New York and she couldn't stand *children*. – I doubt if she ever comes back but she swears she will; and of how Bob Flaharity, who made Na Nook of the North, etc. – and whose broad pink face shines daily with some new vision, is planning with Will James – who looks exactly like his own cowboys – a cowboy picture epic which will probably come to nothing; – but all these things are trivial and I won't bore you with more.

As ever yours and Zelda's,

14 Rue de Tilsitt
Paris, France
[ca. December 27, 1925]

Dear Max:
I write to you from the depths of one of my unholy depressions. The book is wonderful – I honestly think that when its published I shall be the best American novelist (which isn't saying a lot) but the end seems far

away. When its finished I'm coming home for awhile anyhow though the thought revolts me as much as the thought of remaining in France. I wish I were twenty-two again with only my dramatic and feverishly enjoyed miseries. You remember I used to say I wanted to die at thirty – well, I'm now twenty-nine and the prospect is still welcome. My work is the only thing that makes me happy – except to be a little tight – and for those two indulgences I pay a big price in mental and physical hangovers.

. . . . .

. . . I hope the short stories sell seven or eight thousand or so. Is *Gatsby* dead? You don't mention it. Has it reached 25,000? I hardly dare to hope so. Also I deduce from your silence that Tom Boyd's book was a flop. If so I hope he isn't in financial difficulties. Also I gather from reviews that the penciled frown came a croper. I wish Liveright would lose faith in Ernest. Through the whole year only the following American novels have seemed worth a damn to me.

The Spring Flight

Perrenial Bachelor

In Our Time

The Great Gatsby

I thought the books by *Lewis, Van Vechten, Edith Wharton, Floyd Dell, Tom Boyd* and *Sherwood Anderson* were just *lowsy*!

And the ones by *Willa Cather* and *Cyril Hume* almost as bad.

Dos Passos & *Ruth Suckow* I havn't yet read.

The press Anderson got on *Dark Laughter* filled me with a much brighter shade of hilarity. You notice it wasn't from those of us who waited for the Winesburg stories one by one in the *Little Review* but by Harry Hansen, Stallings ect & the other boys who find a new genius once a week and at all cost follow the fashions.

Its good you didn't take my advice about looking up Gertrude Stien's new book (The Making of Americans). Its bigger than Ullyses and only the first parts, the parts published in the Transatlantic are intelligable at all. Its published privately here.

The best English books of the fall are *The Sailor's Return* by David Garnett and *No More Parades* by Ford Maddox Ford (a sequeal to *Some do Not*)

(Speaking of Gertrude Stien I hope you are keeping my precious *Three*

Lives safe for me. Ring's book sounds good. Send me a copy – also the wrap of mine.
. . . . .

No, Zelda's not entirely well yet. We're going south next month to Salies-les-Bains to see if we can cure her there. . . .
. . . . .

My novel should be finished next fall.

Tell me all the gossip that isn't in *The New Yorker* or the *World* – isn't there any regular dirt?

I called on *Chatto and Windus* in London last month & had a nice talk with Swinnerton, their reader (It was he, it seems, who was strong for the book. Saw Leslie* also & went on some very high tone parties with Mountbattens and all that sort of thing. Very impressed, but not very, as I furnished most of the amusement myself. *Please write!* Best to Louise.

Your Friend

. . . . .

14 Rue de Tilsitt
[*New adress*
Guaranty Trust Co.
1 Rue des Italiennes]†
[*ca. December 30, 1925*]

Dear Max:

(1.) To begin with many thanks for all deposits, to you and to the Scribners in general. I have no idea now how I stand with you. To set me straight will you send me my account *now* instead of waiting till February 1st. It must be huge, and I'm miserable about it. The more I get for my trash the less I can bring myself to write. However this year is going to be different.

(2) Hemmingways book (not his novel) is a 28,000 word satire on Sherwood Anderson and his imitators called The *Torrents of Spring*. I loved it, but believe it wouldn't be popular, & Liveright have refused it – *they are backing Anderson* and the book is almost a vicious parody on him. You see I agree with Ernest that Anderson's last two books have let everybody down who believed in him – I think they're cheap, faked, obscurantic and awful. Hemmingway thinks, but isn't yet sure to my satisfaction, that their

---

*Shane Leslie.
†These brackets are Fitzgerald's.

refusal sets him free from his three book (letter) agreement with them. In that case I think he'll give you his novel (on condition you'll publish satire first – probable sale 1000 copies) which he is now revising in Austria. Harcourt has just written Louie Bromfield that to get the novel they'll publish satire, sight unseen (utterly confidential) and Knopf is after him via Aspinwall Bradley.

He and I are very thick & he's marking time until he finds out how much he's bound to Liveright. If he's free I'm almost sure I can get satire to you first & then if you see your way clear you can contract for the novel *tout ensemble.* He's anxious too to get a foothold in your magazine – one story I've sent you – the other, to my horror he'd given for about $40 to an "arty" publication called *This Quarter*, over here.

He's *dead set* on having the satire published first. His idea has always been to come to you & his only hesitation has been that Harcourt might be less conservative in regard to certain somewhat broad scenes. His adress is:

Herr Ernest Hemmingway

Hotel Taube

Schrunns

Vorarlburg

Austria

Don't even tell him I've discussed his Liveright & Harcourt relations with you

As soon as he has definate dope I'll pass it on to you. I wanted a strong wire to show you were as interested, and more, than Harcourt. Did you know your letter just missed by two weeks getting *In Our Time*. It had no sale of course but I think the novel may be something extraordinary – Tom Boyd and E. E. Cummings & Biggs combined.

Wasn't Dos Passos' book* astonishingly good. I'm very fond of him but I had lost faith in his work.

(3.) Tell me all about my play.

(4.) I can't wait to see the book your sending me. Zelda says it might be *Gatsby* but I don't think so.

(5) Poor Eleanor Wylie! Poor Bill Benet! Poor everybody!

(6) My novel is wonderful.

---

* *Manhattan Transfer.*

(7) The translation of Gatsby sounds wonderful.

. . . . .

. . . . .

As Ever

Jan. 13, 1926

Dear Scott:

I enclose three wraps. Don't judge them without putting them around books, because that is the only way in which you can get any idea of how they will look. They are rather shabby specimens but they are all I can get hold of.

I thought Hemingway's stories astonishingly fine and so does everyone who reads them. It seems strange that Liveright has put so little behind them. I speak of this on the assumption that for some reason he is not to publish any more for Hemingway. Otherwise your cable[42] would not have come. I did my best with that cable, but there was a fear that this satire – although in the hands of such a writer it could hardly be rightly so upon any theory – might be suppressible. In fact we could tell nothing about it of course in these respects and it is not the policy obviously of Scribners to publish books of certain types. For instance, if it were even Rabelasian to an extreme degree, it might be objected to. It was only this point that prevented me from wiring you without any qualification because those stories are as invigorating as a cold, fresh wind.

I am afraid though that the qualification was fatal. – But in any case, I think it was bully of you to have acted in our behalf in that way. I was much pleased that you did it. As for Harcourt, I think him an admirable publisher and I haven't any criticism of him. But I believe that as compared with most others, Hemingway would be better off in our hands because we are absolutely true to our authors and support them loyally in the face of losses for a long time, when we believe in their qualities and in them. It is that kind of a publisher that Hemingway probably needs, because I hardly think he could come into a large public immediately. He ought to be published by one who believes in him and is prepared to lose money for a period in enlarging his market. – Although he would certainly, even without much support, get recognition through his own powers.

I have not tried to communicate with him because I did not know how far I ought to go, particularly after getting your second telegram. The fact is that we would publish the satire however certain it might be of financial failure because of our faith in him, – and perhaps also because of the qualities of the work itself, of which I cannot speak.

As ever yours,

129

c/o Guaranty Trust Co.
Paris, France
[ca. January 19, 1926]

Dear Max:

Your thoughtful cablegram[43] came today and I can't imagine how the rumor got started – unless from Zelda using an imaginary illness as a protection against the many transients who demand our time. Somehow if one lives in Paris one is fair game for all the bores one wouldn't look at and who wouldn't look at one in New York. (If there's one thing I hate its a sentence full of "ones")

We have escaped to a small town in the Pyrenes where Zelda is to take a cure. Our adress for cables is

Fitzgerald, Bellevue, Salies-de-Béarn, France

but for letters the Guaranty, Paris is best. We are living in an absolutely deserted hotel. We move on to Nice the first of March. Here are my usual list of things.

(1) Thanks a million times for the bound copy of my book – it is beautiful and, Max, I'm enormously obliged. I wish you'd written in the front – but that will wait till I get home. Your thought of me touched me more than I can say.

(2.) Now about the many deposits. They are past all reckoning but must total $5000 which is a record advance (?) on a book of short stories. I'm terribly sorry, Max. Could he send me my account this year on the 1st of February *really* instead of February 15th. We won't be able to tell about *The Sad Young* anyhow and I'm frantic to know if I'm helplessly in debt.

(3.) What is the date of the book? How are advance sales, compared with Gatsby? Did the latter ever reach 25,000?

(4) Now, confidentially, as to Hemminway. He wrote a satire 28,000 words long on Sherwood Anderson, very funny but very cerebral, called *The Torrents of Spring*. It is *biting* on Anderson – so Liveright turns it down. Hemminways contract *lapses when Liveright turns down a book, so Hemminway says*. But I think Horace will claim this isn't a book and fight it like the devil, according to a letter I saw which he wrote Ernest – because he's crazy to get Ernests almost completed novel *The Sun Also Rises*. It is such a mess that Ernest goes to N.Y. next month.

Meanwhile Harcourt & Knopf are after him but he's favorably disposed toward you because of your letters and of the magazine. He's very excitable, though and I can't promise he'll know his own mind next month. I'll tip you off the moment he arrives. Of course if Bridges likes his work &

if you'll take Torrents he's yours absolutely – contingent, of course, on the fact that he isn't bitched by some terrible contract with Liveright. To hear him talk you'd think Liveright had broken up his home and robbed him of millions – but thats because he knows nothing of publishing, except in the cucoo magazines, is very young and feels helpless so far away. You won't be able to help liking him – he's one of the nicest fellows I ever knew.

. . . . .

Thanks again for my beautiful copy.

As Ever

Jan. 28, 1926

Dear Scott:
You need not feel ashamed of the play, "The Great Gatsby". Far from it. Your ideas and the course of the action have been adhered to far more closely than I ever dreamed they would be. The cast is excellent, especially Gatsby, Buchanan, Daisy, and Wolfshiem. Of course you know all about the changes made in the plot. There is a prologue which seemed to me completely superfluous and therefore bad, – but it may not be so from the popular standpoint, although I should certainly vote against it on even that ground. I saw the performance last night at Stamford, and I know you cannot judge anything by the way those out-of-town audiences take a play, but that one was obviously altogether for it. And all the individuals I saw, like the Burts who went with me, and Bob Benchley, who was in the lobby after the second act, were much pleased. You do, of course, have to make allowances for the presentation of a book upon the stage. But when these are made to a reasonable degree, "The Great Gatsby" is distinctly well done. It is certainly a good play, and highly interesting, and it seems to me it has an excellent chance for success. I thought I would send you this word immediately. I heard nothing about the Great Neck performance, but every indication that the Stamford performance gave was most excellent.

As ever yours,

Feb. 3, 1926

Dear Scott:
I enclose three reviews of "The Great Gatsby". I suppose other people will have sent them, and I suppose other people will have informed you about the apparently undoubted success of the first night. I could not go because of the shift from Monday to Tuesday, but all that went from here were vastly interested and said that the audience was a full one and was impressed. There were many curtain calls. Rennie was liked by everyone.

131

You know how little and how much one can tell from a first night, and we will just have to wait, but the omens all seem to be excellent. As for those whom I have seen since the Stamford night, the least favorable was that of a fairly astute couple who had not read the book. They said they thought it was an extremely entertaining play, but not important. I give that because you never can tell how much one who has read the book reads into the play. . . .

That story of Hemingway's is most excellent.* I do not know what he will make of my letter which I enclose. We are just compelled to ask him to cut, and it will be hard to do. And I judge he is one of those whose interest is much more in producing than in publishing, and he may revolt at the idea of being asked to conform to an artificial specification in length. I wish with his very first story that we did not have to bring this up. I know we can take stories of his though, if he will send them, and I hope he may let us have this. People are beginning to talk about his writing, – those who find things for themselves and appreciate aside from technical literary qualities, a true eye for reality. There is much else to be said of it, but I think that is at the bottom of it, – perhaps it is a real basis of all true writing, when properly understood.

. . . . .

Thanks ever so much for sending the Hemingway. If only we could get the novel!

. . . . .

Yours as ever,

[*c/o Guaranty Trust Co.*]
[*1 Rue des Italiens*]
[*Paris, France*]
[*ca. February 8, 1926*]

Dear Max –

Thanks a million times for your wire and your letter about the Stanford performance. I hope to God it'll make some money for me at last. I agree with you about the prologue.

. . . . .

. . . . .

. . . . .

In regard to my novel. Will you ask somebody what is done if one American murders another in France. Would an American marshall come over for him? From his state of residence? Who would hold him meanwhile

---

*"Fifty Grand," which Hemingway had submitted to *Scribner's Magazine*.

– the consul or the French police? Why isn't that so if one Italien kills another Italien in America.

Its important that I find this out and I can't seem to.

In a certain sense my plot is not unlike Driesers in the American Tragedy. At first this worries me but now it doesn't for our minds are so different.

. . . . .

Do you know I now get 2500 a story from the Post – or did I tell you?

I should be writing this afternoon but I'm nervous as hell and can't. Zelda is much better. My novel will be called either *The World's Fair* or *Our Type*, I don't know which.

As Ever Your Friend

c/o Guaranty Trust Co.
1 Rue des Italiens
Paris, France
[ca. February 13, 1926]

You've been a peach, Max, about writing and wiring news about the play. Here we are in the Pyrenees with the following events taking place in the great world.

(1.) *Gatsby* on the stage

(2) *Gatsby* in England.

(3.) *Gatsby* translation being placed with publisher in Paris.

(4.) *All the Sad Young Men* in New York.

So, in spite of a side trip once a week to Biarritz or Pau or Lourdes or St. Sebastian, we feel a bit out of date. We expect to leave for Nice on March 1st or thereabouts. The letter to Hemminway must have crossed him. By now you've seen him in New York. Your letter was your usual responsive yet tactful self. I hope you get his novel. He's worth 100 Westcotts.

. . . . .

. . . . .

. . . . .

As Ever

South of France
Feb 20th, 1926

Dear Max:
Two things have just occurred to me – or rather three.

(1.) You'll get this letter about the 3d of March. My book of stories may, at that time have been out three weeks or three days – you've not told me the date. Will you in any case write me immediately forcasting roughly the approximate sale? . . . Also, would you send me an income tax blank?

My God! If it should sell 10,000 copies I'd be out of debt to you for the 1st time since 1922. Isn't that a disgrace, when I get $2500. for a story as my regular price. But trash doesn't come as easily as it used to and I've grown to hate the poor old debauched form itself.

How about Tom Boyd? Is he still going to be one of the barnyard boys? Or has he got sense and decided to write about the war, or seducing married women in St. Paul, or life in a bum Kentucky military school, or something he knows about. He has no touch of genius like Hemmingway and Cummings but like Dos Passos he has a strong, valuable talent. He must write about the external world, as vividly and accutely and even brilliantly as he can, but let him stop there. He is almost without the power of clear ratiocination and he has no emotional depths whatsoever. His hide is so thick that only battle itself could really make an impression on him – playing with the almost evanescent spiritual material of Anderson he becomes an ox to public view. I wish to God I could see him & talk to him. For heavens sake, Max, curb your usual (and, generally, sagacious) open-mindedness and don't help him to ruin his future by encouraging his stupidest ambitions. He'll turn bitter with failure.

. . . . .

Now, confidential. T.S. Eliot for whom you know my profound admiration – I think he's the greatest living poet in any language – wrote me he'd read *Gatsby* three times & thought it was *the 1st step forward American fiction had taken since Henry James.*

Wait till they see the new novel!

Did you get Hemmingway?

There was something else I wanted to ask you. What was it? damn it!

We're coming home in the fall, but I don't want to. I'd like to live and die on the French Rivierra

. . . . .

I can't remember my other question and its driving me frantic. Frantic! (Half an hour later) *Frantic!*

FRANTIC!!!

If you see anybody I know tell 'em I hate 'em all, him especially. Never want to see 'em again.

Why shouldn't I go crazy? My father is a moron and my mother is a neurotic, half insane with pathological nervous worry. Between them they havn't and never have had the brains of Calvin Coolidge.

If I knew anything I'd be the best writer in America.

Eureka! Remembered! Refer my movie offers to Reynolds.

> *Hotel Bellevue*
> *Salies-de-Béarn*
> [*ca. March 1, 1926*]

Dear Max:
Ernest will reach N.Y. as soon as this. Apparently he's free so its between you and Harcourt. He'll get in touch with you.

There are several rather but not very Rabelaisian touches in Torrents of Spring (the satire) *No worse than Don Stuart** or Benchley's Anderson parody. Also Harcourt *is said* to have offerred $500. advance [on] *Torrents* and $1000. on almost completed novel. (Strictly confidential.) If Bridges takes *50 Grand* I don't think Ernest would ask you to meet those advances but here I'm getting involved in a diplomacy you can handle better. I don't say hold *50 Grand* over him but in a way he's holding it over you – one of the reasons he verges toward you is the magazine.

In any case he is tempermental in business. Made so by these bogus publishers over here. If you take the other two things *get a signed contract* for The *Sun Also Rises* (novel) Anyhow this is my last word on the subject – confidential between you & me. Please destroy this letter.

. . . . .
. . . . .
. . . . .

> *As Ever*

. . . . .

> *March 4, 1926*

Dear Scott:
I just got your letter today asking for an income tax blank. I enclose one herewith. . . .

As for the sale of "All the Sad Young Men" which only came out last Friday, February 26th, we are already watching it very closely for reprinting. We have printed 10,100, and we have only about 300 on hand now, although of course many that are in the stores have not been sold. I feel

---

*Donald Ogden Stewart, American humorist, playwright and actor.

no hesitancy in saying that you can count absolutely on a sale of 12,000, and the truth is the prospects are excellent. "The Great Gatsby" continues to be successful, markedly so.

I asked Arthur Train about an American who murders another American in France. He is treated as though he were a Frenchman. He is taken in charge by the French police and tried in the French courts by a French judge and jury. I hope this fact won't upset some plan you had for the novel. I asked Arthur if there were any possible way in which there might be some form of American intervention – an envoy of justice, or something, and he said only in case the murderer were in the diplomatic service. Otherwise, he would have the same status as a Frenchman.

I think "Our Type" is the best title. Would "Our Kind" be better? It was used by Louise on a little one-act play, but that would make no difference.

As for Hemingway, whom I enjoyed very much, we have contracted to publish "Torrents of Spring" and the novel. He was willing to give us options on other books, but I never felt well of that way of doing: – if a man does not like us after we have published two of his books, he ought not to be compelled to publish through us, and we do not want to publish for anyone who is not square enough to recognize that what we have done is good, if it is, and to give us the advantage over anybody else. If a writer can get better terms from another publisher on his third or fourth book, it is only fair that he can also demand better terms of us. The relations you have with an author cannot be satisfactory if they are absolutely cut and dried business relations, anyhow. I am extremely grateful to you for intervening about Hemingway. He is a most interesting chap about his bull fights and boxing. His admirable story, "Fifty Grand" was too long to be got into the magazine, and it has been declined by Colliers and the Post, – although Lorimer spoke highly of it. Liberty could not use it because of its length. I do not know exactly what to do with it now. I believe I could sell it to College Humor, but I do not know whether he would like that.

I think your idea about selections from your books of stories primarily for publication in England, is an excellent one; and I do not think there would be much difficulty in bringing it about.[44] Curtis Brown, the agent who has placed your stories for us, could bring it about and would manage it well. Collins would not be in any position to make difficulties because he has sacrificed his opportunity by declining "Gatsby". . . .

I am mighty glad Zelda is better. I am getting off this series of facts as quickly as possible on account of the income tax, etc., but I will write you a *letter* soon.

As ever yours,

P.S. Tom Boyd has a job on the Atlanta Georgian, – I guess a pretty good job. He said he was not going to write another book right away. I agree with you about his powers of ratiocination, quite, but I should not have thought that he was lacking in emotion, and I thought there was great emotion implied throughout "Samuel Drummond" as well as that sensitiveness to the external world. But the total sale was only about five thousand copies.

> *Villa Paquita* ⎫ *adress*
> *Juan-les-Pius* ⎬ *till*
> *Alpes Maritime* ⎬ *June*
> *France* ⎭ *15th*
> [*ca. March 15, 1926*]

Dear Max:

Thanks very much for your nice letter & the income blank. I'm delighted about the short story book. In fact with the play going well & my new novel growing absorbing & with our being back in a nice villa on my beloved Rivierra (between Cannes and Nice) I'm happier than I've been for years. Its one of those strange, precious and all too transitory moments when everything in one's life seems to be going well.

Thanks for the Arthur Train legal advice.

I'm glad you got Hemmingway – I saw him for a day in Paris on his return & he thought you were great. I've brought you two successes (Ring & Tom Boyd) and two failures (Biggs & Woodward Boyd) – Ernest will decide whether my opinions are more of a hindrance or a help.

Why not try *College Humor* for his story. They published one thing of mine.

Poor Tom Boyd! First I was off him for his boneheadedness. Now I'm sorry for him.

> *Your friend*

I am out of debt to you for the first time in four years. . . .

> *Villa Paquita*
> *Juan-les-Pins*
> *France*
> [*ca. April 25, 1926*]

Dear Max:

Why in God's name did the advertising department broadcast a rotten sketch of me that makes me look like a degenerate? Its come to me in a dozen clippings and will probably haunt me the next five years. As it appears in Scribners magazine I suppose Myers sent it out – otherwise I would have thought it originated with some country magazine that needed space in an awful hurry. I know it's partly my own fault for not sending you one and I suppose this sounds vain and unpleasant but if you knew how it has taken the joy out of the press on my book to have that leering, puffy distortion reach me at the head of almost every review you'd know the way I've gotten worked up over it.

Thanks many times for *Our Times.** I read every word of it and loved it. Thoroughly interesting. About Mary Column's article:† I thought that the more solid parts were obvious and pedantic, and that a good half of it was the sort of nonsense I didn't expect from her. What on earth is the connection between Cocteau and Cummings? What does she mean by form. Does she think King Lear lacks it? While Marianne Moore has it? She uses it in the sense of successful conscious organization (so one thinks) and then it develops that she means mere novelty. Says she:

"How profoundly true to their race, period and the needs of their public are the great artists – Goethe, Dante, Shakespeare, Moliere! You can from their work pick out all the qualities, all the thoughts, all the ideals of the time that needed expression."

How in the devil does she know that? How does anyone know that. There may have been whole elements in each of their times (John Donne, Roger Bacon in Shakespeare's and Dante's respective times for example) whose ideals & spirits were not even faintly summed up by the powerful but fallible and all-too-human titan who succeeded in forcing on us his picture. Don't you agree?

I disliked the essay chiefly because its so plausible, and so dead, like (whisper it not, because I like him) the critical work of Ernest Boyd. Perhaps because I've just finished Checkov's *Letters on Literature.* God, there's a book!

You owe me a long letter

As Ever

April 27, 1926

Dear Scott:
The picture is bad and caused us to hesitate. But that it was so widely printed showed the chance there was for a picture, and we could not forego that chance. . . .

Our Times: The United States, 1900–1925, Vol. I, by Mark Sullivan, published by Scribners in 1926.
†"A Critical Credo," *Scribner's Magazine,* April 1926.

As for sales, they are something over 10,000 to date. We have printed 15,000. The prospects are good. I don't enclose reviews, – your clipping agency will furnish them.

The Galsworthys passed through New York on the way to England. I gave them your book and *she* was much pleased. So was he, but he talked of it (between ourselves) with less judgment. He did speak of "Gatsby" as "a great advance"; – but he's not really in sympathy with things today. The books he most admires – I won't mention the one I'm thinking of because it's ours – are laid out on the old lines and are not expressive of present thought and feeling. This is much less true of Mrs. Galsworthy, it seemed to me; – it may be that women, living much more in the present, from day to day, don't get rooted in a period as men almost inevitably do.

. . . . .

. . . . .

Molly Colum's article drew considerable written comment and was vocally much discussed; – which in itself proves nothing except that it was good for Scribner's, as having been in what criticism it has printed, too classical and accademic. I detest argument and though I cannot restrain myself often from a verbal one, I can from a written, and so do now.

I'm almost afraid to tell you about a book that I think incredibly interesting – Spengler's "Decline of the West" – for you'll tell me it's 'old stuff' and that you read it two years ago; – for it was published eight years ago in Germany, and probably six in France, and has been a long time translating into English. I'm trying for a time to read that and Clarendon's "History of the Rebellion" which long ago attracted me through quotations from it I was always encountering in other books.

Our really great success this spring promises to be Thomason's "Fix Bayonets!"; – for, although its price is $3.50, it's already well on toward a sale of ten thousand copies, and we're printing five thousand more. Sullivan is also going strong. I think Hemingway's book* will look well when done: we've made several good cuts to stand on the half title pages; – but it's the novel that I'm most eager to see, "The Sun Also Rises"! They say Dreiser is anxious to leave Liveright, who has certainly done well by him. In fact, there's a story about that he threw a cup of coffee into Liveright's face, – but if it had been true it would have been confirmed, for the Algonquin was the alleged scene of the encounter, – a broadcasting station if ever there was one.

Van Wyck Brooks has been in New Canaan for several months; but although I've seen much of him there was little fun in it because he is so depressed; – and the chief cause is (in confidence) that he's stuck in his book

---

* *The Torrents of Spring*, published by Scribners on May 28th.

on Emerson.* He can't finish it and declares it's a failure. I read it and suggested a scheme to apply to it which would give the structure it totally lacks. But Van Wyck won't adopt it, – at least not as yet. Perhaps he will in the end. – So he says he must get a *job;* and I say, 'What a shame at your age, with a foundation of reputation well laid. Set down the names of ten lesser American writers as titles for articles and I'll sell them at five hundred a piece, and the result will be a book that will outsell any you've done.' But he says he cannot write that way, and so we get no further. What he wants, of course, is a 'part time' job, but such a one if it continues will suck a man under. – Van Wyck could also, and profitably, lecture; for he has a body of ideas all related to U.S. 'civilization' and letters and he could get up a series which would be altogether in line with his literary motives. – But I ought not to bother you with his problem.

We had a grand winter at New Canaan. Skating on most of the weekends and hockey, and over New Years, for three windless days, the whole three-mile lake, a sheet of flexible black ice.

As ever your friend,

Villa Paquita
Juan-les-Pins
France
[ca. May 8, 1926]

Dear Max:
Thanks many times for all the books. The *Hickey*† I loved, having read the other three volumes of it. The war book** too was great – God, what bad luck Tom Boyd had! Stallings made the killing with the play and movie; now Thomason makes a contract with Hearst, for a lot, I guess and Tom who came first came too early, I suppose. Yet *What Price Glory?* would never have been written, I suppose, except for *Through the Wheat.* Not that Tom's novel wasn't a success in a way but to make about $6000. as an originator & see others rake it in like croupiers later – I know how bitter it must make him.

The Biggs book†† was tedious. I'm allowing for having seen it all at least three times but it *was* tedious. Undoubted power and a great gift of prose

*Eventually published by Dutton in 1932 as *The Life of Emerson.*
†*Memoirs of William Hickey.*
**Probably John W. Thomason, Jr.'s *Fix Bayonets*, published by Scribners in the Spring of 1926.
††*Demigods.*

but you cant arbitrarily patch together swads of fine writing and call it a novel. And parts of it were merely sensational bombast. I'm sorry.

Nor, I'm afraid, will Ring's book* add to his reputation. Several stories were fine, none were cheap but – God, I wish he'd write a more or less personal novel. Couldn't you persuade him? The real history of an American manager, say Ziegfeld or a theatrical girl. Think how far Anita Loos got with a mere imitation of him.

. . . . .

. . . . .

The reviews of *All the Sad Young Men* have been pleasant, mostly, but, after the book and the play, rather tame. Did it go to 12,000 as you suggested? We've had some good nibbles for the movie rights of Gatsby but they want $45,000, I hear. I get one third of the gross price.

See my article on Hemmingway in the *Bookman†* – its pretty good.

In *absolute confidence* I've recieved an offer of $3,500 per short story from Liberty. I'm considering it.

My book is *wonderful.* I don't think it'll be interrupted again. I expect to reach New York about Dec 10th with the ms. under my arm. I'll ask between $30,000 & $40,000 for the serial rights and I think Liberty will want it. So book publication would be late Spring 1927 or early fall.

No news. Do write. Tell me if *Torrents of Spring* gets a press. I doubt if it will sell. Again thank you for the books.

Ever and Always Your Friend

. . . . .

> Villa St. Louis
> Juan-les-Pins
> [ca. May 10, 1926]

Dear Max:

The mistral is raging outside like the end of the world and the idea of writing is anathema to me. We are wonderfully situated in a big house on the shore with a beach and The Casino not 100 yds. away and every prospect of a marvellous summer.

I'm sorry about Van Wyke Brookes. You yourself sounded a bit depressed.

Dreiser would be crazy to leave Liveright, tho I can understand how Horace would get on his nerves. I heard that the movie rights of *An American Tragedy* brought $90,000. but I don't believe it. *Gatsby* so it now

---

The Love Nest and Other Stories.
†"How to Waste Material," published in the May issue.

appears sold for $50,000. An agent on the coast got 10% and Davis, Brady & I split the $45,000. Then I had to pay Reynolds 10% more so instead of $16,666.66 I recieved $13,500.000 or $3,166.66 went in agents commissions. However I shouldn't kick. Everybody sells movies through an agent & the Reynolds part was nessessary since I'm away. I thought the drawings for *The Sad Young Men* ads were fine. By the way I'm sending two negatives for pictures. Do send them out right away to replace the others.

. . . . .

I'm not surprised at Galesworthy's not being responsive to my stuff. I've found that if you don't respond to another man's writings the chances are it's mutual – and except for *The Apple Tree* and, oddly enough, *Saints Progress* he leaves me cold. I suspect he had some unfortunate iddylic love affair in his youth and whenever that crops into his work it comes alive to me. The subject matter of *The Forsythe Saga* seemed stuffy to me. I entirely "approve" of him though and liked him personally.

Have you considered coming over?

Always your friend

June 18, 1926

Dear Scott:

"The Torrents" gets praise but not always comprehension. Hemingway sent through me a letter to Anderson. What did he say, I wonder? Not that, as it seemed to me, he need make any apology. I did not think the thing cruel, as Liveright apparently did. There was as much humor in the book as wit. It was not, as we used to say some seasons back – "devastating". I'm waiting impatiently for proof of "The Sun Also Rises". *That* showed more 'genius' than I had inferred from "The Torrents" – which I did not rate so very high – and "In Our Time"; – though I'd inferred much. Your Bookman article I thought excellently done. – . . .

I could come over – and how quickly I'd do it – if it weren't for all these children. We got our French governess who is capable and a good teacher, but as Molly Colum said, "I've yet to see her do any genu*ine* governess-ing." She's fairly young, and, not unnaturally, is chiefly interested in herself. Next year I think we shall go over, but I suppose you won't. Where will you live here? You ought to try to settle in some typical community for quite a long time, not for your future as a citizen so much as for that as a writer: – You'd see a new surface of life that way.

Take Wilmington for instance. Louise and I went down to John's* for a week end and I've been thinking about it ever since. There's a kind of

*John Biggs.

feudalism. The DuPonts, an immense family, mostly female, dominate the town. They marry whom they will. A strong, practical race of vast wealth. We went to a DuPont wedding and saw most of them, and found them fine looking except for an excess of powerful teeth. They are almost the whole show. The talk is always of the doing of one or another. They have the eccentricity and independence – not arrogance for they are simple and natural – that comes from their position, and offer a most interesting subject for conversation.

John has a house on the flat top of a hill at a little distance from a much larger, higher hill which makes a smooth, round ascent. The house is of some Dutch type, of stone covered with light gray cement, which look high and steep, as if they belonged rather in the city. The walls go straight up with no piazzas and as it seems, few windows. Why they should have built such steep-walled, fort-like places, in so mild a climate, I don't know. You see one on every hillside or summit. – But it rained, or dripped all the time we were there and I got a cold, – now an unhappy memory, thank God. There was a most entertaining man named Wiley – author of two novels of a certain quality, but, pale and weak, as I gathered from a fifteen minute survey of them – who gave the most incredible accounts of life in an advertising agency. I was almost hysterical over the ladies who regard Fleischmann's yeast as an opportunity for publicity, and a fine photograph in a fur coat, or a canoe, or on a fine horse, and sometimes get proposed to as a result. You've seen the ads. Did you see that one of Bruce Barton's "The Man Nobody Knows" headed "Christ the Executive" illustrated with two pictures, in juxtaposition, of groups of men around a table? One showed Christ and the twelve apostles; the other a twentieth century "Chairman of the Board" and the directors of a corporation. – I'd meant to send you that and lost it as a genuine whiff of the U.S.A.

It's true John's book was not a success. I mean *he* was not successful with it. But it has astonishing qualities and he may, he should, get command over them, – if he has time. It did make a good impression. I realized long ago, as I saw the manuscript little by little, that he could not fulfill his design, which was too vague in his own mind for one thing, to perfection. And with a tour de force like that perfection is what you need. He's writing another now, is eager to do my story about the biologist and the pernicious insects.

. . . . .

. . . . .

As ever yours,

Villa St. Louis
Juan-les-Pins
A-M.
[*ca. June 25, 1926*]

Dear Max:

Thanks for both letters. We were in Paris having Zelda's appendix neatly but firmly removed or I would have answered before.

First as to Ernests book.* I liked it but with certain qualifications. The fiesta, the fishing trip, the minor characters were fine. The lady I didn't like, perhaps because I don't like the original.† In the mutilated man** I thought Ernest bit off more than can yet be chewn between the covers of a book, then lost his nerve a little and edited the more vitalizing details out. He has since told me that something like this happened. Do ask him for the absolute minimum of necessary changes, Max – he's so discouraged about the previous reception of his work by publishers and magazine editors (tho he loved your letter). From the latter he has had a lot of words and until Bridges offer for the short story (from which he had even before cut out a thousand words on my recommendation) scarcely a single dollar. From the *Torrents* I expect you'll have little response. Do you think the Bookman article did him any good?

· · · · ·

· · · · ·

The novel, in abeyance during Zelda's operation now goes on apace. This is confidential but Liberty, with certain conditions, has offered me $35,000. sight unseen. I hope to have it done in January.

· · · · ·

Ever your Friend

Villa St. Louis
Juan-les-Pins
A-M-
[*ca. August 11, 1926*]

Dear Max:

As to your questions

(1.) Unless the Americans are first driven out of France (as at present seems not unlikely – I'll be home with the finished manuscript of my book about mid-December. We'll be a week in New York, then south to Washington & Montgomery to see our respective parents & spend Xmas – and

---

* The Sun Also Rises.

†Lady Duff Twysden, the model for Lady Brett Ashley in *The Sun Also Rises.*

**Jake Barnes, in *The Sun Also Rises.*

back in New York in mid-January to spend the rest of the winter. Whether the Spring will see us back on Long Island or returning to Europe depends on politics, finances and our personal desires.

(2.) The only censorable thing I found in Ernest's book was the "balls" conversation. I didn't find the James thing objectionable but then he seems to me to have been dead fifty years.

(3.) I'm sorry "Torrents" hasn't done better & delighted about "The Sad Young Men." Have you sounded out Curtiss Brown about an anthology of my stories in England. Still that better wait till my novel. . . .

(4) God, how much I've learned in these two and a half years in Europe. It seems like a decade & I feel pretty old but I wouldn't have missed it, even its most unpleasant & painful aspects.

. . . . .

I do want to see you, Max

Always your Friend

Nov. 4, 1926

Dear Scott:

. . . . .

"The Sun Also Rises" came out a week ago last Friday, and it had excellent reviews in the Times and Tribune, and a number of people of consequence are extremely enthusiastic about it. Hemingway sent me a story called, "The Killers", a very good one, and that Bridges took immediately, and now another has just come which I hope he will take. This is obviously the time to put him to the front, and hold him there, and if we could run several stories close together, we should be helped.

Tom and Peggy Boyd turned up in September at Ridgefield, Conn., about twelve miles from New Canaan. When I came back from a week's vacation, they were settled there more or less, in a rented house but the house has no furnace, and it gets mighty cold in Connecticut. Last week when no furnace had been installed, though long before promised, the real estate man said they were entitled to cancel the lease, and that he would help them get a house that did have a furnace; but on the way they looked at a rather fine old house which was for sale, and Tom bought it. – It has no furnace! But they don't seem to worry much. Anyhow, we are planning to reset and publish in a larger book, with about sixteen full-page pictures by Thomason, a new edition of "Through the Wheat" at $3.50. I believe it will sell that way, and it is entitled to be put forward again in times more propitious to war books.

Louise had a story in last month's Harpers, but not a good one. In

Scribner's she is soon to have one that is far better. She is working on a third. If she could only manage to put writing ahead of a number of other things, I believe she could go pretty far, and so I try to keep her at it, although it is an expensive luxury: – every time she gets a story under way, she feels that she is going to earn some money, and that this entitles her to be a little extravagant; – so long before the story is finished, four or five times the amount of money that it could possibly bring in has been spent.

I have heard that the daughter of Scott and Zelda is extremely sophisticated and so I may have to apologize to her for sending a copy of "Smoky" but it is highly regarded by some who are her elders by a number of years, and so I took a chance. If she does like it, I will get Will James to draw a special picture in it when he comes on again.

I look forward to your coming home as much as almost anything. I hope I shall get a chance to talk to you, but let's not do it at that cafe where they make the double gin rickys. I enjoy them, but I never can seem to talk to any purpose after even a swallow of the liquor.

As ever yours,

Jan. 20, 1927

Dear Scott:

I am under great pressure to tell people two things about you: – where you are, and what is to be the name of your novel. Now the papers have told where you are, so I won't have to refuse as I have been doing because you said confidential in your wire.[45] But how about the title of the novel? And by the way, I guess you are right about "The World's Fair". It is certainly a good title, and I see how it would fit what you told me of the book, the scene and all. There is one good reason for announcing it. It would give you control over it. You would establish a sort of proprietorship. And I think it would help to arouse curiosity and interest in the novel too, which will before so very long begin to appear in Liberty. – But whatever you decide about that, write me a line to tell me when you will be back here.

As ever your friend,

P.S. Love to Zelda.

April 7, 1927

Dear Scott:

I do not know how I ever happened to let you go without getting your address. All I can remember is Brandywine 100, well as I do remember the grand old edifice you are living in, and the broad river roughened by conflict with the tide.*

I do not want to harass you about your book, which might be bad for it. But if we could by any possibility have the title, and some text, and enough of an idea to make an effective wrap, by the middle of April, we could get out a dummy. And even if all these things had to be changed, it would be worth doing this. – It may though, be impossible, and then we won't, because we know perfectly well that all these things are insignificant along side of writing the book undisturbed by mfg. questions.

. . . . .

Love to Zelda.

Yours as ever,

May 10, 1927

Dear Scott:
I had a letter from Hemingway saying that he was about to send off his stories for the book, "Men Without Women" but there is one story there called, "Up in Michigan" I think, which he says Liveright refused to publish in "In Our Time" and that it was on this account that he left Liveright. I think you spoke to Charlie Scribner about this story and said that it was ridiculous that he should think it could be published. Could you tell me about it some time? Certainly we cannot go as far as Liveright is willing to. At least, I look upon him as an extremist in that respect. On the other hand, Mrs. Hemingway told me that the story could be made acceptable even for conservatives, by striking out a few physiological details.

I made an excuse of the loss of your cane to send you a present, which will reach you in a day or two; – may already have reached you.†

I hope the book is going well.

As ever yours,

Ellerslie
Edgemoor
Delaware
[ca. May 12, 1927]

Dear Max:
The cane was marvelous. The nicest one I ever saw and *infinitely* superior

*Early in April, the Fitzgeralds moved into Ellerslie, a Greek-revival mansion outside Wilmington.
†Fitzgerald had apparently lost one of his favorite canes during a visit to New York.

to the one mislaid. Need I say I value the inscription? This is the cane I shall never lose.

It seems a shame to put business into a letter thanking you for such a gift but just a line about Ernest. It is all bull that he left Liveright about that story. One line *at least* is pornographic, though *please* don't bring my name into the discussion. The thing is – what is a seduction story with the seduction left out. Yet if that is softened it is quite printable. However I trust your judgement, as he should.

. . . . .

(Explain to Hemmingway, why don't you, that while such an incident might be lost in a book, a story centering around it *points* it. In other words the material raison d'être as opposed to the artistic raison d'être of the story is, in part, to show the physiological details of a seduction. If that were possible in America 20 publishers would be scrambling for James Joyce tomorrow.)

Thanks many times for looking for the old cane. It doesn't matter. I want to put off the pamphlet* for a month until I make up some misunderstandings with the men who wrote the articles

Many, many sincere thanks Max. I was touched when I found it at the station

June 2, 1927

Dear Scott:

I have been thinking much about the title, "The Boy Who Killed His Mother".† I do not think it is sensational in any objectionable sense whatever, and its very simplicity and directness, almost literalness, give it a value, and a distinction from most of your other titles. At the same time, I am not at all sure about it. You will probably think of other titles in the meantime, so that there will be several to select from.

. . . . .

Yours ever,

---

*Early in March, Fitzgerald had proposed that Scribners put together a pamphlet containing two or three articles on him, "a picture or so, a few appreciations & a short bibliography." Perkins was enthusiastic about the idea and asked Fitzgerald to send along copies of the articles he wanted included.

†Proposed for Fitzgerald's new novel, then in progress.

"Ellersie"
Edgemoor, Delaware
[ca. January 1, 1928]

Dear Max:

Patience yet a little while, I beseech thee and thanks eternally for the deposits.[46] I feel awfully about owing you that money – all I can say is that if book is serialized I'll pay it back immediately. I work at it all the time but that period of sickness set me back – made a break both in the book & financially so that I had to do those Post stories – which made a further break. Please regard it as a safe investment and not as a risk.

I have no news. I liked *Some People* by Nicolson & *The Bridge of San Luis Rey*. Also I loved John's book* and I saw your letter agreeing that its his best thing, & the most likely to go. Its really thought out – oddly enough its least effective moments are the traces of his old manner, tho on [the] whole its steadily & culminatively [cumulatively] effective thoroughout. From the first draft, which was the one I saw I thought he could have cut 2000 or 3000 words that was mere Conradian stalling around. Whether he did or not I don't know.

No news from Ernest. In the latest *transition* (Vol 9.) there is some good stuff by Murray Goodwin (unprintable here) & a fine German play.

Always Your Afft. Friend

Except for a three day break last week (Xmas) I have been on the absolute wagon since the middle of October. Feel simply grand. Smoke only Sanos. God help us all.

Jan. 3, 1928

Dear Scott:

I was delighted to get your letter. I heard from John Biggs that you were making a splendid come back. Did you get the game of deck tennis? That would put on the final touches. I think we ought all to be proud of the way you climbed on the water wagon. It is enormously harder for a man who has no office hours and has control of his own time, – and it is hard enough for anybody.

We feel no anxiety whatever about the novel. I have worried a little about the length of time elapsing between that and "The Great Gatsby". By the way, I was talking to Conrad Aiken whose opinions are worth something, and his opinion of "The Great Gatsby" is as high as any. I told him how depressed we were at the first reviews, and how I really thought

---

Seven Days Whipping by John Biggs.

the book had been injured by them because it did not gain the immediate impetus that good reviews would have given. He said, "Well now everybody knows anyhow what it was, and what 'Gatsby' means."

Wishing you and Zelda the best of New Years, I am,

Ever your friend,

Jan. 24, 1928

Dear Scott:

We have just agreed to take on a collection of Morley Callaghan's stories.* Some of them are very good, and they are all the genuine thing. And so is he himself. He wants particularly to see you, and I told him to let me know two or three days in advance before he came down again, and that I felt pretty sure I could get you to come over. He has interesting ideas about writing, and a remarkably just sense of things. At the first glance he is not very prepossessing, but one sees after a couple of minutes of talk, that he is highly intelligent and responsive. He is writing a novel which I have seen in unfinished form, and believe will turn out well.

I was immensely impressed with John's story, and that in the face of a great deal of scepticism. I thought it would be good, but that it would lack the same things which "Demigods" did, – and those things are really essential to any sort of a success. I thought he might never acquire them. But this story is magnificently written, far better than "Demigods". Who but John would ever attempt to make a story out of such materials. . . .

I have not read "The Bridge of San Luis Rey" myself, although when it came out I sent copies to a number of people who I thought would know a good thing. Between ourselves, the extravagant praise of a certain contributor to the columns of the Magazine, rather put me off it.† As he likes it, I suspect I might not. I did read "The Caballa" when it came out, and thought it most promising.

We can surely count on your novel for the fall, can't we? It must be very nearly finished now.

Ever your friend,

June 28, 1928

Dear Scott:

I am off tomorrow to Windsor for a month, but if you want anything from

---

*Published later in 1928 as *Strange Fugitive*.

†Perkins may be referring here to William Lyon Phelps, then a regular book reviewer for *Scribner's Magazine*.

us, I think the most direct way to get it done would be to communicate with C.S., Jr. He will be here and will see to it.

I got from Ober your three boys' stories,[47] and read them with great interest. Won't you have a book of them sometime? I thought the best part of any of them was that account of how the boys and girls met in a certain yard at dusk. That was beautifully done. That magical quality of summer dusk for young boys I have never before seen evoked. I hope you will be doing some more of these stories. I have just been having lunch with John Biggs, who said that Zelda wrote you were thinking of coming home,* he seemed to think, right away. I did not believe it though.

Ever your friend,

58 Rue de Vaugirard
[Paris, France]
[ca. July 15, 1928]

Dear Max:
I read John Bishops novel. Of course its impossible. All the people who were impressed with Norman Douglass *South Wind* & Beerbohm's *Zulieka Dobson* tried to follow them in their wretched organization of material – without having either the brilliant intelligence of Douglass or the wit of Beerbohm. Vide the total collapse of Aldous Huxley. Conrad has been, after all, the healthy influence on the technique of the novel.

Anyhow at the same time Bishop gave me a novellette to read – and to my great astonishment, as a document of the Civil War its right up to Bierce & Stephen Crane – beautifully written, thrilling and water tight as to construction & interest. He's been so discouraged over the hash he made of the novel that he's been half afraid to send it anywhere & I told him that now that tales of violence are so popular I thought Scribners magazine would love to have a look at it.

So I'm sending it – no one has seen it but me. His adress is
   Chateau de Tressancourt
   Orgeval, Seine et Oise
I'm working hard as hell

As Ever your friend

*After unsuccessfully trying to finish his novel at Ellerslie, Fitzgerald and his family had gone to Europe for the summer.

[*58 rue de Vaugirard*]
[*Paris, France*]
[*ca. July 21, 1928*]

Dear Max

(1) The novel goes fine. I think its quite wonderful & I think those who've seen it (for I've read it around a little) have been quite excited. I was encouraged the other day, when James Joyce came to dinner, when he said, "Yes, I expect to finish my novel in three or four years more at the *latest*" & he works 11 hrs a day to my intermittent 8. Mine will be done *sure* in September.[48]

(2) Did you get my letter about *André Chamson?*[49] Really, Max, you're missing a great opportunity if you don't take that up. Radiguet was perhaps obscene – Chamson is absolutely *not* – he's head over heels the best young man here, like Ernest & Thornton Wilder rolled into one. This *Hommes de la Route* (Road Menders) is his 2nd novel & all but won the Prix Goncourt – the story of men building a road, with all the force of K. Hamsun's *Growth of the Soil* – not a bit like Tom Boyds bogus American husbandmen. Moreover, tho I know him only slightly and have no axe to grind, I have every faith in him as an extraordinary personality like France & Proust. Incidently King Vidor (who made *The Crowd* & *The Big Parade*) is making a picture of it next summer. If you have any confidence in my judgement do at least get a report on it & let me know what you decide. Ten years from now he'll be beyond price.

(3) I plan to publish a book of those *Basil Lee* Stories after the novel. Perhaps one or two more serious ones to be published in the Mercury or with Scribners if you'd want them, combined with the total of about six in the Post Series, would make a nice *light* novel, almost, to follow my novel in the season *immediately* after, so as not to seem in the direct line of my so-called "work." It would run to perhaps 50 or 60 thousand words.

(4) Do let me know any plans of a) Ernest b) Ring c) Tom (reviews poor, I notice) d) John Biggs

(5) Did you like Bishops story? I thought it was grand.

(6) Home Sept 15th I think. Best to Louise

. . . . .

Ever yr Devoted & Grateful Friend,

Aug. 6, 1928

Dear Scott: –

I was delighted to get that letter in which you said the novel was going so well. I returned from my vacation last Monday and would have written immediately except that I wanted also to have gotten somewhere with Chamson. The delay was not that I did not take action on your first mention of this, but that the book was in the hands of Mrs. Boyd* and she could not bring me a copy here. I finally got one myself through the bookstore. I ordered one from Paris on first hearing from you but they sent the wrong book, – "Essay, Man and History". I have had the "Road Menders" read and shall now merely read enough of it to confirm, as I expect to do, the opinion of the reader which is high. Then we will try to make a deal with Mrs. Boyd. Mr. Scribner and all of us are most grateful to you for suggestions like this and we certainly do value your opinion. You never yet fell wrong that I know of.[50] As for the "Bishop" I think it very fine but the magazine certainly cannot use it because of its length and I don't know what to do about it. I will write you fully within a few days. Ring's book will not come out until 1929, early. We thought it best to wait for a full collection and there are four copies that we can get into it by postponement. John Biggs has had good reviews but does not look like much of a sale. I am to see him on Thursday for lunch.

There are many more things I want to write you about but I am being as brief as I can because Miss Wyckoff† is away and the stenographers here are all terribly over-worked.

Love to Zelda.

Ever your friend,

Edgemoor**
Nov '28

Dear Max:
It seems fine to be sending you something again, even though its only the first fourth of the book (2 chapters, 18,000 words). Now comes another short story, then I'll patch up Chaps. 3 & 4 the same way, and send them, I hope, about the 1st of December.

Chap. I. here is good

Chap II. has caused me more trouble than anything in the book. You'll realize this when I tell you it was once 27,000 words long! It started its career as Chap I. I am far from satisfied with it even now, but won't go into its obvious faults. I would appreciate it if you jotted down any criticisms – and *saved them until* I've sent you the whole book, because I want to *feel* that each part is finished and not worry about it any longer, even

*Probably literary agent Madeleine Boyd.
†Irma Wyckoff (Mrs. Osmer Muench), Perkins' secretary.
**The Fitzgeralds had returned home late in September.

though I may change it enormously at the very last minute. All I want to know now is if, in general, you like it & this will have to wait, I suppose, until you've seen the next batch which finishes the first half. (My God its good to see those chapters lying in an envelope!

I think I have found you a new prospect of really extraordinary talent in a Carl Van Vechten way. I have his first novel at hand – unfortunately its about Lesbians. More of this later.

I think Bunny's title* is *wonderful!*

Remember novel is confidential, even to Ernest.

Always Yrs.

Nov. 13, 1928

Dear Scott:

I have just finished the two chapters. About the first we fully agree. It is excellent. The second I think contains some of the best writing you have ever done – some lovely scenes, and impressions briefly and beautifully conveyed. Besides it is very entertaining, including the duel. There are certain things one could say of it in criticism, but anyhow I will make no criticism until I read the whole book, and so see the relationships of the chapters. I think this is a wonderfully promising start off. Send on others as soon as you can.

I wish it might be possible to get this book out this spring, if only because it promises so much that it makes me impatient to see it completed.

Ever yours,

[Ellerslie]
[Edgemoor, Delaware]
[ca. March 1, 1929]

Dear Max:

I am sneaking away like a thief without leaving the chapters – there is a weeks work to straighten them out & in the confusion of influenza & leaving, I havn't been able to do it. I'll do it on the boat & send it from Genoa. A thousand thanks for your patience – just trust me a few months longer, Max – its been a discouraging time for me too but I will never forget your kindness and the fact that you've never reproached me.

I'm delighted about Ernest's book – I bow to your decision on the modern library without agreeing at all. $100 or $50 advance is better than ⅛ of $40 for a years royalty, & the Scribner collection sounds vague & arbi-

---

* *I Thought of Daisy,* a novel by Edmund Wilson, published by Scribners in 1929.

trary to me. But its a trifle & I'll give them a new & much inferior story instead as I want to be represented with those men, i e Forster, Conrad, Mansfield ect.[51]

. . . . .

Will you watch for some stories from a young Holger Lundberg who has appeared in the Mercury, he is a man of some promise & I headed him your way.

I hate to leave without seeing you – and I hate to see you without the ability to put the finished ms in your hands. So for a few months good bye & my affection & gratitude always

[Paris]
[ca. April 1, 1929]

Dear Max:

This letter is too hurried to thank you for the very kind & encouraging one you wrote me. Its only to say – watch for a book on *Baudelaire* by Pierre Loving which Madeliene Boyd will bring you. I believe another one has been published but this man once did me a service & I promised to call your attention to it, before knowing it had a rival in the market.

I'm delighted about Ernest's novel.* Will be here in Paris trying as usual to finish mine, till July 1st. c/o The Guaranty Trust, Rue des Italiennes. Then the seashore.

A French man here (unfortunately I havn't his book at hand, but he's a well known writer on aviation) has written a book called "Evasions d'Aviateurs" dealing with aviators escapes during the war – all true & to me facinating. It's a best seller here now. In three months will come a sequel which will include some escapes of German & American aviators (as you know it was the tradition of all aviators to escape) which will include that of Tommy Hitchcock.

What would you say to the two in one oversized volume profusely illustrated with photographs? I believe Liberty had a great success with Richthoven & as a record of human ingenuity Les Evasions d'Aviateurs is astounding. To swell the thing a 3d book he has just published called *Special Missions of Aviators during the War* might be added. What do you think? It might just make a great killing like *Trader Horn* – it has a certain bizzare quality to divert the bored.

Unfortunately I havn't the man's name.

Again thank you for your kind and understanding letter. I'm ashamed of myself for whining about nothing & never will again.

* *A Farewell to Arms*, published by Scribners in September, 1929.

155

April 12, 1929

Dear Scott:

I was certainly glad to get a letter from you and I immediately wrote Madeline Boyd to see if she could get through Bradley, an option on the book about the escapes of aviators. The Chamson has got beautiful reviews, but so far has not sold much; – but we are bringing out "Roux le Bandit" in the fall, and shall follow it by the other. I think we shall get the right results in the end. Don't think I do not – or that we do not – realize how much you have done for us apart from your own books. We fully appreciate it as a very great thing for us. – But the book we really want to publish is your book.

As for the last sentence of your letter, it ought not to have been written. You never did it so far as I know. You have always been to me the very model of courage.

Ever yours,

Villa Fleur des Bois
Boulevard Eugene Gazagnaire
(Till Oct 1st)
Cannes.
[ca. June 1929]

Dear Max:
A line in haste to say

(1.) I am working night & day on novel from new angle that I think will solve previous difficulties

(2.) Dotty Parker, whos *Big Blonde* won O. Henry prize is writing a novelette or novel. She has been getting bad prices & I think, if she interested you she'd be glad to find a market in Scribners. Just now she's at a high point as a producer & as to reputation. . . .
I wouldn't lose any time about this if it interests you.

(3.) Ernest's last letter a little worried, but I don't see why. . . . I hope to god *All Quiet on the Western Front* won't cut in on his sales. My bet is the book will pass 50,000.

(4) Deeply sorry about Ring.* *Why* won't he write about Great Neck, a sort of Oddysee of man starting in theatre business.

---

*Perkins had written on May 31st that Lardner's new book, *Round Up*, had sold 10,000 copies, with a prospect of 10,000 more, but that he seemed "dreadfully discouraged."

(5.) Do send me Bunny's book. I heard about his breakdown. I hope his poems include "Our Autumns were unreal with the new – "*Please* ask him about it – its haunted me for 12 years.

(6) Sorry about John's* leg – am writing him as I want news of the play.

(7) Tom Boyd has apparently dropped from sight, hasn't he. Do give me any news

Always Yr. Afft. Friend

October 30, 1929

Dear Scott:

Weeks ago I began to hear rumors that you were about to sail for America, – in fact that you were then probably actually on the ocean. Then John Biggs began to think you would arrive any day, – probably at New Orleans. – But yesterday I had a letter from Ernest which spoke about you in a way which made me think you must be in Paris, and said nothing about your sailing at all, and so I am in hopes this letter may get there before you leave.

You will have heard about Ernest's book from him: it has sold just about 36,000 to date, and the only obstacle to a really big sale is that which may come from the collapse of the market, – what effect that will have nobody can tell. It may have a very bad effect on all retail business including that of books. No book could have been better received than his, and it has been the outstanding seller ever since it appeared. It has been pre-eminent. You may also have heard that Ring's play, "June Moon" based upon "Some Like 'Em Cold" and having songs for which Ring wrote both words and music, is a distinct success. – But this does not encourage me so much, because I am sure if Ring made a lot of money, he would do even less writing of the kind we can use, than even now. – And he is writing another play too, and once a man gets going at that, it is a question if he will ever do anything else, except by necessity. I hope you and Ernest will keep out of it.

I have seen several people lately who have seen you. One was Robert McAlmon.† Ernest sent me a letter telling me he was coming, and so far as I could see the letter was entirely designed to help him, and there was no advantage to Ernest whatever in his meeting me. Ernest simply hoped that we would be able to do something for McAlmon as publishers, and yet when we got out to dinner what does McAlmon do but start in to say

---

*John Biggs.

†American writer and editor.

mean things about Ernest (this is absolutely between you and me) both as a man and as a writer. I can see that he might be envious, and that that was all the significance his talk had, but you would think even so, that when Ernest had brought us together, he might have laid off on him.

Another who had seen you was Callaghan. – He had seen you, he said, out of the corner of his eye while boxing with Ernest. He said you were meant to be keeping time, but that you were evidently thinking of something quite remote from boxing, and that he wondered if you ever would call the end of the round.

Bunny Wilson's book has sold about 3,000 and it is not going to have a large sale. What did you think of it? It did get excellent reviews and among a certain crowd made quite a hit, – but for the general public there is too much thought in it, or rather the thought and theory are too important and conspicuous elements in it. At least I suppose that is the trouble. We have been having quite an active and exciting season here with the life of Mrs. Eddy and the Christian Scientists living up to their great motto "All is love" by boycott and intimidation, which we have countered by advertising the fact that they were using these methods. You would have been much interested in this whole affair if you had been on hand. I sent Ernest a copy of the book, – or did I send you one? Then of course there was a certain amount of controversy over the "Farewell" out of which we seem to have come very successfully; – and the Wolfe book* of which I told you before you left here, is also stirring things up quite a bit.†

10 Rue Pergolèse
[Paris, France]
[ca. November 15, 1929]

Dear Max:

For the first time since August I see my way clear to a long stretch on the novel, so I'm writing you as I can't bear to do when its in one of its states of postponement & seems so in the air. We are not coming home for Xmas, because of expense & because it'd be an awful interruption now. Both our families are raising hell but I can't compromise the remains of my future for that.

I'm glad of Ring's success tho – at least its for something new & will make him think he's still alive & not a defunct semi-classic. Also Ernest's press has been marvellous & I hope it sells. By the way, McAlmon is a bitter rat and I'm not surprised at anything he does or says. He's failed as

*Later published as *Look Homeward, Angel*, by Thomas Wolfe.
†Letter breaks off here, unsigned.

a writer and tries to fortify himself by tieing up to the big boys like Joyce and Stien and despising everything else. Part of his quarrel with Ernest some years ago was because he assured Ernest that I was a fairy – God knows he shows more creative imagination in his malice than in his work. Next he told Callaghan that Ernest was a fairy. He's a pretty good person to avoid

Sorry Bunny's book didn't go – I thought it was fine, & more interesting than better or at least more achieved novels.

. . . . .

Oh, and what the *hell* is this book I keep getting clippings about with me and Struthers Burt and Ernest ect. As I remember you refused to let *The Rich Boy* be published in the *Modern Library* in a representative collection where it would have helped me & here it is in a book obviously fordoomed to oblivion that can serve no purpose than to fatigue reviewers with the stories. I know its a small matter but I am disturbed by the fact that you didn't see fit to discuss it with me.

However that's a rather disagreeable note to close on when I am forever in your debt for countless favors and valuable advice. It is because so little has happened to me lately that it seems magnified. . . .

Ever Yr. Afft Friend

Nov. 30, 1929

Dear Scott:

I am sorry you feel as you do – and I understand why you feel as you do – about the collection of stories. The truth is I did not care much about the venture myself, but I see no harm in it at all, and the idea was that a collection like this could sell in school and college courses. . . .I did speak to you about this collection, and you acquiesced in it in a letter you wrote me just before you sailed.

You may be right about wanting stories in the Modern Library, and it has been much on my mind that you should not have one of your best ones in if you have a story in at all. But what are regular publishers to do if all kinds of special sorts of publishers get out anthologies all the time, and come to them for their material and pay practically nothing for it, either to them or to the author. There are more of these demands for material for anthologies every year. – When a new publisher sets up, the very first thing he does is to try to get up an anthology of stories. I realize that the Modern Library is in a different position from others. It is a fine enterprise too, and good for the book business as a whole, in the long run. – But they come down upon us all the time with these requests, and it is hard to be making exceptions, and this book of theirs as originally planned, was over fifty percent made up of material published by Scribners.

I could not be glader of anything than of hearing how well you are going forward now. I know the book will be a great book, and you will have the most ardent support from every man here when it is ready.

Remembrances to Zelda. I am sending Scotty a copy of "American Folk and Fairy Tales".

Ever your friend,

Dec. 17, 1929

Dear Scott:

I am enclosing a letter I got from Callaghan, and a note which he sent to the Herald Tribune, and which was printed there. They will show you how things stand. The girl who started this story is one Caroline Bancroft. She wanders around Europe every year and picks up what she can in the way of gossip, and prints it in the Denver paper, and it spreads from there. Callaghan told me the whole story about boxing with Ernest, and the point he put the most emphasis on was your time-keeping. That impressed him a great deal. He did say that he knew he was more adept in boxing than Ernest, and that he had been practising for several years with fighters. He was all right about the whole matter. He is much better than he looks.[52]

. . . . .

Ernest's book should have sold very close to 70,000 by Christmas, and then the question is whether we can carry it actively on into the next season; – and that is chiefly a question because of the fact that we are evidently in for a period of depression. We have come out well here for the year – probably the best year we have had – but it is largely because of four or five very good books. Most books have failed this year, and most publishers have had bad years because of the fall season.

I hope you and Zelda will be coming back sometime early in 1930. Why don't you think of going down to Key West if I go in the spring?

Ever your friend,

10 Rue Pergolèse
Paris, France
Jan 21st 1930

This has run to seven long close-written pages so you better not read it when you're in a hurry.*

Dear Max: There is so much to write you – or rather so many small

---

*This note appeared above the salutation.

things that I'll write 1st the personal things and then on another sheet a series of suggestions about books and authors that have accumulated in me in the last six months.

(1.) To begin with, because I don't mention my novel it isn't because it isn't finishing up or that I'm neglecting it – but only that I'm weary of setting dates for it till the moment when it is in the Post Office Box.

(2) I was very grateful for the money* – it won't happen again but I'd managed to get horribly into debt & I hated to call on Ober, who's just getting started, for another cent†

(3.) Thank you for the documents in the Callaghan case. I'd rather not discuss it except to say that I don't like him and that I wrote him a formal letter of apology. I never thought he started the rumor & never said nor implied such a thing to Ernest.

(4.) Delighted with the success of Ernest's book. I took the responsibility of telling him that McAlmon was at his old dirty work around New York. McAlmon, by the way, didn't have anything to do with founding *Transition.* He published Ernest's first book over here & some books of his own & did found some little magazine but of no importance.

(5) Thank you for getting Gatsby for me in foreign languages

(6) Sorry about John Biggs but it will probably do him good in the end. *The Stranger in Soul Country* had something & the *Seven Days Whipping* was respectable but colorless. *Demigods* was simply oratorical twirp. How is his play going?

(7.) Tom Boyd seems far away. I'll tell you one awful thing tho. Lawrence Stallings was in the West with King Vidor at a *huge* salary to write an equivalent of *What Price Glory.* King Vidor told me that Stallings in despair of showing Vidor what the war was about gave him a copy of *Through the Wheat.* And that's how Vidor so he told me made the big scenes of the *Big Parade.* Tom Boyd's profits were a few thousand – Stallings were a few hundred thousands. Please don't connect my name with this story but it is the truth and it seems to me rather horrible.

(8) Lastly & most important. For the English rights of my next book Knopf** made me an offer so much better than any in England (ad-

---

*On January 13th, Perkins had deposited $500 for Fitzgerald.
†Harold Ober had recently disassociated himself from Paul Reynolds and was now starting on his own.
**Alfred A. Knopf, Ltd.

vance $500.00; royal[t]ies sliding from ten to fifteen & twenty; guaranty to publish next book of short stories at same rate) that I accepted of course.[53] . . .

. . . Incidentally he [Knopf] said to me as Harcourt once did to Ernest that you were the best publishers in America. I told him he was wrong – that you were just a lot of royalty doctorers & short changers.

No more for the moment. . . .

Ever Your Devoted Friend

I append the sheet of brilliant ideas of which you may find one or two worth considering. . . .

(Suggestion List)

(1.) Certainly if the ubiquitous and ruined McAlmon deserves a hearing then John Bishop, a poet and a man of really great talents and intelligence does. I am sending you under another cover a sister story of the novelette you refused, which together with the first one and three shorter ones will form his Civil-War-civilian-in-invaded-Virginia-book, a simply grand idea & a new, rich field. The enclosed is the best thing he has ever done and the best thing about the *non-combatant* or rather behind-the-lines war I've ever read. I *hope* to God you can use this in the magazine – couldn't it be run into small type carried over like Sew Collins did with *Boston* & you *Farewell to Arms*? He *needs* the encouragement & is *so* worth it.

(2) In the new American Caravan amid much sandwiching of Joyce and Co is the first work of a 21 year old named *Robert Cantwell*. Mark it well, for my guess is that he's learned a better lesson from Proust than Thornton Wilder did and has a destiny of no mean star.

(3.) Another young man therein named *Gerald Sykes* has an extraordinary talent in the line of heaven knows what, but very memorable and distinguished.

(4) Thirdly (and these three are all in the whole damn book) there is a man named Erskine Caldwell, who interested me less than the others because of the usual derivations from Hemmingway and even Callaghan – still read him. He & Sykes are 26 yrs old. I don't know any of them.

If you decide to act in any of these last three cases I'd do it within a few weeks. I know none of the men but Cantwell will go quick with his next stuff if he hasn't gone already. For some reason young writers come in groups – Cummings, Dos Passos & me in 1920–21; Hemmingway, Callaghan & Wilder in 1926–27 and no one in between and no one since. This looks to me like a really new generation

(5) Now a personal friend (but he knows not that I'm [writing] you) – Cary Ross (Yale 1925) – poorly represented in this *American Caravan*, but rather brilliantly by poems in the *Mercury* & *Transition*, studying medicine at Johns Hopkins & one who at the price of publication or at least examination of his poems might prove a valuable man. Distincly *younger* that [than] *post* war, later than my generation, sure to turn to fiction & worth corresponding with. I believe these are the cream of the young people

(6) [general]* Dos Passos wrote me about the ms. of some protegée of his but as I didn't see the ms. or know the man the letter seemed meaningless. Did you do anything about Murray Godwin (or Goodwin?). Shortly I'm sending you some memoirs by an ex-marine, doorman at my bank here. They might have some documentary value as true stories of the Nicaraguan expedition ect.

(7.) In the foreign (French) field there is besides Chamson one man, and at the opposite pole, of great great talent. It is not Cocteau nor Arragon but young René Crevel. I am opposed to him for being a fairy but in the last *Transition* (number 18.) there is a translation of the beginning of his current novel which simply knocked me cold with its beauty. The part in *Transition* is called *Mr. Knife and Miss Fork* and I wish to God you'd read it immediately. Incedently the novel is a great current success here. I know its not yet placed in America & if you're interested *please* communicate with me *before* you write Bradley.

(8) Now, one last, much more elaborate idea. In France any military book of real tactical or strategical importance, theoretical or fully documented (& usually the latter) (and I'm not referring to the one-company battles between "Red" & "Blue" taught us in the army under the name of Small Problems for Infantry). They are mostly published by Payots here & include such works as *Ludendorf's Memoirs*; and the *Documentary Preparations for the German break-thru in 1918* – how the men were massed, trained, brought up to the line in 12 hours in 150 different technical groups from flame throwers to field kitchens, the whole inside story *from captured orders* of the greatest *tactical* attack in history; a study of *Tannenburg* (German); several, both French & German of the 1st Marne; a thorough study of gas warfare, another of Tanks, no dogmatic distillations compiled by some old dotart, but original documents.

Now – believing that so long as we have service schools and not much preparation (I am a political cynic and a big-navy-man, like all Europeans) English Translations should be available in all academies, army service

---

*These brackets are Fitzgerald's.

schools, staff schools ect (I'll bet there are American army officers with the rank of Captain that don't know what "infiltration in depth" is or what Colonel Bruckmüller's idea of artillery employment was.) It seems to me that it would be a great patriotic service to consult the war-department bookbuyers on some subsidy plan to bring out a tentative dozen of the most important as "an original scource [source] tactical library of the lessons of the great war." . . . This, in view of some millions of amateurs of battle now in America might be an enormous popular success as well as a patriotic service. Let me know about this because if you shouldn't be interested I'd like to for my own satisfaction make the suggestion to someone else. Some that I've underlined may be already published.

My God – this is 7 pages & you're asleep & I want to catch the Olympic with this so I'll close. Please tell me your response to *each* idea.

Does Chamson sell at all? Oh, for my income tax will you have the usual statement of lack of royalties sent me – & for my curiosity to see if I've sold a book this year except to myself.

Feb. 11, 1930

Dear Scott:

I enclose the royalty report. It was mighty good to get your long letter and all the suggestions, and I shall write you in detail about them this week. But as for the John Bishop story, I think it is a very, very fine thing, and although you must not say anything yet to him about it, I do hope we can work out a way of getting it into the Magazine. It is a hard proposition, for in a sense it is not a magazine kind of thing even in character. But it is a most unusual and impressive piece of work.

The Chamson stories have sold only about 2500 copies apiece. "The Crime of the Just" comes out pretty soon, and we may do better; – but anyhow, I am in hopes of publishing them all in one volume, and the very faint hope that we may be able to interest the Guild in the one volume. The stories are so short that they are at a disadvantage as separate books anyhow, and although they have had very warm reviews, they did not strike with a sufficient impact to get through to a sizeable public. – But when put together, they may well do more. Chamson tells us that he is writing a larger, and altogether different sort of novel. We have had very nice, sympathetic letters from him always.

I am trying to get in touch with Cantrell and Erskine Caldwell, and I shall let you know what comes of it.

I have here Crevell's "Etes-vous Fous" and I shall have the Transition, and I shall certainly communicate with you before the week is done. The military books I do not think we can go in for. We are pretty heavily embarked in literature relating to war, although quite different, of course, from that you speak of. – And there is even a large book on the whole military conduct of the war that we are involved with. – A fine book too, but a very large and difficult one. Besides, the American people do not believe there is ever going to be another war, apparently, – at least outside the Union Club and the Brevoort.

This letter is just a preliminary to a real answer. I have been so excessively busy that I have not been able to round things up as quickly as I had hoped.

Ernest went through, and seemed in fine shape. I swore I would go down to Key West in March, – and I do hope to do it for I have seldom liked a place as well.

Always your friend,

March 14, 1930

Dear Scott:

I am off tomorrow for Key West where Mike Strater* also is, for two weeks. I wish you were here and could come too. Ernest is planning for a cruise up to the Everglades. If I ever go down there again after this year, and you are in this country, I shall keep after you until I get you to come along.

John Bishop writes that he told you about our accepting his story, but I wrote to you about it at the same time that I wrote to him. Since then I have seen both Cantwell, who is a very interesting fellow, and Caldwell. In fact we have taken two stories by Caldwell, though they are not up to his best. Cantwell submitted one which I enjoyed immensely in reading, but which we could not take partly because it was very long, and partly because it was one of those stories which do not make a clear, definite impression, – more of the sort that Katherine Mansfield often wrote in that respect. But it was beautifully done. I had lunch with him, and he is to send us others, but some friend of his had led him long ago to Farrar and Rhinehart, and they had accepted his first novel without seeing a line of it, which I do not think we could have done. Caldwell is also writing a novel, and although other publishers are after him now, I think we can probably have it.

Harold Ober yesterday gave me reason to hope that a large part of your novel would be here before long. I'll tell you when we get that into our hands, and a publication date set, we'll let loose everything we have got in the way of salesmanship and advertising. Everyone here is impatient to

*A painter and friend of Hemingway.

get that book and what is more, there is no author who commands a more complete loyalty than you do.

Ever your friend,

Dear Max:

I was delighted about the Bishop story – the acceptance has done wonders for him. The other night I read him a good deal of my novel & I think he liked it. Harold Ober wrote me that if it couldn't be published this fall I should publish the Basil Lee stories, but I know too well by whom reputations are made & broken to ruin myself completely by such a move – I've seen Tom Boyd, Michael Arlen & too many others fall through the eternal trapdoor of trying [to] cheat the public, no matter what their public is, with substitutes – better to let four years go by. I wrote young & I wrote a lot & the pot takes longer to fill up now but the novel, my novel, is a different matter than if I'd hurriedly finished it up a year and a half ago. If you think Callahgan hasn't completely blown himself up with this death house masterpiece just wait and see the pieces fall. I don't know why I'm saying this to you who have never been anything but my most loyal and confident encourager and friend but Ober's letter annoyed me today & put me in a wretched humor. *I know what I'm doing* – honestly, Max. How much time between *The Cabala* & *The Bridge of St. Luis Rey*, between *The Genius* & *The American Tragedy* between *The Wisdom Tooth* & *Green Pastures.** I think time seems to go by quicker there in America but time put in is time eventually taken out – and whatever this thing of mine is its certainly not a mediocrity like *The Woman of Andros* & *The Forty Second Parallel*. "He [is] through" is an easy cry to raise but its safer for the critics to raise it at the evidence in print than at a long silence.

Ever yours

Dear Max:

I'm asking Harold Ober to offer you these three stories† which Zelda wrote in the dark middle of her nervous breakdown. I think you'll see that

---

*Two plays by Marc Connelly.
†"A Workman," "The Drouth and the Flood" and "The House."

apart from the beauty & richness of the writing they have a strange haunting and evocative quality that is absolutely new. I think too that there is
a certain unity apparent in them – their actual unity is a fact because each
of them is the story of her life when things for awhile seemed to have
brought her to the edge of madness and despair. In my opinion they are
literature tho I may in this case read so much between the lines that my
opinion is valueless. (By the way Caldwell's stories were a throrough
disappointment, wern't they – more crimes committed in Hemmingway's
name)

Ever yours

July 8, 1930

Dear Scott:
There is nothing so futile as telling a person you are sorry for things that
have happened, – particularly when the person is one who knows how
sorry you would be. I do hope Zelda is getting on. It is too bad. You
certainly have a lot on your hands. We got the cable, and have replied that
the fifteen hundred was deposited.

Ernest was here a while ago to meet Bumby,* who had come over with
Ernest's sister-in-law. Ernest was very well, and we had some good times.
We managed to take over from Liveright "In Our Time" and we shall
re-issue that, and I believe will do quite well with it. On account of the
circumstances it was published in, it never had a good show, and I think
we could almost give it the effect of a new book, for the general public.

John Bishop sent over another story which was too long, and was not
otherwise quite right for magazine publication, but he shortened it, and
changed it in the other ways, and I think it is a very fine story. – Certainly
it is a beautiful piece of writing.

Business never was worse, but people begin to think it will pick up in
the fall. . . . We came out much better than most people this spring because
of S. S. Van Dine,† whose books seem not to have been affected by the
depression, – in fact, almost to have gained by it. The booksellers seemed
to think that they could sell it, and only it, and concentrated upon it.

Hoping that things will soon be better with you all, and that you may
be back here, I am,

Ever your friend,

---

*Nickname of John, Hemingway's oldest son.
†Pen-name of Willard Huntington Wright, author of the Philo Vance mystery stories.

Dear Scott:

I have read Zelda's manuscripts over several times – they came to me while I was away – and I do think they show an astonishing power of expression, and have and convey a curiously effective and strange quality. – But they are for a selected audience, and not a large one, and the magazine thinks that on that account, they cannot use them. One would think that if she did enough more they might make a book. Descriptively they are very rare, and the description is not just description. It has a curious emotional content in itself. But for the present I shall have to send them back to Ober. I think one of the little magazines might use them. I wish we could.

I am terribly sorry about Zelda herself.* But if she has made progress maybe it should become more rapid, and everything will come out right.

Wolfe wrote me that he had seen you and greatly enjoyed it, but said he feared he had been bad company for you, – that he had felt worried and morose.

Ernest writes from Wyoming saying that he had wanted to write to you, but that he was working well on his book, and did not dare stop, and giving all kings of regards, etc.

I have been away for two weeks and am terribly jammed up with work, and it is as hot as can be.

Always yours,

Geneva, Switzerland†
[ca. September 1, 1930]

Dear Max:

All the world seems to end up in this flat and antiseptic smelling land – with an overlay of flowers. Tom Wolfe is the only man I've met here who isn't sick or hasn't sickness to deal with. You have a great find in him – what he'll do is incalculable. He has a deeper culture than Ernest and more vitality, if he is slightly less of a poet that goes with the immense surface he wants to cover. Also he lacks Ernests quality of a stick hardened in the fire – he is more susceptible to the world. John Bishop told me he needed advice about cutting ect, but after reading his book I thought that was nonsense. He strikes me as a man who should be let alone as to length, if he has to be published in five volumes. I liked him enormously.

I was sorry of course about Zelda's stories – possibly they mean more to me than is implicit to the reader who doesn't know from what depths

---

*Fitzgerald had written, late in July, that "Zelda is still sick as hell."

†Fitzgerald was in Switzerland so that he could be near Zelda, who was in Les Rives de Prangins sanitarium on Lake Geneva.

of misery and effort they sprang. One of them, I think now, would be incomprehensible without a Waste-Land footnote. She has those series of eight portraits that attracted so much attention in *College Humor* and I think in view of the success of Dotty Parkers *Laments* (25,000 copies) I think a book might be got together for next Spring if Zelda can add a few more during the winter.

Wasn't that a nice tribute to C.S. from Mencken in the Mercury?*

The royalty advance or the national debt as it might be called shocked me.† The usual vicious circle is here – I am now exactly $3000. ahead which means 2 months on the Encyclopedia. I'd prefer to have all above the $10,000 paid back to you off my next story (in October). You've been so damn nice to me.

Zelda is almost well. The doctor says she can never drink again (not that drink in any way contributed to her collapse), and that I must not drink anything, not even wine, for a year, because drinking in the past was one of the things that haunted her in her delerium.

Do please send me things like Wolfe's book when they appear. Is Ernest's book a history of bull-fighting? I'm sending you a curious illiterate ms written by a chasseur at my bank here. Will you skim it & see if any parts, like the marines in Central America, are interesting as pure data? And return it, if not, directly to him? . . .

Always yours

This illness has cost me a fortune – hence that telegram in July.** The biggest man in Switzerland gave all his time to her – & saved her reason by a split second.

Nov. 12, 1930

Dear Scott:
I am terribly ashamed about the David Livingston manuscript.†† I read quite a bit of it and found there was a great deal to be said for the way it was written, in detail. Very spirited and graphic. But then I gave it to Meyer here who read it all through, and one other looked it over, and in the end we decided we could not do it. – But in the rush of things I never did get to writing about it. If you tell me though, I will explain it all to Ober, and he may place it.

---

*Charles Scribner, Senior, President of Charles Scribner's Sons, had died in May.
†Perkins had sent Fitzgerald the royalty report on August 12th.
**Fitzgerald had wired Perkins for $1500 on July 7th.
††Apparently the book by the chasseur at his bank which Fitzgerald had mentioned that he was sending Perkins. Early in November Fitzgerald wrote asking whether the manuscript had ever arrived.

He sent us the other day a story by Zelda called "Miss Bessie". We took it, – if the price we offered, which was not very high, is acceptable. I suppose you must have read it so there is not much need of my saying anything about it, but it did give a very complete strong sense of a character in this Southern old maid. It was moving in that way, but it had another quality that was still more moving. – In some way it made the reader share the feelings of the young girl through whose eyes Miss Bessie was seen, so that she was not only real, and in some degree was not real, but was as the young girl saw her.

But when we send the proof I was going to ask Zelda if she would consider whether her figures of speech – I suppose they would be called similes – were not too numerous, and sometimes too remote. – That is, sometimes she likens something in the story to something too distant from it; and this has the effect sometimes of putting the emphasis on the figure of the simile instead of the thing to which it is likened. Then too, there is a little point at the end as to how the man met his death which needs clarification, I thought.

Zelda probably knows just as much about writing as anybody hereabouts, but few writers can get sufficiently away from their own work to know how it will strike a reader. So I did not think she would mind the raising of these points.

I have heard that you are to come back before Christmas. Is this so? I wish it were. I only saw John Bishop when he was here once, but enjoyed that. Ernest, having escaped all the dangers involved in killing grizzlies and elk, in Montana, then got badly hurt in a motor accident. Dos Passos was with him. They were driving at night and in the glare of coming headlights Ernest got too far over to the right and ran off the road into a gulley. His upper right arm was so badly broken that they had to operate and tie the bone. Pauline* wired me that he had been in great pain, but that it ought not to last long. – But evidently she was worried about him. It was something very unusual in the way of a broken arm.

Always your friend,

Grand Hôtel de la Paix
Lausanne
[ca. May 15, 1931]

Dear Max:
An idea:
Princeton has had lots of books – too many in the last ten years (on a

*Mrs. Ernest Hemingway.

cursory inspection I'm not so much impressed with Burnham's book which leans heavily on so many of us greybeards) but –

There's been no Harvard book since Charlie Flandrau & Philosophy Four.* I'm very impressed with a series of Harvard-Boston Society stories by Bernard de Voto which have been running in the Post the last year. They're light, romantic & *exceedingly witty*. I think that under some such title as "Outside the Yard" the as yet unsaturated Harvard public would lap them up. (I don't dare suggest you call them "Recent Researches at Cambridge.")

The new avant-garde magazines are not up to *Transition*, & this *Caravan* has nothing new except some good poetry. The Jazz Age is over. If Mark Sullivan is going on† you might tell him I claim credit for naming it & that it extended from the suppression of the riots on May Day 1919 to the crash of the Stock Market in 1929 – almost exactly one decade.

Zelda is *so* much better. I'm taking her on a trip tomorrow – only for the day. But she's herself again now, tho not yet strong. *Please* send that proof of hers.

Yours always

May 21, 1931

Dear Scott:

You are certainly entitled to credit for the phrase, "The Jazz Age". I shall tell Sullivan about it too. What you say is extremely interesting, and significant, and Dashiell** is writing you to ask for an article about it. If you could possibly squeeze it in, I think there might be advantage in it for you, – apart from the price paid, which would look pretty small, I know. It may be hard to believe, but the fact is that an article in Scribner's has a much greater effect in the real book reading public, than one in the Post. Arthur Train, who has written millions of articles in the Post, put one on Boston in Scribner's, and was astonished at the effect. I thought you might well have something important to say in such a paper as this which might be of very marked value indirectly to sale.

I am awfully glad to hear about Zelda and hope to Heaven she may go on well. We shall soon send you proof. I have spoken to Dashiell.

I had meant to write you about Key West, but now so much time has

---

*Charles Flandrau wrote two novels based on his undergraduate days at Harvard, *Harvard Episodes* (1897) and *The Diary of a Freshman* (1901).

†With his history of the United States between 1900–1925. Entitled *Our Times*, the history was published, in six volumes, by Scribners between 1927 and 1935.

**Alfred Dashiell, Managing Editor of *Scribner's Magazine*. Fitzgerald wrote the piece and it was published, under the title "Echoes of the Jazz Age," in the November, 1931, issue.

elapsed that it seems hardly worthwhile. Ernest was in grand shape except for his arm, and that enabled him to fish, which is quite a piece of work. He could not straighten his arm on account of adhesions, and these may have to be cut, but that seems to be thought a trifle, and in the end he is sure to be practically what he was before the break.

Molly Colum seems to be in a bad way. Weeks ago I heard she had sprained her ankle, but yesterday I got a letter speaking of a bone having to set, and of its being worse now than it was in the beginning. She cannot move her foot. I know she would be mighty keen to see you if you had time to drop in at 1 bis rue de Vaugirard.

Now Ernest has gone off to Spain, and in view of his talent for getting hurt, I think he is mighty likely to run into a bomb or something. – But then, he seems to get hurt under conditions when you would never dream of such a thing, such as when he is standing under a skylight, and not under those in which anybody else would get hurt.

I am looking up the De Voto stories. I know him somewhat, and favorably, and I am told the stories are pretty good. He is a promising man.

Always yours,

Oct. 21, 1931

Dear Scott:

I think there is no doubt that Zelda has a great deal of talent, and of a very colorful, almost poetic kind. In the case of the particular story, "The Two Nuts"[54] I think perhaps the color and all that, rather overwhelmed the story. Zelda has a marvellous instinct for metaphors, or whatever they called them. They are always remarkably good in themselves, – those places where she likens something to something else, but I think that sometimes they are so effective that the thing she likens a thing to, out-shines the thing she means to illuminate. It was that way with this story often, I thought. It would not so much have mattered if there had not been so much of a story in one way, – that is, the career of those poor nuts who were so very representative of the time and the point of view. I thought the story got rather buried. I do not doubt she could easily place it anyhow, but if it ever should get revised, I do not doubt she could place it here, – but I know there is more money elsewhere.

I am glad the depression seems a long way off. People feel a little more cheerful hereabouts. Ernest was in great shape, – never saw him better. He has gone to Kansas City until after the event, and thereafter to Key West. I do not believe I am going to be able to get to Key West, but if I do, I wish to thunder you could do it too.

Always yours,

Don Ce-Sar Hotel   For three days only
Pass-a-grille Beach, St. Petersburg, Florida*
[ca. January 15, 1932]

Dear Max:

At last for the first time in two years & ½ I am going to spend five
consecutive months on my novel. I am actually six thousand dollars ahead
Am replanning it to include what's good in what I have, adding 41,000 new
words & publishing. Don't tell Ernest or anyone – let them think what
they want – you're the only one whose ever consistently felt faith in me
anyhow.

Your letters still sound sad. For God's sake take your vacation this
winter. Nobody could quite ruin the house† in your absense, or would
dare to take any important steps. Give them a chance to see how much they
depend on you & when you come back cut off an empty head or two.
Thalberg did that with Metro-Goldwyn-Mayer.

Which reminds me that I'm doing that "Hollywood Revisited"[55] in the
evenings & it will be along in, I think, six days – maybe ten.

Have Nunnally Johnston's [Johnson's] humorous stories from the Post
been collected? Everybody reads them. Please at least look into this. Ask
Myers – he ought to search back at least a year which is as long as I've been
meaning to write you about it.

Where in hell are my Scandanavian copies of *The Great Gatsby?*

You couldn't have sent me anything I enjoyed more than the Churchill
book.

Always Yours Devotedly

Hotel Rennert
Baltimore**
[ca. April 30, 1932]

Dear Max:

. . . . .

Zelda's novel†† is now good, improved in every way. It is new. She has
largely eliminated the speakeasy-nights-and-our-trip-to-Paris atmosphere.
You'll like it. It should reach you in ten days. I am too close to it to judge
it but it may be even better than I think. *But* I must urge you two things

---

*The Fitzgeralds had returned to the United States in September, 1931, after Zelda's
release from Pragins.
†Charles Scribner's Sons.
**Fitzgerald had come to Baltimore to be near Zelda, who was in the Phipps Clinic there.
††*Save Me the Waltz*, published by Scribners in October, 1932.

173

(1.) If you like it please *don't* wire her congratulations, and please keep whatever praise you may see fit to give *on the staid side* – I mean, *as you naturally would*, rather than yield to a tendency one has with invalids to be extra nice to cheer them up. This seems a nuance but it is rather important at present to the doctors that Zelda does not feel that the acceptance (always granted you like it) means immediate fame and money. I'm afraid all our critical tendencies in the last decade got bullish; we discovered one Hemmingway to a dozen Callaghans and Caldwells (I think the latter is a wash-out) & probably created a lot of spoiled geniuses who might have been good workmen. Not that I regret it – if the last five years uncovered Ernest, Tom Wolfe & Faulkner it would have been worth while, but I'm not certain enough of Zelda's present stability of character to expose her to any superlatives. If she has a success coming she must associate it with work done in a workmanlike manner for its own sake, & part of it done fatigued and uninspired, and part of it done when even to remember the original inspiration and impetus is a psychological trick. She is not twenty-one and she is not strong, and she must not try to follow the pattern of my trail which is of course blazed distinctly on her mind.

(2.) Don't discuss contract with her until I have talked to you.

Ring's last story in the *Post** was pathetic, a shade of himself, but I'm glad they ran it first and I hope it'll stir up his professional pride to repeat.

Beginning the article† for you on Monday. You can count on it for the end of next week.

Now *very important.*

(1.) I must have a royalty report for 1931 for my income tax – they insist.

(2.) I borrowed $600 in 1931. $500 of this was redeemed by my article.** The other hundred should show in royalty report.

(3.) Since *Gatsby* was not placed with *Grosset* or *Burt* I'd like to have it in the *Modern Library*. This is my own idea & have had no approach but imagine I can negotiate it. Once they are interested would of course turn negotiations over to you. But I feel, should you put obstacles in the way

*"One Hit, One Error, One Left," which appeared in the April 23rd issue.
†The article on Hollywood.
**"Echoes of the Jazz Age."

you would be doing me a great harm and injustice. *Gatsby* is constantly mentioned among memorable books but the man who asks for it in a store on the basis of such mention does not ask twice. Booksellers do not keep such an item in stock & there is a whole new generation who cannot obtain it. This has been on my mind for two years and I must insist that you give me an answer that doesn't keep me awake nights wondering why it possibly benefited the Scribners to have me represented in such an impersonal short story collection as that of *The Modern Library* by a weak story & Ring ect by none at all. That "they would almost all have been Scribner authors" was a most curious perversion of what should have been a matter of pride into an attitude of dog-in-the-manger.

Excuse that outburst, Max. Please write, answering all questions. Tell Louise I liked her story & hope she's better. Things go all right with me now. What news of Ernest? And his book?*

Ever Your friend

May 2, 1932

Dear Scott:
I had to be away for a few days so all I did when your letter came was to see that you got the royalty information.

As to "The Great Gatsby", we are perfectly willing to have that go into the Modern Library, and in fact I had once or twice mentioned it to Cerf as something they might take. His inclination seemed to be to wait until another novel had been published, or another book of some kind, which would bring you forward again. I understand perfectly how you feel about the stories, and I understood it at the time. But really the great defect in the publishing business – the thing that underlies all its troubles is that it lets rights to its own books get into the hands of reprint publishers. . . .

Ernest's book is a very very fine book. In some ways it is his best and biggest book. It is very revealing too because it gives a whole point of view about life in giving one about bull fighting. It says wonderfully interesting things about writing, directly, and much more by inference. And there are beautiful things in it about America, as well as about Spain.

You tell me when I ought to say anything to Zelda. In not writing to her I have not been showing anything like the interest we feel in her novel, and I do not want to discourage her by thinking we are not anxious to get

---

* *Death in the Afternoon.*

the manuscript back. But I shall do nothing without word from you. I am mighty glad things look pretty fair now.

Always yours,

[*Hotel Rennert*]
[*Baltimore, Md.*]
[*ca. May 14, 1932*]

Dear Max:
Here is Zelda's novel. It is a good novel now, perhaps a very good novel – I am too close to it to tell. It has the faults & virtues of a first novel. It is more the expression of a powerful personality, like *Look Homeward Angel* than the work of a finished artist like Ernest Hemmingway. It should interest the many thousands interested in dancing. It is *about something* & absolutely new, & should sell.

Now, about its reception. If you refuse it, which I don't think you will, all communication should come through me. If you accept it write her directly and I withdraw all restraints on whatever meed of praise you may see fit to give.[56] The strain of writing it was bad for her but it had to be written – she needed relaxation afterwards and I was afraid that praise might encourage the incipient egomania the doctors noticed, but she has taken such a sane common sense view lately (at first she refused to revise – then she revised completely, added on her own suggestion & has changed what was a rather flashy and self-justifying "true confessions" that wasn't worthy of her into an honest piece of work. She can do more with the galley but I cant ask her to do more now.) – but now praise will do her good within reason. But she musn't write anything more on the *personal* side for six months or so until she is stronger.

Now a second thing, more important than you think. You havn't been in the publishing business over twenty years without noticing the streaks of smallness in very large personalities. Ernest told me once he would "never publish a book in the same season with me", meaning it would lead to ill-feeling. I advise you, if he is in New York, (and always granting you like Zelda's book) *do not praise it, or even talk about it to him!* The finer the thing he has written, the more he'll expect your entire allegiance to it as this is one of the few pleasures, rich & full & new, he'll get out of it. I know this, & I think you do too & probably there's no use warning you. There is no posssible conflict between the books but there has always been a subtle struggle between Ernest & Zelda, & any apposition might have curiously grave consequences – curious, that is, to un-jealous men like you and me.

One more thing. Please, in your letter to Zelda (if of acceptance) do not mention contracts or terms. I will take it up immediately on hearing from you.

Thanks about the *Modern Library*. I don't know exactly what I shall do. Five years have rolled away from me and I can't decide exactly who I am, if anyone.

. . . . .

Ever your Friend

"La Paix," Rodgers' Forge,
*Towson, Maryland,**
January 19, 1933.

Dear Max:

I was in New York for three days last week on a terrible bat. I was about to call you up when I completely collapsed and laid in bed for twenty-four hours groaning. Without a doubt the boy is getting too old for such tricks. Ernest told me he concealed from you the fact that I was in such rotten shape. I send you this, less to write you a *Rousseau's Confession* than to let you know why I came to town without calling you, thus violating a custom of many years standing.

Thanks for the books that you have had sent to me from time to time. They comprise most of the reading I do because like everybody else I gradually cut down on expenses. When you have a line on the sale of Zelda's book let us know.

Found New York in a high state of neurosis, as does everybody else, and met no one who didn't convey the fact to me: it possibly proves that the neurosis is in me. All goes serenely down here. Am going on the water-wagon from the first of February to the first of April but don't tell Ernest because he has long convinced himself that I am an incurable alcoholic, due to the fact that we almost always meet on parties. I am *his* alcoholic just like Ring is mine and do not want to disillusion him, tho even Post stories must be done in a state of sobriety. I thought he seemed in good shape, Bunny less so, rather gloomy. A decision to adopt Communism definitely, no matter how good for the soul, must of necessity be a saddening process for anyone who has ever tasted the intellectual pleasures of the world we live in.

*During the summer, Fitzgerald had moved into "La Paix," a rented Victorian house on the Bayard Turnbull estate outside Baltimore.

For God's sake can't you lighten that pall of gloom which has settled over Scribner's?* – Erskine Caldwell's imitations of Morley Callaghan's imitations of Ernest, and Stuart Chase's imitations of Earl Browder imitating Lenine. Maybe Ring would lighten your volume with a monthly article. I see he has perked up a little in the New Yorker.

All goes acceptably in Maryland, at least from the window of my study, with distant gun flashes on the horizon if you walk far out of the door.

Ever your old friend,

Jan. 27, 1933

Dear Scott:

Those were fine photographs you sent me, and you look mighty well and happy in them. – And it is time you were happy, and I am prophesying to myself that you will have a book published within the next eighteen months, – that allows for serialization. Those ducks, or whatever you have there, look a great sight bigger than the ones we got. You must be shooting over the grounds where your ancestors shot. – Every now and then I have come across something about them.

You think that Ernest thinks very differently about you from what he does, I guess. He told me about having a very long talk with you. You did call me up, by the way. I was out and did not get back until after five, and then I called up the Plaza but you were out. I left a message that you were to get in touch with Ernest at the Brevoort. I thought you had gone back the next day until later I heard you had not, and the day after that, I think it was, I called up Harold Ober and he told me you had just gone, and that you did not feel too good.

I am sending you a couple more books in case you are out of "reading matter". There are plenty of good people we could get like Ring Lardner if we could pay the price, but we cannot touch them. Ring's prices are frightful. I wish we could find somebody with humor.

I have been waiting about Zelda's book in the hope that copies sent on consignment (we had to distribute a great many books that way since the booksellers would not take any chance on anything) would turn out to have sold. They did not though, and I think the sale will amount to about 1400 copies. That is way above the average for a first novel in that bad year, but you are use[d] to such big numbers that it will seem mighty bad to you. As soon as I can get the accurate figures, I shall send them to Zelda.

Always yours,

*Scribner's Magazine.

DEAR SCOTT / DEAR MAX

Dear Max:

I meant to ask you when I last wrote but forgot about it: do you remember (you couldn't possibly) that when I submitted the manuscript of *Flappers and Philosophers* thirteen years ago I sent with it some poems which were to be interpolated between the text of the stories. You advised against publishing the poems but they were not returned and I have no copies of them. Would you have somebody go through your manuscript files and find them and send them on?

I was sorry I said that about the magazine which, in spite of everything, is one of the best in America. Probably I was still smarting under your refusal of *Crazy Sunday* though I understand exactly why you had to turn it down.* Incidentally, you must have been right about it for O'Brien took it for one of his *Best Short Stories* of the year and you know my unutterably low opinion of that gent.

I do not think the sale of Zelda's book was bad when I have just learned that Dos Passos' 1919 [*Nineteen Nineteen*] only sold 9,000 copies. At that rate I don't see how my book is even going to pay the debt I owe you because he is certainly more in the public eye at present than I am.

Will be getting in touch with you within the next few months on what I hope will be important business.

Ever your friend,

Feb. 3, 1933

Dear Scott:

I have hunted up the poems and here they are. – Also a memorandum that may serve as a souvenir, in Zelda's writing I think.

I look forward to your getting in touch with me. If only this world will settle down on some kind of stable basis so that a man can attend to his own affairs I think that you will soon begin to do steady and consistent work. Let the basis be anything so long as it is a basis, – a relatively fixed point from which a man can view things.

I do not think that the outcome with Dos Passos means very much. His sales have steadily dropped. I suppose he might have sold 20,000 or more in this case if it had not been for the depression. But the truth is I do not think his way of writing, and his theory makes books that people care to

* *Scribner's Magazine* had turned down Fitzgerald's story because of its length.

read unless they are interested objectively in society, or in literature purely for its own sake. His whole theory is that books should be sociological documents, or something approaching that. I know I never have taken one of them up without feeling that I was in for three or four hours of agony only relieved by admiration of his ability. They are fascinating, but they do make you suffer like the deuce, and people cannot want to do that.

I am sending Zelda a novel that I believe she will enjoy, – "South Moon Under".*

Always yours,

August 4, 1933

Dear Scott:

When do you think I shall see you? I don't want to be away when you are likely to turn up, but I don't want to pin you down to a date, either. I hope things are going on well. You have had a mighty hard pull, but it may end rightly. Whenever any of these new writers come up who are brilliant, I always realize that you have more talent and more skill than any of them; – but circumstances have prevented you from realizing upon the fact for a long time.

I wish we could have sent Zelda a larger check.† When I see you, I'll speak to you about it. I would have written to her encouraging her to write more because I think she really could do a great deal, except that the result did not give much in a practical sense, with which to back the argument. Many of the reviews too are bad, but they were all based upon that one point of over-writing in the matter of figures of speech.

Ernest is on the point of sailing from Havana for Spain, where he and Sidney Franklin** and a man named Whitney, are to make a movie to fit the title "Death in the Afternoon". We are to publish a collection of his stories this fall. He fished for some months off the coast of Cuba, and with results that made what we used to get off the Tortugas look like sardines.

I think things are bad with Ring. I hate to inquire. He is at Easthampton and nobody ever seems to see him.

I guess I can hope to see you in a few weeks.

Always yours,

---

*By Marjorie Kinnan Rawlings.
†For royalties on *Save Me the Waltz*.
**Bull-fighter and friend of Hemingway.

DEAR SCOTT / DEAR MAX

Dear Max:

The novel has gone ahead faster than I thought. There was a little set back when I went to the hospital for four days but since then things have gone ahead of my schedule, which you will remember, promised you the whole manuscript for reading November 1, with the first one-fourth ready to shoot into the magazine (in case you can use it) and the other three-fourths to undergo further revision. I now figure that this can be achieved by about the 25th of October. I will appear in person carrying the manuscript and wearing a spiked helmet.

There are several points and I wish you would answer them categorically.

1. Did you mean that you could get the first fourth of the story into the copy of the magazine appearing late in December and therefore that the book could appear early in April? I gathered that on the phone but want to be sure. I don't know what the ocean travel statistics promise for the spring but it seems to me that a May publication would be too late if there was a great exodus and I should miss being a proper gift book for it. The story, as you know, is laid entirely in Europe – I wish I could have gotten as far as China but Europe was the best I could do, Max (to get into Ernest's rhythm).

2. I would not want a magazine proof of the first part, though of course I would expect your own proof readers to check up on blatant errors, but would want to talk over with you any small changes that would have to be made for magazine publication – in any case, to make them myself.

3. Will publication with you absolutely preclude that the book will be chosen by the Literary Guild or the Book of the Month? Whatever the answer the serial will serve the purpose of bringing my book to the memory and attention of my old public and of getting straight financially with you. On the other hand, it is to both our advantages to capitalize if possible such facts as that the editors of those book leagues might take a fancy to such a curious idea that the author, Fitzgerald, actually wrote a book after all these years (this is all said with the reservation that the book is good.) Please answer this as it is of importance to me to know whether I must expect my big returns from serial and possibly theatrical and picture rights or whether I have as good a chance at a book sale, launched by one of those organizations, as any other best seller.

Ober is advancing me the money to go through with it (it will probably not need more than $2,000 though he has promised to go as far as $4,000) and in return I am giving him 10% of the serial rights. I plan to raise the money to repay him (if I have not already paid him by *Post* stories) by asking a further advance on the book royalties or on my next book which might be an omnibus collection of short stories or those two long serial stories about young people that I published some time ago in the *Post* as the Basil stories and the Josephine stories – this to be published in the fall.

You are the only person who knows how near the novel is to being finished, *please don't say a word to anyone.*

4. How will you give a month's advance notice of the story – slip a band on the jacket of the December issue? I want to talk to you about advertising when I see you in late October so please don't put even the publicity man at any work yet. As to the photographs . . . I don't want any of the old ones sent out and I don't want any horrors to be dug up out of newspaper morgues.
. . . . .

5. My plan, and I think it is very important, is to prevail upon the *Modern Library*, even with a subsidy, to bring out *Gatsby* a few weeks after the book publication of this novel. Please don't say that anybody would possibly have the psychology of saying to themselves "One of his is in the *Modern Library* therefore I will not buy another", or that the two books could be confused. The people who buy the *Modern Library* are not at all the people who buy the new books. *Gatsby* – in its present form, not actually available in sight to book buyers, will only get a scattering sale as a result of the success of this book. I feel that every time your business department has taken a short-sighted view of our community of interest in this matter, which is my reputation, there has been no profit on your part and something less than that on mine. As for example, a novel of Ernest's in the *Modern Library* and no novel of mine, a good short story of Ernest's in their collection of the Great Modern Short Stories and a purely commercial story of mine. I want to do this almost as much as I want to publish this novel and will cooperate to the extent of sharing the cost.

There will be other points when I see you in October, but I will be greatly reassured to have some sort of idea about these points so that I can make my plans accordingly.[57] I will let you know two or three days in advance when you may expect me.

One last point: Unlike Ernest I am perfectly agreeable to making any necessary cuts *for serial publication* but naturally insist that I shall do them myself.

You can imagine the pride with which I will enter your office a month from now. *Please do not have a band as I do not care for music.*

Ever yours,

La Paix, Rodgers' Forge,
Towson, Maryland,
September 29, 1933.

Dear Max:

Since talking to you and getting your letter another angle has come up. Ober tells me that Burton of *Cosmopolitan* is very interested in the novel and if he took it would, in Ober's opinion, pay between $30,000 and $40,000 for it. Now against that there are the following factors:

1. The fact that though Burton professes great lust for my work the one case in which I wrote a story specifically for him, that movie story that you turned down and that Mencken published,* he showed that he really can't put his taste into action; in that case the Hearst policy man smeared it.

2. The tremendous pleasure I would get from appearing in *Scribners.*

3. The spring publication.

4. My old standby, the *Post,* would not be too pleased to have my work running serially all spring and summer in the *Cosmopolitan.*

On the other hand, the reasons why it must be considered are between thirty and forty thousand, and all of them backed by the credit of the U.S. Treasury. It is a purely hypothetical sum I admit and certainly no serial is worth it, yet if Willie Hearst is still pouring gold back into the desert in the manner of 1929 would I be stupid not to take some or would I be stupid not to take some? My own opinion is that if the thing is offered to Burton, he will read it, be enthusiastic, and immediately an Obstacle will appear. On the other hand, should I even offer it to them? Should I give him a copy on the same day I give you a copy asking an answer from him within three days? Would the fact that he refused it diminish your interest in the book or influence it? Or, even, considering my relations with you would it be a dirty trick to show it to him at all? What worries me is the possibility of being condemned to go back to the *Saturday Evening Post* grind at the exact moment when the book is finished. I suppose I could and probably will need a damn good month's rest outdoors or traveling before I can even do that.

---

*"Crazy Sunday," *American Mercury,* October, 1932.

Can you give me any estimate as to how much I could expect from you as to payment for the serial and how much of that will be in actual cash? It seems terrible to ask you this when it is not even decided yet whether or not you want it; but what I want to do is to see if I can *not* offer it at all to Burton; I wish to God I had never talked to Harold about it and got these upsetting commercial ideas in my head.

I am taking care of the picture matter. I certainly would like to be on your cover and stare down Greta Garbo on the news stands. I figure now that it should reach you, at the latest, on the 25th, though I am trying for the 23rd.

Ring's death was a terrible blow. Have written a short appreciation of him for the *New Republic.* *

Please answer.

Ever yours,

September 30, 1933.

Dear Scott:

If the *Cosmop* would give you $30 or $40,000 for the serial, I think the only strong argument that could be advanced against taking it would be the quality of the magazine. The fact that you have not had a novel since so long and have been writing stories only for popular magazines makes it somewhat desirable that you should now appear in a high-class magazine. I know Harold Ober has said that, but my honest opinion, given against a natural tendency toward wishful thinking to the contrary, is that this element is exaggerated. I don't think the prospects of the novel would be injured by its appearing in the *Cosmop* enough to overcome the financial advantages. I think when the novel came out it would soon ride over any of the possible prejudices there might be in the upper levels of readers. In fact I doubt if the prejudices exist at all. It would be difficult if it were a question of Liberty which is so horribly cheap now. As to all the other points you make such as the one about your relations with us, – they, and in particular that one, ought not to figure at all. Our relations with you wouldn't be right if they let you do something to your disadvantage, but I honestly don't think there is anything in that point whatever.

As to the arrangements we should make, I haven't been able to talk about it enough to figure it out. We'll have to do that quickly if the serial does come to us. We'll do the best we can you can be sure. But I think you

*Ring Lardner died on September 25th. Fitzgerald's "Ring" appeared on October 11th in the *New Republic*.

ought in the circumstances to give them a copy of the novel at the time you give it to us. There does exist the risk you mention of having to go back to the S.E.P. grind. Escape from that is the main thing. –[58]

. . . . .

. . . . .

I was in hopes that you might do us an article on Ring. I thought you could do one about Ring, himself.

Always yours,

Oct. 6, 1933

Dear Scott:

I just read your piece on Ring. Of course you could not do anything for Scribner's now. I thought it might have been only on one phase of him alone, but it says a great deal. I thought it was a very fine piece.

I am now writing to ask your advice. – I want to have us publish some sort of volume of Ring's material. The only possibilities I can think of are either a selection from his stories by somebody qualified to take out the best, and those most representative of his talent; or a selection from all of his writings, which would let in something from "You Know Me Al" and those little plays that you speak of, and some of the best of his lighter things. But whether we followed one of these plans, or the other, we would need an introduction, and I think only one that was written by someone really appreciative of him as a writer, and at the same time knew him well as a man, and was appreciative of him that way too, would do. – Grantland Rice would not do therefore, and the usual literary critic certainly would not. – So who would? Would you, do you think? And if so, would you be willing to undertake it? It is true that you only knew Ring after what was the most typical part of his career was over, – when he was a sports writer, and a newspaperman, and all that. I suppose people like Grantland Rice might say, why didn't they ask someone who went through all those days with him? Anyhow, I wish you would either write me about this matter (it is a pure favor I am asking you) or else think it over until you appear here in the latter part of this month. – We could not publish a book until 1934. If we did it, I would want to get a really fine picture of Ring. I would almost rather have it after the Great Neck days because, although he did look terribly gaunt and ill, even before he went to the hospital, I do think that you could see better what a remarkable creature he was then.[59]

John Bishop is back, – has a house in Connecticut.

Always yours,

*La Paix, Rodgers' Forge,
Towson, Maryland,
October 19, 1933.*

Dear Max:

All goes well here. The first two chapters are in shape and am starting the third one this afternoon. So the first section comprising about 26,000 words will be mailed to you Friday night or Saturday morning.

Naturally I was delighted by your gesture of coming up two thousand. I hope to God results will show in the circulation of the magazine and I have an idea they will. Negotiations with *Cosmopolitan* were of course stopped and Ober is sure that getting the release from *Liberty* is merely a matter of form which he is attending to. I think I will need the money a little quicker than by the month, say $1000 on delivery of the first section and then the other 3 $1000s every fortnight after that. This may not be necessary but the first $2000 will. As you know, I now owe Ober two or three thousand and he should be reimbursed so he can advance me more to carry me through the second section and a *Post* story. Naturally, payments on the serial should be made to him.

I am saying this now and will remind you later. My idea is that the *book* form of the novel should be set up *from the corrected proof of the serial,* – in that I will reinsert the excisions which I am making for the serial.

If you have any way of getting French or Swiss railroad posters it would be well for you to try to. Now as to the blurbs:* I think there should not be too many; I am sending you nine.†

"The Great Gatsby is undoubtedly a work of art."

London Times

As to T. S. Eliot: what he said was in a letter to me – that he'd read it several times, it had interested and excited him more than any novel he had seen, either English or American, for a number of years, and he also said that it seemed to him that it was the first step forward in the American novel since Henry James.

I know him slightly but I would not dare ask him for an endorsement. If it can be managed in any way without getting a rebuff, even some more qualified statement would be the next best thing to an endorsement by Joyce or Gertrude Stein.

Of course I think blurbs have gotten to be pretty much the bunk, but maybe that is a writer's point of view and the lay reader does not understand the back-scratching that is at the root of most of them. However, I

*Perkins had asked Fitzgerald for statements about *Gatsby* for publicity purposes.
†The first eight are missing.

leave it in your hands. Don't quote all of these unless you think it is advisable.

We can talk over the matter of *Gatsby* in the Modern Library after your announcement has appeared.

Again thanks for the boost in price and remember the title is a secret to the last.

Ever your friend,

I should say to be careful in saying it's my first book in seven years *not to imply that it contains seven years* work. People would expect too much in bulk & scope.

This novel, my 4th, completes my story of the boom years. It might be wise to accentuate the fact that it does *not* deal with the depression. *Don't* accentuate that it deals with Americans abroad – there's been too much trash under that banner.

No exclamatory "At last, the long awaited ect." That merely creates the "Oh yeah" mood in people.

La Paix, Rodgers' Forge,
Towson, Maryland,
October 20, 1933.

Dear Max:
Made not only the changes agreed upon but also cut out several other small indelicacies that I happened upon. I think this is now damn good.*

How is this for an advertising approach:

"For several years the impression has prevailed that Scott Fitzgerald had abandoned the writing of novels and in the future would continue to write only popular short stories. His publishers knew different and they are very glad now to be able to present a book which is in line with his three other highly successful and highly esteemed novels, thus demonstrating that Scott Fitzgerald is anything but through as a serious novelist."

I don't mean necessarily these exact words but something on that general line, I mean something politic enough not to disparage the *Post* stories but saying quite definitely that this is a horse of another color.

If Dashiell likes this section of the book ask him to drop me a line. Am starting the revision of the second section Monday.

Ever your friend,

*Fitzgerald is referring to *Tender Is the Night* in serial form.

La Paix, Rodgers' Forge,
Towson, Maryland,
November 13, 1933.

Dear Max:

I was too sanguine in estimating the natural divisions of the novel. As it turns out in the reworking the line up is as follows:

    I. The first triangle story, which you have

(26,000 words)

    II. Completion of that story, plus the throw-back to courtship of doctor and his wife (19,000 words)

    III. The doctor's struggles with his problem, concluding with his debacle in Rome.

    IV. The doctor's decline after he has given up.

    These two last parts are going to be *long as hell*, especially IV, Section III, as you may remember, includes the part about his journeying around Europe, which we agreed could be considerably cut, but Section IV could not be cut much without omission of such key incidents as would cripple the timing of the whole plan. That Section is liable to amount to as much as forty thousand words – could you handle it? Or must I divide it, and lose a month on spring publication?

    By that time reader interest in the serial will be thoroughly aroused (or thoroughly killed) so I think the idea of the book publication should be paramount if you can arrange the material factor of such a long installment.

Ever yours,

P. S. By the way: where in hell is the proof? And will you have two struck off? This is important for Section II where the medical part begins, but how can I ask a doctor to judge fairly upon Section II unless he can read Section I?[60]

1307 Park Avenue,
Baltimore, Maryland,
January 13, 1934.

Dear Max:

What do you think of the idea of using twenty-four of those wood-cuts, which illustrate the serial, as head and tail pieces for chapters in the book or, alternatively, interspersing them through the novel? I think it is comparatively an innovation in recent fiction and might give the book a certain distinction. I've gotten very fond of the illustrations. Who the hell is the illustrator? If it is too expensive a process let me know, but since the cuts are already made I thought it might not be.

. . . . .

I did not thank you over the phone for the further advance, which does not mean that I did not appreciate it, but only that I have so much to thank you for.[61]

Tell Dashiell that I cannot promise not to make changes in Section III, but under no conditions will it be lengthened. Section IV is taking longer than I thought and it may be the middle of next week before you get it.

Ever Yours

P.S. 1. Will you ask Dashiell to strike off as many as half a dozen additional proofs because I have always a use for them in passing them around for technical advice. . . .

P.S. 2. Don't forget my suggestion that the jacket flap should carry an implication that though the book starts in a lyrical way, heavy drama will presently develop.

P.S. 3. Any contract you suggest will probably be O.K. . . .

P.S. 4. Also remember that upon due consideration I would prefer the binding to be uniform with my other books. If these were prosperous times and there were any prospect of a superior reissue of my whole tribe I'd say "let it begin here" to quote the famous commander of the Minute men, but there isn't, so I prefer to stick to my undistinguished green uniform – I mean even to the point of the guilt stampings being uniform to the others.

P.S. 5. I don't want to bore you by reiterating but I do think the matter of Gatsby in the Modern Library should be taken up as shortly as possible after the appearance of installment II.[62]

P.S. 6. Am getting responses only from a few writers and from the movies. The novel will certainly have *success d'estime* but it may be slow in coming – alas, I may again have written a novel for novelists with little chance of its lining anybody's pockets with gold. The thing is perhaps too crowded for story reachers to search it through for the story but it can't be helped, there are times when you have to get every edge of your finger-nails on paper. Anyhow I think this serial publication will give it the best chance it can possibly have because it is a book that only gives its full effect on its second reading. Almost every part of it now has been revised and thought out from three to six times.

. . . . .

Jan. 15, 1934

Dear Scott:

. . . I'll think about the points you bring up. – But I think everything is coming out mighty well. That is my belief.

I am giving Dashiell your message. The blurb should be and will be as you say, and I am not forgetting about Gatsby.

Unless for some reason the book is above the general public's head – for some reason I cannot see in view of its fascination – it ought to be more than a *sucess d'estime.*

. . . . .

I know that you are having a hell of a time jumping from iron to iron to keep them all at the right temperature, but I think you might consider (I say it with much hesitation and doubt) the possibility of reducing in length what was in the first installment and the first part of the second. It is probably impossible, and perhaps unwise anyhow. I thought you might conceivably cut out the shooting in the station. The purpose would be only that as soon as people get to Dick Diver their interest in the book, and their perception of its importance increases some thirty to forty percent. People do read a book differently from a serial though. I merely suggest the idea in order that your subconscious mind may work upon it a little without distracting you at all from anything else. – To be considered if at all, only when you come to the book proof.

Ever yours,

1307 Park Avenue,
Baltimore, Maryland,
January 18, 1934.

Dear Max:

. . . . .

Much as I value your advice, by which I profited in the revision of Gatsby, I can't see cutting out the "shooting at the train-side." It serves all sorts of subtle purposes and since I have decided that the plan of the book is best as originally conceived, the small paring away would be very little help and I think would do more harm than good. I intend to think over this question once more but at the moment I am satisfied with the book as it stands, as well as being pretty dead on it. I want to hear some reactions on Section II, but I like the slow approach, which I think has a psychological significance affecting not only the work in question, but also having a bearing on my career in general. Is that too damn egotistical an association?

Ever yours,

1307 Park Avenue,
Baltimore, Maryland,
February 5, 1934.

Dear Max:

Isn't there any mechanical means by which you can arrange to include the 1400 words of the arrest in Cannes?* The more I think of it the more I think that it is absolutely necessary for the unity of the book and the effectiveness of the finale to show Dick in the dignified and responsible aspect toward the world and his neighbors that was implied so strongly in the first half of the book. It is all very well to say that this can be remedied in book publication but it has transpired that at least two dozen important writers and newspaper men are reading the book in the serial and will form their impressions from that. I have made cuts in Section IV – a good bit of the last scene between Dick and Tommy but also the proof has swollen somewhat in revision which counteracts that, nor can I reduce the 1250 words of that scene to 800. I am saying 1400 because I know there will be a slight expansion. Couldn't you take out some short piece from the number? Surely it hasn't crystallized at this early date. Even with this addition the installment is shorter than the others, as I promised Fritz.†

If I do not hold these two characters to the end of the book it might as well never have been written. It is legitimate to ruin Dick but it is by no means legitimate to make him an ineffectual. In the proof I am pointing up the fact that his intention dominated all this last part but it is not enough and the foreshortening without the use of this scene, which was a part of the book structure from the first, does not contain enough of him for the reader to reconstruct his whole personality as viewed as a unit throughout – and the reason for this is my attempt to tell the last part entirely through Nicole's eyes. I was even going to have her in on the Cannes episode but decided against it because of the necessity of seeing Dick alone.

My feeling about this was precipitated by the remarks of the young psychiatrist who is the only person who had read all the magazine proof and only the magazine proof. He felt a sharp lesion at the end which those who had read the whole novel did not feel.

While I am writing you I may as well cover some other points:

1. Please don't forget the indentation of title and author on the front

---

*Perkins wired Fitzgerald on February 5th asking whether he could condense the arrest to eight-hundred words as that was all that could be fitted into the magazine installment. On the same day, presumably before he wrote this letter, Fitzgerald replied by telegram, expressing the hope that the entire scene could be retained.

†Alfred Dashiell.

cover as in previous books. There are other Fitzgeralds writing and I would like my whole name on the outside of the book, and also I would prefer uniformity.

2. Would you please strike off at least three book proofs for me, all to be used for revisions such as medical, linguistic, etc? . . .

3. In advertising the book some important points are: Please do not use the phrase "Riviera" or "gay resorts." Not only does it sound like the triviality of which I am so often accused, but also the Riviera has been thoroughly exploited by E. Phillips Oppenheim and a whole generation of writers and its very mention invokes a feeling of unreality and unsubstantiality. So I think it would be best to watch this and reduce it only to the statement that the scenes of the book are laid in Europe. If it could be done, a suggestion that, after a romantic start, a serious story unfolds, would not be amiss; also it might be mentionable that for exigencies of serialization, a scene or two was cut. In general, as you know, I don't approve of great ballyhoo advertisements, even of much quoted praise. The public is very, very, very weary of being sold bogus goods and this inevitably reacts on solider manufactures.

I find that revising in this case is pulling up the weakest section of the book and then the next weakest, etc. First, Section III was the weakest and Section IV the strongest, so I bucked up III, then IV was the weakest and is still but when I have fixed that Section I will be the weakest. The section that has best held up is Section II.

I was tremendously impressed with "South Moon Under" until I read her prize short story, "Gal Young Un." I suddenly saw the face of Ethan Fromme peering out from under a palmetto hat. The heroine is even called Matt in tribute to the power of the subconscious. Well, well, well, I often think of Picasso's remark "You do it first then other people can come along and do it pretty and get off with a big proportion of the spoils. When you do it first you can't do it pretty." So I guess Miss Rawlings is just another writer after all, just when I was prepared to welcome her to the class of 1896 with Ernest, Dos Passos and myself.

Please wire about the inclusion of the Cannes episode,* and *don't* sidetrack these advertising points.

Ever yours,

---

*Perkins agreed to retain the arrest scene in its entirety in a telegram on February 5th, before he even received this letter.

Feb. 14, 1934

Dear Scott:

I am planning to see you on Saturday.

Now I enclose a letter (keep it for me) from Bennet Cerf whom I supplied with complete magazine proofs of "Tender Is the Night". . . . Here are comments from Marjorie Rawlings: "I hear much talk already of 'Tender Is the Night'. I thought, beginning to read it after I had written you, that Fitzgerald had filled the contract I was setting up for myself – a book disturbing, bitter and beautiful. I am totally unable to analyze the almost overpowering effect that some of his passages create – some of them about quite trivial people and dealing with trivial situations. There is something terrifying about it when it happens, and the closest I can come to understanding it is to think that he does, successfully at such times, what I want to do – that is, visualizes people not in their immediate setting, from the human point of view – but in time and space – almost, you might say, with the divine detachment. The effect is very weird when he does it with unimportant people moving in a superficial and sophisticated setting. I shouldn't put it that way, for of course importance and un-importance are relative – if they exist at all."

I hope you can get through the book proof pretty fast. We are mighty crowded for time, – I have said nothing about it because I knew you had to have the way clear for magazine proof. We want to publish as close to the end of the serial as we possibly can, and there is a lot of work to be done by the printers in make-up, etc.

Always yours,

. . . . .

1307 Park Avenue,
Baltimore, Maryland,
March 4, 1934.

Dear Max:

Confirming our conversation on the phone this morning, I wish you could get some word to the printers that they should not interfere with my use of italics. If I had made a mess of a type face, that would be another matter. I know exactly what I am doing, and I want to use italics for *emphasis*, and not waste them on the newspaper convention laid down by Mr. Munsey in 1858. . . .

Going over the other points, I hope both (1) that the review copies will go out in plenty of time, and (2) that they will get the version of the novel as it will be published because there is no doubt that each revision makes a tremendous difference in the impression that the book will leave. After all, Max, I am a plodder. One time I had a talk with Ernest Hemingway, and I told him, against all the logic that was then current, that I was the tortoise and he was the hare, and that's the truth of the matter, that everything that I have ever attained has been through long and persistent struggle while it is Ernest who has a touch of genius which enables him to bring off extraordinary things with facility. I have no facility. I have a facility for being cheap, if I wanted to indulge that. I can do cheap things. I changed Clark Gable's act at the moving picture theatre here the other day. I can do that kind of thing as quickly as anybody but when I decided to be a serious man, I tried to struggle over every point until I have made myself into a slow moving Behemoth (if that is the correct spelling), and so there I am for the rest of my life. Anyhow, these points of proof reading, etc, are of tremendous importance to me, and you can charge it all to my account, and I will realize all the work you have had on it.

As I told you on the phone, I enjoyed Marjory Rawlin's praise, but it was somewhat qualified by her calling my people trivial people. Other stuff has drifted in from writers all over America, some of it by telegram, which has been complimentary.

Now, about advertising. Again I want to tell you my theory that everybody is absolutely dead on ballyhoo of any kind, and for your advertising department to take up any interest that the intellectuals have so far shown toward the book and exploit that, would be absolutely disastrous. The reputation of a book must grow from within upward, must be a natural growth. I don't think there is a comparison between this book and The Great Gatsby as a seller. The Great Gatsby had against it its length and its purely masculine interest. This book, on the contrary, is a woman's book. I think, given a decent chance, it will make its own way in so far as fiction is selling under present conditions.

Excuse me if this letter has a dogmatic ring. I have lived so long within the circle of this book and with these characters that often it seems to me that the real world does not exist but that only these characters exist, and, however pretentious that remark sounds (and my God, that I should have to be pretentious about my work), it is an absolute fact – so much so that their glees and woes are just exactly as important to me as what happens in life.[63]

Zelda is better. There is even a chance of her getting up for the exhibition of her paintings at Easter, but nothing certain. Do you still think that idea of piling the accumulated manuscript in the window* is a valid one?

---

*Fitzgerald had proposed exhibiting the accumulated drafts and manuscripts of *Tender Is the Night* in Scribners Fifth Avenue display window, as a publicity gimmick.

My instinct does not quite solve the problem. What do you think? Would it seem a little phoney?

With best wishes,

1307 Park Avenue,
Baltimore, Maryland,
March 5, 1934.

Dear Max:

The stout arrived this morning and I am sampling it for lunch. I think I'd better have my photograph taken first for if I become as swollen as you intend my thousands and thousands of younger admirers will just leave the sinking ship.

By the way, when you and Louise left here did you, by any chance, take with you 12 spoons, 12 forks, 12 knives (fish), 12 knives (dinner), 1 silver salver, 1 revolver, 1 platinum and diamond wrist-watch? I don't like to accuse *anybody* of *anything* but there is a very curious coincidence. I may say if it's all sent back within the week I shall take no further steps in the matter. We assure you, sir, that we returned the wrong trousers and we are having our agent look into the matter. With a business as large as ours and trousers as small as yours such things will happen.

In any case, Max, if the stout kills me I protected myself by a new clause in my will based on the old Maryland Poison Act – Md.362 XX: 1, 47.*

Yours very truly,

1307 Park Avenue,
Baltimore, Maryland,
May 15, 1934.

Dear Max:

In reference to our conversation: I have roughly about four plans for a book to be published this autumn.† Now I think that we must, to some extent, set aside the idea that a diffuse collection stands much chance of a decent sale, no matter what previous records Ernest and I have made. Of course I shall make every attempt to unify what I prepare by an inclusive and definitive title, which is even more important with short stories than with a novel, for it is necessary to bind them together and appeal to one mood in a buyer. Moreover, with so much material to choose from I think the collection should have some real inner unity, even in preference to

---

*This letter is signed "F. Scott Fitzgerald (Bart.)."
† *Tender Is the Night* had been published on April 12th.

195

having it include selected stories of many types. Roughly here are my ideas:

Plan 1.   The idea of a big omnibus including both new stories and the pick of the other three collections. You must tell me what luck you've had with the omnibus volumes of Lardner, Galsworthy, etc.

Plan 2   The Basil Lee stories, about 60,000 words, and the Josephine stories, 37,500 – with one or two stories added, the last of which will bring Basil and Josephine together – making a book of about 120,000 words under some simple title such as "Basil and Josephine." This would in some ways look like the best commercial bet because it might be taken like Tarkington's "Gentle Julia," "Penrod," etc. almost as a novel, *and the most dangerous artistically for the same reason* – for the people who buy my books might think that I was stringing them by selling them watered goods under a false name.

Plan 3.   A collection of new short stories. Of these there are about forty, of which about twenty-nine are possible and say fifteen might be chosen, with the addition of one or two very serious, non-commercial stories, which I have long planned but have yet to write, to heighten the tone of the volume. This might be unified under some title which would express that they are tales of the golden twenties, or even specifically, "More Tales of the Jazz Age." The table of contents would be something like this:

The dates are not the dates written but the period each story might represent.

1918 – *The Last of the Belles* or else *The Love Boat*
1919 – *Presumption*
1920 – *The Adolescent Marriage* or else *One Trip Abroad*
1921 – *Outside the Cabinet Makers* or else *A short Trip Home*
1922 – *Two Wrongs* or else *A Freeze-out*
1923 – *At Your Age* or else *In a Little Town*
1924 – *Crazy Sunday* or else *Jacob's Ladder*
1925 – *Rough Crossing* or else *Family in the Wind*
1926 – *The Bowl* or else *Interne*

1927 – *Swimmers* or else
     A New Leaf
1928 – *Hotel Child* or else
1929 – *Change of Class*
     Majesty or else
1930 – *The Bridal Party*
     I Got Shoes
1931 – *Babylon Revisited* or else
     More Than Just a House
1932 – *Between Three and Four*

and three others, *Two for a Cent, The Pusher-in-the-Face* and *One of My Oldest Friends* which makes up the twenty-nine, excluding the Basil and Josephine stories, the unwritten ones and a couple of new ones I have just finished and can't judge.

I don't know how many of these you remember but of course I would ask you and perhaps a few other people to read over a selection and give some opinions, though among these twenty-nine there is scarcely one which *everybody* has enjoyed and scarcely one which *nobody* has enjoyed.

Plan 4. This is an idea founded on the success of such books as Alexander Woollcott's "While Rome Burns." As you know I have never published any personal stuff between covers because I have needed it all for my fiction; nevertheless, a good many of my articles and random pieces have attracted a really quite wide attention, and might again if we could get a tie-up of title and matter, which should contain wit and a soupçon of wisdom and not look like a collection of what the cat brought in, or be haunted by the bogey of all articles in a changing world, of being hilariously dated. It might be the best idea of all. Let me give you a rough idea as to what I have in that line:

There are my two articles for the *Post* which attracted such wide attention in their day that I have yet to hear the last of them, "How to Live on $36,000 a Year" and "How to Live on Practically Nothing a Year." There are "Echoes of the Jazz Age" from *Scribner's* and "My Lost City" which the *Cosmopolitan* has been holding up but wouldn't sell back to me to publish in the *American*. Other articles which have attracted attention are "Princeton" in *College Humor*, "One Hundred False Starts" in the *Post*, "The Cruise of the Rolling Junk," a long, supposedly humorous account of an automobile journey that appeared in *Motor*, an article called "Girls Believe in Girls" in *Liberty*, and two articles called "Making Monagomy Work" and "Are [Our] Irresponsible Rich?" published by the Metropolitan Syndicate in the early twenties, and an article called "On Being Twenty-five" in the *American*. And these also from the early twenties, "Wait till you have children of your own" (Woman's Home Companion), "Imagination" and "A Few Mothers" in the *Ladies Home Journal* and "The Little Brother of the Flapper" in *McCalls*.

This, or a good part of it, would have to comprise the backbone of the book and would be about 57,000 words. In addition there are some literary reviews, etc. of which nothing should be preserved except the elegy on Ring and an article in the *Bookman* on "How to Waste Material" welcoming Ernest's arrival. Beyond this there are a few hors d'oeuvres such as "A Short Autobiography" and "Salesmanship in the Champs Elysees" both in the *New Yorker* and a few other short sketches from *Vanity Fair, College Humor,* etc. and some light verse. There are also a couple of articles in which Zelda and I collaborated – idea, editing and padding being mine and most of the writing being hers – but I am not sure I would be justified in using it. Also I have some of my very first stories written at twelve and thirteen, some of which are funny enough to be reprinted.

Looking this over it doesn't seem very voluminous. I haven't seen Woollcott's book (by the way, did he get a copy of the novel?) and don't know how thick it is, but there seems to be some audience somewhere for collections (Dorothy Parker, etc.) as didn't exist in the 1920s.

The above [is] all that I could count on getting ready for next fall. The "dark age" novel could not possibly be ready inside of a year, that is to say, for the autumn of 1935.

Would you please think over this line-up carefully and let me hear your advice, also I will ask Zelda's, which is often pretty good in what does not concern herself and which is always, strangely enough, conservative. A fifth idea of sandwiching some of my stuff in with hers, her old sketches of girls in *College Humor*, her short phantasies, etc. has occurred to me but I don't know that I think it's advisable.

I may come up but probably not. Thanks a lot for the money.*

Ever yours,

May 17, 1934

Dear Scott:

We are all strongly in favor of Plan #2, Basil and Josephine. The only point against it might be that of the time you would need to get it right. If you feel confident about that not being too great, – not more than six weeks say – we are very strongly for it. I see the danger of misleading the public into thinking of it as a novel in the same sense that "Tender Is the Night" is, and we ought to be sure that there is no mistake made. I think

---

*Perkins had deposited $600 for Fitzgerald on May 15th.

we could surely do it with safety and I believe the book would be very much liked and admired.

After Plan #2, we favor Plan #3. I am writing you immediately without going into the matter at any great length, in order to get a decision. We want to put you into the fall list right away.

Always yours,

1307 Park Avenue,
Baltimore, Maryland,
May 21, 1934.

Dear Max:

On thinking it over and in going over the Basil and Josephine stories the business seems impossible. They are not as good as I thought. They are full of Tarkington and as he is now writing a new series of juveniles there would be inevitable comparisons and perhaps not to my advantage.

Secondly, they would require a tremendous amount of work and a good deal of new invention to make them presentable.

Thirdly, I have not quite enough faith in the Business Department to believe that they would not exploit it to some extent as a novel (as in their using a private letter to me from T.S. Eliot on the jacket of "Tender" when they swore they only wanted it to show to the trade) and any such misconception would just ruin what position I have reconstituted with the critics. The ones who like "Tender" would be disgusted; the ones who were baffled by it or dislike my work would take full advantage to goose-pile on me. It's too damn risky and I am too old for such a chance and the penalty might be too high. What it amounts to is that if it is presented as a novel it wrecks me and if it were presented as short stories then what is the advantage of it over a better collection of short stories? I admit there is some.

Fourthly, I find that I have bled too many of them of their best phrases and ideas for "Tender Is the Night."

However, I have decided to bust up the series and use some of them in this book (Kipling busted up his "Soldiers Three" stories in the same way and ran them through several books.)

So that leaves Plan 3. I have picked out eight stories that I *know* I want to republish and I am submitting to you now fifteen others from which I wish you would select (perhaps collecting several opinions) about six or seven or eight to join to the original eight. I can meanwhile start evening work revising the first eight.

The working title will be "More Tales of the Jazz Age" though I will keep thinking on that subject. Barring accidents you can certainly count on the stories in six weeks.

Ever yours,

June 4, 1934

Dear Scott:

I am returning the stories. I divided them into three groups according to my preference, but of course you will consider in the selection anyhow, the question of variety of kinds which I have not done.

Into the first group I have put:

Last of the Belles

Two Wrongs

Majesty (especially because the ending is fine)

He Thinks He's Wonderful ⎫

A Perfect Life   ⎬ Basil and Josephine

Woman With a Past   ⎭

In the next group:

I Got Shoes (which I think comes mighty near to being a very fine story but did not seem to me to be completely successful)

Presumption (which I thought was one of the few stories that ever got away completely with a surprise at the end)

More Than a House

A New Leaf

In the third group I put:

At Your Age

Change of Class

Between Three and Four

A Freeze Out

The Bowl

This grouping is pretty arbitrary and will only help you because it is some other person's judgment.

Always yours,

Dear Max:
I have pretty well lined up the book. It comes to sixteen stories as you will
see from enclosure (1).[64] You seem to like the Basil Lee and Josephine
stories so well that I am sending you herewith the others of the series and
if there is any of these that you like equally I can include them. Of course
the book is 120,000 words long now and you may want me to take out one
or two of the others. I hate to impose on you when I know you are so busy
but I will be greatly obliged if you would look over these seven within the
next fortnight and send them back. As I say, I have sixteen stories and each
one you choose of these adds about 7500 words. Appended also is a list of
titles, enclosure (2)[65] I am not crazy about any of them but I don't seem
very fertile in that direction at present.

As I wired you I did not care for the jacket. My suggestion is to carry
out an idea you used in the advertising of "All the Sad Young Men" which
makes a virtue of the diversity of the material rather than an attempt to
conceal it, briefly, a set of figures typifying eight or ten of the principle
characters spread over the jacket. John Held, Jr. did that in the "Vegetable" if you will remember. Here we might have Basil, Josephine, a movie
star, an army officer, a little girl, a sinister ghostly man (as in "A Short Trip
Home"), a girl wearing a crown as in "Majesty." ect. These should not be
caricatures like Held's figures nor yet decorations like Shenton's designs
but somewhere in between. Perhaps you know someone who could dope
up such a scheme. They might be cloud-like figures swirling along with
only their faces and busts showing. I can see the idea but can't quite picture
it but I have no doubt that a clever man could. As you know the biggest
short story success of late has been in a book that called itself frankly
"Seven Gothic Tales."*

The following is a burlesque of the idea but may illustrate: Supposing
these figures were seen like souls coming out of the smoke of the torch of
the Statue of Liberty, or seen in the windows of a fast express bounding
over a precipice, or they might all be rising from the smoke of a devastated
battlefield, or they might all be placed over some sweating workmen who
make their adventures possible. Anyhow, you'll get the idea.

Ever yours,

P.S. Shall I feed in the stories as I correct them so the setting up can begin?

*By Isak Dinesen.

1307 Park Avenue,
Baltimore, Maryland,
June 26, 1934.

Dear Max:

Am sending along No. 1 of the stories because I feel it's going to be the devil to set up. There are two others all corrected, but the slow thing is to look through "Tender Is the Night" and see what phrases I took out of the stories. This is confused by the fact that there were so many revisions of "Tender" that I don't know what I left in it and what I didn't leave in it finally. I am going to have trouble with two of the stories you suggested.[66] In "The Captured Shadow" I'll have to make up a whole new ending which is almost like writing a new story. Secondly, the Josephine story, "A Nice Quiet Place," has some awfully phoney stuff in the middle that I'll have to find a substitute for. So can't I send the stories in their original order, and have them set up *separately*, and then sandwich between them the last two if I can think of some way of fixing them in time.

Nothing new about the title.[67]

By the time you get this you will have gotten a begging telegram asking for a thousand dollars. How I ever got so deep in debt I don't know unless it's been this clinic business,* because I've written regularly a story a month since finishing the last proof of "Tender" and they have been sold. I have also fixed up and sold some of Zelda's little articles besides. Debt is an odd thing and it seems if you ever get started in it it is very difficult to get disentangled. I have put the movie possibilites of the novel out of mind for the present though the young man I told you about who went from here to the coast is still trying further treatments in hopes that they will buy it. My best chance now is that if Phyllis Bottome's psychiatric story† goes they may all rush to buy whatever else is available in that line. Looks now as if I will be here until well into the summer, but I am going to try damn hard to get a month off somewhere if I can get clear of debt and clear of the work to which I committed myself. I can well understand all your difficulties working in the office by day and with Tom Wolfe by night because until ten days ago, when I collapsed and took to my bed I have been doing about the same thing. I am all right now and once I get this "Post" story off should be out of the worst.

Zelda does much better. Morrow read her stuff but turned down the plan.

Ever yours,

---

*Fitzgerald is referring to the cost of having Zelda treated at the Phipps Clinic.
†*Private Worlds* (1934).

DEAR SCOTT / DEAR MAX

1307 Park Avenue,
Baltimore, Mayland,
July 30, 1934.

Dear Max:

The bottom sort of fell out of things after you left.* We sat around for a few hours and talked a lot about you. The only flaw in the evening was the fact that afterwards I didn't seem to be able to sleep any better in Virginia than I did in Maryland, so after reading an old account of Stuart's battles for an hour or so, I got dressed in despair and spent the small hours of the morning prowling around the place, finally snatching two hours of sleep between seven and nine. The next day – it being our hostess' custom to sleep late – Anne took me over to meet the fabled Harden, who was as interesting as promised by the discussions of him. Returning to "Welbourne" a whole slew of Virginians appeared and to my regret I didn't have much more chance to talk to Elizabeth, because my conscience had begun to worry me and I decided to take the three o'clock bus back to Washington. However, one of the guests took dictation and I managed to have my joke about Grant and Lee taken down on paper. Then last night I had it faked up by the "Sun" here in Baltimore and I am going to send one to Elizabeth framed. Please return the one herewith enclosed for your inspection.

I thought Elizabeth Lemon was charming – I wonder why the hell she never married. The whole atmosphere of that countryside made me wonder about many things. It seems to me more detached than any place I have ever visited in the Union except a few remote towns in Alabama and Georgia during the war before the radio came. By the way, I had never ridden in a bus before and thought it was rather a horrible experience after the spacious grace of that house.

This morning before breakfast I read Tom Wolfe's story in *Scribner's.*† I thought it was perfectly beautiful and it had a subtlety often absent from his work, an intense poetry rather akin to Ernest (though naturally you won't tell Tom that because he wouldn't take it as a compliment.) What family resemblance there is between we three as writers is the attempt that crops up in our fiction from time to time to recapture the exact feel of a moment in time and space exemplified by people rather than by things – that is, an attempt at what Wordsworth was trying to do rather than what Keats did with such magnificent ease, an attempt at a mature memory

---

*Perkins and Fitzgerald had made a trip to Middleburg, Virginia, where they had visited some of Perkins' relatives who lived in a pre–Civil War mansion called "Welbourne."
†"The House of the Far and Lost."

203

of a deep experience. Anyhow please congratulate him for me with all my heart.

This letter is dragging out. Hope you found Louise all right. A thousand thanks for taking me into that very novel and stimulating atmosphere. I had been in a hell of a rut.

Ever yours,

P.S. Here's the money I owe you. I made it twelve instead of eleven because I had forgotten that expensive wine that I insisted upon ordering and which I drank most of, and anyhow twelve is a more symmetrical number than eleven.

July 30, 1934

Dear Scott:

I am sending you the Memoirs of Baron de Marbot. I know you will enjoy reading it, and what we are doing is to select about 100,000 words from it and publishing it under the title of "The Adventures of General Marbot". John Thomason has made very many pictures, and better ones than he ever made before, even better than the Crockett. Maybe reading this book between two and four would take you out of things. I have known of it since childhood because my father used to translate it to me directly from the French, and I find that Thomason had always known it too.

I hope you got a good rest down there in Virginia. – Or did Elizabeth take you next day around to see all the rich people? I came back comfortably in an air-cooled car, and worked last night with Thomas Wolfe, but I could not get that place out of my head.

Yours always,

1307 Park Avenue
August 17, 1934.

Dear Max,

I can't possibly see cleaning up the proofs of "Taps at Reveille"* before October 1st, and I suppose that means publication would be delayed until November 1st. I am sorry as Hell that it has to be this way; perhaps, even, you would better list it as a February book, although I do *think* that I should be able to do it before the first of October under normal circumstances. Working in ill health, however, slows up everything, and the

---

*The title finally decided upon for the short story collection.

harder I try to work, the more the ultimate effect for the *present* makes me incapable of more work. Remember, one is no longer twenty-one.

You wouldn't want to put out the book in December, would you? A book of short stories, I shouldn't imagine, could not compete with the rush of novels offered at that time. I have had the feeling lately that the people that buy books – mostly women – do it when their husbands spare them the money; so that some pronouncement by our Current Dictator might be more significant in sales than the old seasonal rules. You couldn't sell such an idea to an old Tory like Whitney.* But you might remember this prophecy a year from now.

I hope all goes well with you. Everything here is somewhat confused by an accumulation of work and the fact that my secretary went off for two weeks' vacation – I had abandoned so much detail to her that I can hardly feel my way around – and by the fact that affairs do not go well with Zelda.

Beth† dropped me a line to say that she had got the framed Appommatox clipping, and in the same note asked me if I could come down there for two days early next week, but I can't think at the moment how it can be worked in. If I took work down with me, I know I wouldn't do it; and if I didn't, I would be too woried to have a good time. However, it *might* be practical by the week-end of the 27th, and how about your joining me in such a pilgrimage?

Best wishes,

Aug. 20, 1934

Dear Scott:
My personal idea of it would be that we should publish the book of stories as soon as we could, whenever it was. I think it urgently important that you should bring out these stories close to "Tender Is the Night" for I think that the reviewers will be impressed by them, and that it will lead to a new discussion of "Tender Is the Night" and give a good many of them a chance to speak out more clearly than they did before. "Tender Is the Night" will have had time to sink in, and they will have had more conviction about it. Besides, the stories themselves show more sides of you than "Tender Is the Night". – They show that you understand more different sorts of people than are in that. I am very anxious to get them out for those reasons, especially.

You are in a position where you are compelled to think of immediate financial return beyond anything else. But if there is any conceivable way

*Probably Whitney Darrow.
†Elizabeth Lemon.

by which you could get these proofs read quickly and let us get the book out in October, it would in every other respect than that of immediate financial return be worth doing. You are smart about organizing your work, so you must have thought of everything. Is there any way that another person could work with you? The only question seems to be that of what you have used from the stories in "Tender Is the Night." I several times did notice things you had used. This ought to be avoided, of course, but I think it need not be avoided to the very uttermost. There is no reason a writer should not repeat a little in those respects. Hem has done it. Anyhow, whatever would hasten the publication of this book would, I think, be worth doing if it could be done.

Always yours,

P.S. Just got your telegram about Pat O'Mara.[68] I know he has written well, and we shall look after his manuscripts well.

1307 Park Avenue
Baltimore, Md.
[August 23, 1934]

Dear Max,

I have considered everything about the book very carefully and decided that it would be too difficult – I don't mean considered it in a hasty way, but considered it just as carefully as anything can be considered, looking at every possible angle. I am not in the proper condition either physically or financially to put over the kind of rush job that this would be. It would be an attempt to do what I did with "Tender" and would leave me in exactly the same spot that "Tender Is the Night" did. I see your reasoning about the critics; nevertheless, I have a feeling that this is not as important as it might seem.

I have got to get myself out of this morass of debt and I see my way clear now to doing it, to a great extent, having reduced it from the twenty thousand dollars in the red, where I was wallowing when I started the last lap on the book, to the two or three thousand that I am in now; but I am terribly unhappy in debt and do not get much comfort out of my personal life if I feel any such shadow over me.

To speak of brighter matters, went down for a day with Elizabeth, after all. She was as usual, *but* almost at the moment that I had got there, she got word that her sister and brother-in-law were due home from a sickness (I never can straighten up their family relationships). And so I decided th[a]t my part was to leave, though I had planned to stay there another few hours and Elizabeth and I had, in addition, planned to howl for you over

206

the telegraph to see if you could possibly break your week in the middle.
. . . . .

. . . . .

   She is a sweet person and I can understand your feeling of affection for her.

Best wishes always,

1307 Park Avenue
August 24, 1934.

Dear Max,
This is sort of a postscript to my letter of yesterday: I do think that you were doing specious reasoning in part of your letter. The fact that Ernest has let himself repeat here and there a phrase would be no possible justification for my doing the same. Each of us has his virtues and one of mine happens to be a great sense of exactitude about my work. He might be able to afford a lapse in that line where I wouldn't be and after all I have got to be the final judge of what is appropriate in these cases. Max, to repeat for the third time, this is in no way a question of laziness. It is a question absolutely of self-preservation. It is not going to be a money book in any case and is not going to go very far toward reimbursing the money I still owe you, and so I think in view of everything that my suggestion of waiting until after Christmas is the best.

   Besides, it is not only the question of the repetitions but there are certain other stories in the collection that I couldn't possibly *think* of letting go out in their current form. I fully realize that this may be a very serious inconvenience to you but for me to undertake anything like that at this moment would just mean sudden death and nothing less than that.

Ever yours,

. . . . .

Oct. 17, 1934

Dear Scott:
. . . . .

I am enclosing a royalty report because you always want to see it. We deposited the hundred, but you know, Scott, it is not quite the same here as in the old days when we had a dictatorship. We may be getting out of tune with the times, but now we have more or less of a republic. The house has half a dozen different departments, and the heads of all of them have an interest in the entire business. Charlie and I understand this situation, but it is impossible to make such a one, for instance, as the head of the educational department (which, by the way, does better than we do in the depression) understand it. He would think we were just crazy, having all but cleared up your indebtedness by the way we arranged for "Tender Is the Night" to let it all pile up again. I wish to Heaven – and I know you do too – that we could work the thing out some way. But you have had a run of mighty bad luck, and have struggled against it very valiantly, and it still is true, "as the feller says" that the only sure thing about luck is that it will change.

Always yours,

1307 Park Avenue
Baltimore, Maryland
October 30, 1934

Dear Max:

I don't know what legends I have left in Lowden County.[69] I went down and behaved myself well on all occasions but one, when I did my usual act, which is – to seem perfectly all right up to five minutes before collapse and then to go completely black. On this occasion, my chauffer was at hand and let me sleep. The strain on Elizabeth was nul. I have got to like Charlie and Missy very much, but whether it is reciprocated is still another story.

And still another story is whether it *does* rest me to go down there. I get excited because of the gaiety – Mary Rumsey was there but she seemed wearied from her affairs in Washington, and not the woman I had known on Long Island. She seemed to be continually be calling the butler. Although she was perfectly sweet to me – ordered a special supper, had guests to tea – (to which, because of circumstances, we couldn't get to) – and was sore about it and, with her usual good manners, expressed no resentment.

Came back and finished the *Red Book* story,* which I think is good (& is accepted) This is twelve o'clock in the morning and I worked till twelve last night getting off this *Red Book* affair. I am going to sleep for half an hour, after that if I have any energy, I'm going out and get a hair-cut.

I'm going to do at least two stories more but until I get some money from the *Red Book* Business, which should be by Wednesday, I don't know whether I can begin again the serious correction of the stories. God knows, you should know how conscientious I am. And when you say we are likely to be ready for Spring, you under-estimate my ideas of current conditions

*"In the Darkest Hour," Part I of *The Count of Darkness*, Fitzgerald's planned novel of medieval life.

in pub. business. What the devil, Max – your Spring list isn't made till Xmas is it?

I have never had to ask you to stick with me, but after that mood of terrible discouragement I was in last month, you might have taken literally what I said. I am, in point of fact, never really discouraged; nevertheless to *communicate* it were a crime indeed.

After getting off the mediaeval story I am taking a day's rest-up.

Thanks a million times for the "Art of the Novel" by Henry James. I thought Calverton's book* was very poor but told him the opposite.

Ever yours,

1307 Park Avenue
Baltimore, Maryland
November 1, 1934

Dear Max:
This is only to tell you that the story about Welbourne† is in this week's copy of the Post. Didn't want you to miss it.

I'm relieved that the legends that Tom Wolf told you are harmless – but I accuse Elizabeth of a semi-attempt to make legendary figures of all literary characters, and people her region with a new mythology.[70]

Glad Tom Wolf had a good time there and I hope all progresses well in that direction.

About the stories: All I can say is that I am doing my best and think I can get the full proof to you before Christmas. Will you have the proof-readers set up "Her Last Case" from the Sat. Eve. Post and send me galleys of that – though there is very little I want to change. I will try to get you two or three stories by the middle of next week which will release more much [much more] type. This is contingent upon my third mediaeval story (Balmer** has just taken the second) which I have embarked upon and which sounds good to me. I have decided to do a string of these, at least two more after this one, and then do a Post story. They bring approximately half as much money but I can do them faster because of the feeling of enthusiasm, probably the feeling of escape from the modern world. I am going to sandwich in the stories between this next mediaeval event and the one following.

Best always,

---

*Probably *The Passing of the Gods* (1934), by V. F. Calverton, penname of George Goetz.
†"Her Last Case."
**Edwin Balmer, editor of *Redbook*.

1307 Park Avenue,
Baltimore, Mayland,
November 8, 1934.

Dear Max:

. . . . .

My big mistake was in thinking I could possibly deliver this collection for this fall. I should have known perfectly well that, in debt as I was to the tune of about $12,000 on finishing "Tender," I should have to devote the summer and most of the fall to getting out of it. My plan was to do my regular work in the daytime and do one story every night, but as it works out, after a good day's work I am so exhausted that I drag out the work on a story to two hours when it should be done in one and go to bed so tired and wrought up, toss around sleepless, and am good for nothing next morning except dictating letters, signing checks, tending to business matters ect; but to work up a creative mood there is nothing doing until about four o'clock in the afternoon. Part of this is because of ill health. It would not have seemed so difficult for me ten years, or even five years ago, but now just one more straw would break the camel's back.

. . . . .

As you may have seen I took out "A New Leaf" and put in "Her Last Case." You didn't tell me whether or not you read it or liked it.

I know you have the sense that I have loafed lately but that is absolutely not so. I have drunk too much and that is certainly slowing me up. On the other hand, without drink I do not know whether I could have survived this time. In actual work since I finished the last proof of the novel in the middle of March, eight months ago, I have written and sold three stories for the *Post*, written another which was refused, written two and a half stories for the *Redbook*, rewritten three articles of Zelda's for *Esquire* and one original for them to get emergency money, collaborated on a 10,000 word treatment of "Tender Is the Night," which was no go, written an 8,000 word story for Gracie Allen, which was also no go, and made about five false starts on stories which went from 1,000 to 5,000 words, and a preface to the Modern Library edition of "The Great Gatsby," which equalizes very well what I have done in other years. I am good for just about one good story a month or two articles. I took no vacation this summer except three or four one-night trips to Virginia and two business trips to New York, each of which lasted about four or five days. Of course this is no excuse for not making more money, because in harder times you've got to work harder, but as it happens I am in a condition at the moment where to work extra hard means inevitably that I am laid up for a compensitory time either here or in the hospital. All I can say is that I will try to do two or three of these all at once after finishing each piece of work, and as I am now working at the rate of a story each ten days for the *Redbook* series I should finish up the ten I have left to do in about one hundred days and deliver the last of them in mid-February. Perhaps if things break better it may be a month sooner.

Thanks immensely for the Henry James which I thought was wonderful and which is difficult reading as it must have been to write and for "At Sea."*

. . . . .

I hope you'll be down here soon. It was rather melancholy to think of "Welbourne" being closed for the winter, but the last time I saw Elizabeth she seemed quite reconciled at visiting here and there, though such a prospect would drive me nuts. . . .

Best ever,

1307 Park Avenue,
Baltimore, Maryland,
November 10, 1934.

Dear Max:

Supplementing my letter of a few days ago, remember that the thing which has been delaying the stories is not only the internal difficulties (such as replacing the high points removed and inserted in "Tender") but also the work on the medieval series, which is going along steadily and now has reached almost 30,000 words! I know a bird in the hand is worth two in the bush but if this should be ready, as I firmly believe it will, for a year from now, it is much more likely to make money than this spring's collection of stories. Remember it is a novel and not merely a string of episodes about a single character as in the case of the Basil stories. It just happens that it does divide itself into fairly complete units and that Balmer, thank God, is sold on it.

. . . . .

Ever yours,

1307 Park Avenue,
Baltimore, Maryland,
November 20, 1934.

Dear Max:

Your letter did not cover the junking of "Her Last Case"† but I presume

---

*A novel by Arthur Calder-Marshall, published by Scribners in 1934.

†On November 15th, Fitzgerald had wired Perkins that he was removing both "Her Last Case" and "A New Leaf" from the book.

that you had not yet started to set it up. (I wish you'd return it to me.) Anyhow, here is the substitute for it and this is *final.** It will be published in the January issue of "Esquire.". . .

I don't know how good this story is, but a certain type of reader will like it, and it can scarcely be accused of any crimes such as being "well made" with which some of the others might be charged. It's been in my mind a long time and rather *had* to be written and it makes a break in the rather uniform length and structure of the commercial numbers.

However, it is just off the stove and I have not had any opinions on it so if you do not like its savor please tell me! In that case I would provide no substitute but publish seventeen instead of eighteen stories. If you *do* like it, will you have it set up in galley immediately and send it to me?

Ever yours,

P.S. That was good news about Ernest. Needless to say I am highly curious about the setting of his novel. I hope to God it isn't the crusading story that he once had in mind, for I would hate like hell for my 9th century novel to have to compete with *that.*

P.S. 2. I particularly don't want the *Basil* or *Josephine* stories run together as units – that is, as if they were two novelettes. The only indication that each is a series should be provided by the table of contents and by the heading of each story such as:

BASIL

IV The Captured Shadow etc.

In other words, each story should start on a new page.

Excuse me for being so finicky but in the pressure of doing many things at once I am slipping into the old psychology that if I don't do it myself it will be all wrong – a fault that *you*, young man, are inclined to share with me. This Lee biography† is shooting me in that direction. Again and again his weakness in trusting others, when he carried only the main scheme in his head, is emphasized.

. . . . .

. . . . .

Nov. 22, 1934

Dear Scott:

I am returning "Her Last Case". I don't know why you dropped it. I thought you were going to send that story I read a good part of about

---

*"The Fiend."

†*Robert E. Lee* by Douglas Southall Freeman, published by Scribners in four volumes in 1934 and 1935.

plagiarism which I did think was better than "Her Last Case" as a complete story. I know what this story is after glancing at it. I shall read it after five. You could have kept it and made a much bigger and finer story. You are profligate with your material as Ring told you about "The Rich Boy".

Hem's story is not the one you speak of. I think that is something he is keeping for a remote future. This story is "The Highlands of Africa".* It is 75,000 words by his estimate, which is likely to be too short. It is not a novel in form, but rather, a story. He raises all kinds of complicated questions about how it should be published, and I have got to think them all over and write him so I do not know when it will be published. He is very happy about it, – says in quality it is more like "Big Two Hearted River" and that it does what he always did have a wonderful talent for, paint landscapes.

Honestly, Scott, I think you are going to have a fine book of stories, and it is going to look well, and you may be fooled on the way it sells. I shall send you the jacket soon, but it is coming along well. I hope you stay keen about the mediaeval book. The way things are going makes it seem more and more a happy idea.

Always yours,

1307 Park Avenue,
Baltimore, Maryland,
November 26, 1934.

Dear Max:
The real thing that decided me about "Her Last Case" was that it was a *place* story and just before seeing it in *published form* I ran across Thomas Wolfe's "The House of the Far and Lost" and I thought there was no chance of competing with him on the same subject, when he had brought off such a triumph. There would inevitably have been invidious comparisons. If my story had anything to redeem it, except atmosphere, I would not hesitate to include it but most of it depends on a mixture of hysteria and sentiment – anyhow, I did not decide without some thought.

I think by this time you will have read and liked "The Fiend" which, spare and meager as it may be, has, I believe, a haunting quality. At least the tale in itself had enough poignancy to haunt me long enough, to keep in my skull for six years. Whether I've given it the right treatment, or disparaged it by too much peeling away of accessories, I can't say. That's one reason that I asked you to set it up, because maybe I am not too clear about it myself and maybe I can do something with the proof if it seems advisable.

*Published by Scribners in 1935 as *The Green Hills of Africa*.

I throw out most of the stuff in me with delight that it is gone. That statement might be interesting to consider in relation with Ernest's article in last month's *Esquire*,* an unexpressed idea is often a torment, even though its expression is liable to leave an almost crazy gap in the continuity of one's thoughts. And it would have been absolutely impossible for me to have stretched "The Rich Boy" into anything bigger than a novelette.

That statement was something that Ring got off; he never knew anything about composition, except as it concerned the shorter forms; that is why he always needed advice from us as to how to organize his material; it was his greatest fault the fault of many men brought up in the school of journalism – while a novelist with his sempiternal sigh can cut a few breaths. It is a hell of a lot more difficult to build up a long groan than to develop a couple of short coughs!

Glad Ernest isn't doing the Crusading story, now, because it would be an unfortunate competition.

Josephine† goes along and I think I will be in the clear about her this week, and – as I told you – two or three of the others have already been done and just have to be glanced at.

Your suggestion to go to Key West is tempting as hell but I don't know whether it would be advisable on either Ernest's account or mine. We can talk about that later.

A short note from Beth acknowledged an invitation that I gave her to meet Gertrude Stein is she if she should be in the vicinity, and said that she had a long letter from you. Outside of that, life has gone along at what would seem to most people a monotonous routine: entertained Lovestone; "The Opposition Communist" Saturday and put him up for the night but haven't quite made up my mind about what I think of him.

Am so fascinated with the medieval series that my problem is making them into proper butcher's cuts for monthly consumption. I have thought of the subject so long that the actual fertility of invention has become even a liability.

Ever yours,

1307 Park Avenue,
Baltimore, Maryland,
December 17, 1934.

Dear Max:
Enclosed are two galleys and also a short story called "The Night Before

---

*"Genio After Josie: A Havana Letter."
†The Josephine stories.

Chancellorsville" which I wish could be included into the book. This story and "The Fiend" together are not as long as "Her Last Case" so I think they would fit in your space originally allowed for that.

2. On original galley 84 six lines from the bottom (in story "First Blood") there occurs the phrase "their eyes were blazing windows across the court of the same house." This phrase I find occurs in *Tender is the Night* and I am *very anxious* to cut it if I haven't already done it on the galley I returned to you. This is awfully important to me and I wish you would have it checked up before you put it into page proof. Certain people I know read my books over and over again and I can't think of anything that would more annoy or disillusion a reader than to find an author using a phrase over and over as if his imagination were starving. *Please let me know if you find it!*

. . . . .
. . . . .
. . . . .
. . . . .

Ever yours,

P.S. If you do not like "The Night Before Chancellorsville" please tell me frankly. My idea is that this and "The Fiend" would give people less chance to say they are all standardized *Saturday Evening Post* stories, because, whatever can be said about them, they are not that. . . .[71]

1307 Park Avenue,
Baltimore, Maryland,
December 18, 1934.

Dear Max:

Tremendously obliged for the fifty dollars.* The *Redbook* is stalling on these Medieval stories, much to my disgust, and that is slowing up things and also it may put a crimp in the series so far as serialization is concerned. They have taken three and can't seem to decide about the fourth so temporarily I am going to return to the *Post* and make some larger money until that straightens out. This was the reason for the financial emergency.

Now I've got to blow up because an incident of this proof has upset my entire morning. You know how irascible I am when I am working and it increases with the years, but I have never seen a proof reader quite as dumb as the one who has looked over this second galley. In the first place I did not *want* a second galley and did not ask for it – these stories have been

---

*Deposited by Perkins on December 18th.

corrected *once* for myself, *once* for the *Post* and the third time on your first galleys and *that is all I can do. . . .*[72]

Example: This proof reader calmly suggests that I correct certain mistakes of construction in the character's dialogue. My God, he must be the kind who would rewrite Ring Lardner, correcting his grammar, or fix up the speeches of Penrod to sound like Little Lord Fauntleroy. Who is it? Robert Bridges?

His second brilliant stroke of Victorian genius was to query all the split infinitives. If, on a fourth version, I choose to let them stand I am old enough to know what I am doing. On this proof I simply struck off the queries and am sending the rest back without looking at it. My worry is that I didn't look at the Basil stories at all before returning them, and if he has corrected all Basil's language, spoiling some of my jokes – well it just gives me the feeling of wanting to send back the whole mass of first galleys and saying set it up.

Honestly, Max, I have worked like a dog on these galleys and it is costing me money to make these changes, and to have some cluck fool with them again is exasperating beyond measure. They should have gone right into page proof from my first galleys – I would a hundred times rather have half a dozen errors creep in than have half a dozen humorous points & carefully considered rhythms, spoiled by some school marm. This may seem vehement but I tell you it will haunt me in my sleep until you write reassuring me that no such thing happened in the case of the *Basil* stories.

Again thanks for the money. It was a life-saver. There will be another story coming along tomorrow.

Ever yours,

Feb. 18, 1935

Dear Scott:

I guess you are probably back in Baltimore by now, and I hope I shall hear from you soon. I did not agree with you about the change of title at all.[73] I think you have a good title. I cannot believe that "Reveille" which is known to every man who was ever in the national guard, the army, military school, boys' camp or girls' camp, is a difficult word for people, and even if it is, "Taps" is not. It would not be one of those titles they cannot speak of from embarrassment, – which is what the salesmen say about some difficult ones to pronounce. But anyhow, it really would be wrong to begin to make any further changes after so many have been made. I want to do as you want, and only do not when it seems impossible.

I hope the rest* did you a lot of good, but if I had known you were going

---

*Fitzgerald had gone to North Carolina.

to take a vacation I would have tried to bring you to Key West. Hem was quite mad that I did not, because I had intimated to him before that I might be able to get you to come.

I am sending a copy of "Of Time and the River" which is to be published on March 8th.

Always yours,

1307 Park Avenue,
Baltimore, Maryland,
February 26, 1935.

Dar Max:
Just heard from reading "Time" that Tom Boyd is dead and it is quite a shock. Do you know anything about the attendant circumstances?[74]

Looking forward eagerly for Tom Wolfe's book.*

Got in this morning from North Carolina and am at hard work again on short stories. (I've been on the absolute wagon for a month, not even beer or wine, and feel fine.) As soon as you get a copy of "Taps" even if unbound, or a jacket, please send them to me. I am very anxious to see how it lines up *especially the jacket.* What publication date have you?

Ever yours,

P.S. I am sure that nothing Tom has said in his dedication[75] could exaggerate the debt that he owes you – and that stands for all of us who have been privileged to be your authors.

1307 Park Avenue,
Baltimore, Maryland,
March 9, 1935.

Dear Max:
The book† arrived. It was fine to see. I liked the get up and thought it was an excellent blurb on the back, but –

– is it, alas, too late to do anything about the jacket? It is pretty God-awful and about six people have commented on it. I don't know who Miss Doris Spiegal is but it's rather discouraging to spend many hours trying to make the creatures in a book charming and then have someone who can't draw as well as Scottie cover five square inches with daubs that make them look like morons. The first jacket was very much better.

This sounds ungrateful in view of the trouble my books have always

---

* *Of Time and the River.*
† *Taps at Reveille.*

been, but I do want to record the fact that of late I have been badly served by your art department. To take a perfectly good photograph and debauch it into a toothless old man on the back of "Tender" was not so good, but I do think a jacket like this has the absolute opposite effect of those fine attractive jackets that Hill and Held used to draw for my books. I always believed that eternal care about titles and presentation was a real element in their success.

I've seen Jim Boyd and we've had several meals together. He's an awfully nice fellow.

. . . . .

Ever yours,

P.S. I was glad that Tom* got nice reviews in *Time* and the *New Yorker* and that they gave him space in proportion to the time and effort that went into his volume. I'm going to give it a more thorough reading next week.

1307 Park Avenue,
Baltimore, Maryland,
March 11, 1935.

Dear Max:

The second annoyance to you in two days – pretty soon I'm going to be your most popular author. (By the way we had sort of a Scribner congerie here last night. Jim Boyd and Elizabeth came to supper and George Calverton dropped in afterwards. Your name came up frequently and you would have probably wriggled more than at Wolfe's dedication. To prolong this parenthesis unduly I am sorry I mentioned Tom's book. I hope to God I won't be set up as the opposition for there are fine things in it, and I loved reading it, and I am delighted that it's a wow, and it may be a bridge for something finer. I simply feel a certain disappointment which I would, on no account, want Tom to know about, for, responding as he does to criticism, I know it would make us life long enemies and we might do untold needless damage to each other, so please be careful how you quote me. This is in view of Calverton's saying he heard from you that I didn't like it. It has become increasingly plain to me that the very excellent organization of a long book or the finest perceptions and judgment in time of revision do not go well with liquor. A short story can be written on a bottle, but for a novel you need the mental speed that enables you to keep the whole pattern in your head and ruthlessly sacrifice the sideshows as Ernest did in "A Farewell to Arms." If a mind is slowed up ever so little

*Thomas Wolfe.

it lives in the individual part of a book rather than in a book as a whole; memory is dulled. I would give anything if I hadn't had to write Part III of "Tender is the Night" entirely on stimulant. If I had one more crack at it cold sober I believe it might have made a great difference. Even Ernest commented on sections that were needlessly included and as an artist he is as near as I know for a final reference. Of course, having struggled with Tom Wolfe as you did this is old hat to you. I will conclude this enormous parenthesis with the news that Elizabeth has gone to Middleburg to help Mrs. White open up her newly acquired house.)

. . . . .

. . . . .

Ever yours,

P.S. I haven't had a drink for almost six weeks and haven't had the faintest temptation as yet. Feel fine in spite of the fact that business affairs and Zelda's health have never been worse.

April 8, 1935

Dear Scott:
I sent Hem a copy of "Taps at Reveille",* but not in time for him to read it before he started on a trip for Bimini with Dos† and Make [Mike] Strater. But I just had a letter from him in which he says: "How is Scott? I wish I could see him. A strange thing is that in retrospect his Tender is the Night gets better and better. I wish you would tell him I said so."

Always yours,

1307 Park Avenue,
Baltimore, Maryland,
April 15, 1935.

Dear Max:
You don't say anything about "Taps" so I gather it hasn't caught on at all. I hope at least it will pay for itself and its corrections. There was a swell review in *The Nation;*** did you see it?

I went away for another week but history didn't repeat itself and the trip was rather a waste. Thanks for the message from Ernest. I'd like to see him too and I always think of my friendship with him as being one of the high spots of life. But I still believe that such things have a mortality,

*Published late in March.
†John Dos Passos.
**By William Troy.

perhaps in reaction to their very excessive life, and that we will never again see very much of each other. I appreciate what he said about "Tender is the Night." Things happen all the time which make me think that it is not destined to die quite as easily as the boys-in-a-hurry prophesied. However, I made many mistakes about it from its delay onward, the biggest of which was to refuse the Literary Guild subsidy.

Haven't seen Beth since I got back and am calling her up today to see if she's here. I am waiting eagerly for a first installment of Ernest's book.* When are you coming south? Zelda, after a terrible crisis, is somewhat better. I am, of course, on the wagon as always, but life moves at an uninspiring gait and there is less progress than I could wish on the Mediae-val series – all in all an annoying situation as these should be my most productive years. I've simply got to arrange something for this summer that will bring me to life again, but what it should be is by no means apparent.

. . . . .
. . . . .
. . . . .

Ever yours,

1307 *Park Avenue,*
Baltimore, Maryland,
April 17, 1935.

Dear Max:
Reading Tom Wolfe's story† in the current *Mondern Monthly* makes me wish he was the sort of person you could talk to about his stuff. It has all his faults and virtues. It seems to me that with any sense of humor he could see the Dreiserian absurdities of how the circus people "ate the cod, bass, mackerel, halibut, clams and oysters of the New England coast, the terra-pin of Maryland, the fat beeves, porks and cereals of the middle west" etc. etc. down to "the pink meated lobsters that grope their way along the sea-floors of America." And then (after one of his fine paragraphs which sounds a note to be expanded later) he remarks that they leave nothing behind except "the droppings of the camel and the elephant in Illinois." A few pages further on his redundance ruined some paragraphs (see the last complete paragraph on page 103) that might have been gorgeous. I

---

* *The Green Hills of Africa*, which ran serially, in seven installments, in *Scribner's Magazine* (prior to its book publication), beginning in May 1935.
†"Circus at Dawn."

sympathize with his use of repetition, of Joyce-like words, endless metaphor, but I wish he could have seen the disgust in Edmund Wilson's face
when I once tried to interpolate part of a rhymed sonnet in the middle of
a novel, disguised as prose. How he can put side by side such a mess as
"With chitterling tricker fast-fluttering skirrs of sound the palmy honied
birderies came" and such fine phrases as "tongue-trilling chirrs, plum-
bellied smoothness, sweet lucidity" I don't know. He who has such infinite
power of suggestion and delicacy has absolutely no right to glut people on
whole meals of caviar. I hope to Christ he isn't taking all these emasculated
paeans to his vitality seriously. I'd hate to see such an exquisite talent turn
into one of those muscle-bound and useless giants seen in a circus. Athletes
have got to learn their games; they shouldn't just be content to tense their
muscles, and if they do they suddenly find when called upon to bring off
a necessary effect they are simply liable to hurl the shot into the crowd and
not break any records at all. The metaphor is mixed but I think you will
understand what I mean, and that he would too – save for his tendency to
almost feminine horror if he thinks anyone is going to lay hands on his
precious talent. I think his lack of humility is his most difficult characteristic, a lack oddly enough which I associate only with second or third rate
writers. He was badly taught by bad teachers and now he hates learning.

There is another side of him that I find myself doubting, but this is
something that no one could ever teach or tell him. His lack of feeling other
people's passions, the lyrical value of Eugene Gant's love affair with the
universe – is that going to last through a whole saga? God, I wish he could
discipline himself and really plan a novel.

I wrote you the other day and the only other point of this letter is that
I've now made a careful plan of the Mediaeval novel as a whole (tentatively
called "Philippe, Count of Darkness" *confidential*) including the planning
of the parts which I can sell and the parts which I can't. I think you could
publish it either late in the spring of '36 or early in the fall of the same year.
This depends entirely on how the money question goes this year. It will
run to about 90,000 words and will be a novel in every sense with the
episodes unrecognizable as such. That is my only plan. I wish I had these
great masses of manuscripts stored away like Wolfe and Hemingway but
this goose is beginning to be pretty thoroughly plucked I am afraid.

A young man has dramatized "Tender is the Night" and I am hoping
something may come of it. I may be in New York for a day and a night
within the next fortnight.

Ever yours,

Later – Went to N.Y. as you know, but one day only. Didn't think I would like Cape that day.* Sorry you & Nora Flynn† didn't meet. No news here – I think Beth is leaving soon.

April 25, 1935

Dear Scott:

I was just having lunch with Jim Boyd, who, by the way, will be in Baltimore tomorrow. I happened to tell him that you were doing that mediaeval series (but I did not mention the title of the novel, and won't) which was especially in my mind since I had just read your letter. Jim was simply delighted. He has the greatest admiration for your talents, and he said that he had not known about this, but that he himself had thought that the best thing you could do for the moment was a historical novel. I told you that Ned Sheldon** had said the same thing. It is curious they both should have thought of it, – and both of them think that no one surpasses you in possibilities.

It would be a grand thing if some time it should come about that you could talk to Tom. Of course everything you say is true as truth can be. But even if one had an utterly free hand, instead of being subject to constant abuse (God damned Harvard English, grovelling at the feet of Henry James, etc.) it would be a matter of editing inside sentences even, and that would be a dangerous business. But gradually criticism, and age too, may make an impression. By the way. – That Calverton story to the effect that Tom thought he was better than so and so, and so and so, while true in a literal sense, was not true in spirit. I think it is right enough Tom should feel the way he does, which is that what he has to say is so overwhelmingly important that it is all he can see. It is not that he thinks he is better than anyone else. He just does not think about the other people at all. When he reads them he is quite keen about them for a while, but it does not seem to him to be the important thing that they are doing because what he is doing seems to him momentous.

I swear I do not see why a good man could not make a grand play out of "Tender Is the Night".

Always yours,

---

*Perkins was having lunch with Jonathan Cape, the English publisher, and had asked Fitzgerald to join them.

†Nora Langhorne Flynn, who, with her husband, Lefty, befriended Fitzgerald during 1935 and 1936.

**Probably American dramatist Edward Sheldon.

1307 Park Avenue,
Baltimore, Maryland,
April 29, 1935.

Dear Max:

Jim Boyd called me up on race-day[76] but I missed him as he pulled out of the Belvedere before the race was over. Elizabeth, by the way, left yesterday or today.

I got "Roll River"* and in the same mail another book called "Deep Dark River,"† (Farrar & Rhinehart), so Max, if you don't mind I want the names of my books changed to fit in with this new mode. They should be called "This Side of the River," "Rivers and Philosophers," "Tender is the River," and "Rivers at Reveille." Please see to this immediately because dat ol' debbil certainly does make sales.

Zelda is better. I am thinking of closing up shop here and going to North Carolina for a real physical rest as I am God damned tired of being half sick and half well. I will be writing all the time of course.

I would rather you didn't mention the *century* of my novel or advise people that some of it is in the *Red Book*. Let it just stand for the present as an historical novel.

. . . . .

Ever yours,

. . . . .

1307 Park Avenue,
Baltimore, Maryland,
May 11, 1935.

Dear Max:

It was fine seeing you but I was in a scrappy mood about Tom Wolfe. I simply cannot see the sign of achievement there yet, but I see that you are very close to the book and you don't particularly relish such an attitude.

I am closing the house and going away somewhere for a couple of months and will send you an address when I get one.

. . . . .

I'd like to see Ernest but it seems a long way and I would not like to see him except under the most favorable of circumstances because I don't think I am the pleasantest company of late.** Zelda is in very bad condition and my own mood always somehow reflects it.

*A novel by James Boyd, published by Scribners in 1935.
†A novel by Robert Rylee.
**Perkins, on May 6th, had written that Hemingway, who was recovering from a bullet wound in his leg, had invited Fitzgerald to visit him in Bimini.

Katy Dos Passos was here and in *her* version the bullet bounced off the side of the boat, but I suppose when Ernest's legend approaches the Bunyan type it will have bounced off the moon, so it is much the same thing.
. . . . .

Ever yours,

Hotel Stafford
Baltimore, Md.
Sunday evening
[ca. June 25, 1935]

Dear Max:
I feel I owe you a word of explanation; 1st: As to the health business, I was given what amounted to a death sentence about 3 months ago. It was just before I last saw you – which was why, I think, I got into that silly quarrel with you about Tom Wolfe that I've regretted ever since. I was a good deal dismayed & probably jealous, so forget all I said that night. You know I've always thought there was plenty room in America for more than one good writer, & you'll admit it wasn't like me.

. . . . .

2nd Came up to Baltimore for five days* to see Zelda who seems hopeless & send Scotty to camp, I had 24 hrs with nothing to do and went to N.Y. to see a woman I'm very fond of – its a long peculiar story (. . . – one of the curious series of relationships that run thru a man's life). Anyhow she'd given up the wk. end at the last minute to meet me & it was impossible to leave her to see you.
Putting Scotty on train in 10 minutes.

In haste, always yrs.

I wish Struthers Burt would decide on a name – I call him everything but Katherine!†

Sept. 28, 1935

Dear Scott:
I have got to go for a two weeks' vacation beginning Tuesday, but I expect to come to Baltimore sometime after that.
Ernest is here now, in fine shape. He is going to be in this region

---

*Fitzgerald had been spending the summer at the Grove Park Inn, in Asheville, North Carolina.

†Burt's full name was Maxwell Struthers Burt. His wife's name was Katherine.

probably for some time because he wants to wait until it gets cool enough to return to Key West. He means to go somewhere in the country. He has speculated several times about seeing you, but he is bent upon writing stories, – has done a couple.

Every writer seems to have to go through a period when the tide runs against him strongly, and at the worst it is better that it should have done this when Ernest was writing books that are in a general sense minor ones. That is, the kind that the trade and the run of the public are bound to regard that way. I hope we can think of something to be done about it between now and October 25th.

I am sorry we did not get Scotty, but Harold did not seem to want to let her go at the beginning, and then Nance had to have her tonsils out.[77] The whole family is back from Europe, and we are all in New York.

Yours always,

Cambridge Arms,
Baltimore, Maryland,
October 24, 1935.

Dear Max:

Thank you again.* I haven't realized on either of the two stories but will hear from one this week end and from the other the beginning of next week.

Have you got any suggestions about the Red Book series? I now have about 30,000 words (in the 4 written stories) but Balmer of the *Red Book* is noncommittal about whether he wants any more or not. What could Scribner's pay in cash for the rest of the series? Or have you read the last two and did you like them? The fourth isn't published yet. I know this is a wild idea and even granted that the material fitted Scribner's you wouldn't have the advantage of featuring it as a serial from the beginning, but of course it is to your advantage to have me finish the book.

The original plan was to have been a book of over 100,000 words, but supposing instead, I published two books of 60,000 words each about my noble Philippe, the first book dealing with his youth. That book you see would be half done now.

This all sounds like a make-shift arrangement but I can't see how in the next six months I can raise enough money to continue the mediaeval theme unless it is somehow subsidized by serialization. Have you any ideas?

Ever yours,

*Perkins had deposited $300 in Fitzgerald's Baltimore bank on October 18th.

Oct. 26, 1935

Dear Scott:

It seems to me most unlikely that we could do anything through the magazine about stories you began with the Red Book, but if you have copies of those that have been published, I wish I could read them. I only read the first one. Anyhow, by doing that, I could have more idea of the advisability of breaking the scheme into two books. It might be a good thing to do.

Ernest got a first-rate review* in the Sunday Times Supplement, a very good review in the Tribune Supplement, excellent short reviews in the Atlantic and in Time, a bad review in the Saturday Review (which does not count for much) and mostly unfavorable comment from Gannett,† and very unfavorable from Chamberlain,** but the review in the Times is more important than all the others put together, generally speaking. The unfavorable reviews are mostly colored by this prevalent idea that you ought to be writing only about the troubles of the day, and are disapproving of anything so remote from present social problems as a hunting expedition.

I had lunch with Bunny Wilson, who seems better and happier than in years, and very enthusiastic about Russia as a country, and a people. I got the impression that his views on Communism were somewhat sobered and more philosophical, and that he thought better of his own country. I suspect he now feels that whatever form of society Russians and Americans are revolving toward is a long slow process. He also told me that he had inherited from an uncle enough money to make his situation considerably more comfortable.

Always yours,

1 East 34th Street,
Baltimore, Maryland,
March 17, 1936.

Dear Max:

A kid named Vincent McHugh has written me asking me to recommend him to you. Ordinarily I would not do such things any more but he has been a sort of unknown protegé of mine for some time. He has published

---

*Of *The Green Hills of Africa.*

†Critic Lewis Gannett, whose book reviews appeared daily in the New York *Herald Tribune.*

**Critic John Chamberlain, whose book reviews appeared in the daily New York *Times.*

a book called *Sing Before Breakfast* which I thought was a remarkable book and showed a very definite temperament. I'm not promising you that he is as strong a personality as Ernest or Caldwell or Cantwell or the men that I have previously recommended, but I do wish you would get hold of this earlier book *Sing Before Breakfast* published by Simon and Schuster in 1933 and consider that as much as what he has to offer at the moment in making your decision.

I know, that due to your experience with Tom Boyd, you place a great deal of emphasis on vitality, but remember that a great deal of the work in this world has been done by sick men and people who at first sight seem to have no vitality will suddenly exhibit great streaks of it. I've never seen this young man but potentially he seems capable of great efforts.[78]

Things are standing still here. I am waiting to hear this afternoon about a *Saturday Evening Post* story, which, if it is successful, will continue a series.

Best wishes always,

1 East 34th Street,
Baltimore, Maryland,
March 25, 1936.

Dear Max:
In regard to the enclosed letter from Simon and Schuster* do you remember my proposing some years ago to gather up such of my non-fiction as is definitely autobiographical – "How to Live on $36,000 a Year," etc., "My Relations with Ring Lardner," a *Post* article called "A Hundred False Starts," of hotels stayed at that I did with Zelda and about a half dozen others and making them into a book? At the time you didn't like the idea and I'm quite aware that there's not a penny in it unless it was somehow joined together and given the kind of lift that Gertrude Stein's autobiography† had. Some of it will be inevitably dated, but there is so much of it and the interest in this *Esquire* series has been so big that I thought you might reconsider the subject on the chance that there might be money in it. If you don't like the idea what would you think of letting Simon and Schuster try it?

I don't want to spend any time at all on it until I am absolutely sure of publication and, as you know, of course I would prefer to keep identified

---

*Simon and Schuster had written Fitzgerald expressing interest in publishing in book form the autobiographical articles which he was publishing in *Esquire*.
† *The Autobiography of Alice B. Toklas.*

with the house of Scribner, but in view of the success of the Gertrude Stein book and the Seabrook* book it just might be done with profit.

Ever yours,

March 26, 1936

Dear Scott:

I remember your speaking to me about a collection of non-fiction. I did not think well of it as a collection. But do you remember at the time when you were struggling desperately with "Tender Is the Night" and it seemed as if you might not get through with it for long, that I suggested a reminiscent book? It might even have been before you published "Echoes of the Jazz Age" in 1931, which was a beautiful article. I have been reading that again lately, and have been hesitating on the question of asking you to do a reminiscent book, – not autobiographical, but reminiscent. Gertrude Stein's autobiography is an apt one to mention in connection with the idea. I even talked to Gilbert Seldes about it, and he was favorable. I do not think the Esquire pieces ought to be published alone. But as for an autobiographical book which would comprehend what is in them, I would be very much for it. Couldn't you make a really well integrated book? You write non-fiction wonderfully well, your observations are brilliant and acute, and your presentations of real characters like Ring, most admirable. I always wanted you to do such a book as that. Whatever you decide, we want to do, but it would be so much better to make a book out of the materials than merely to take the articles and trim them, and join them up, etc.

Always yours,

1 East 34th Street,
Baltimore, Maryland,
April 2, 1936.

Dear Max:

Your letter really begs the question because it would be one thing to join those articles together and another to write a book. The list would include the following:

1. A short autobiography I wrote for the *Saturday Evening Post* "Who's Who and How."

---

*Probably *Asylum* by William B. Seabrook (1934), in which the author recounted his experiences in a mental hospital for alcoholics.

2. An article on Princeton for *College Humor.**

3. An article on being twenty-five for the *American.*†

4. "How to Live on $36,000 a Year" for the *Post.*

5. "How to Live on Practically Nothing a Year" for the *Post.*

6. "Imagination and a Few Mothers" for the *Ladies Home Journal.*

7. "Wait Till You Have Children of Your Own" for the *Woman's Home Companion.*

8. "How to Waste Material" for *Bookman.*

9. "One Hundred False Starts" for *Post.*

10. "Ring Lardner" *New Republic.*

11. A short autobiography for *New Yorker.***

12. "Girls Believe in Girls" *Liberty.*

13. "My Lost City" *Cosmopolitan* (still unpublished, but very good I think.)

14. "Show Mr. and Mrs. F—to—" *Esquire.*

15. Echoes from [of] the Jazz Age.

16. The three articles about cracking up from *Esquire.*††

This would total 60,000 words. I would expect to revise it and add certain links, perhaps in some sort of telegraphic flashes between each article.

Whether the book would have the cohesion to sell or not I don't know. It makes a difference whether people think they are getting some real inside stuff or whether they think a collection is thrown together. As it happens the greater part of these articles are intensely personal, that is to say, while a newspaper man has to find something to write his daily or weekly article about, I have written articles entirely when the impetus came from within, in fact, I have cleaner hands in the case of non-fiction than in fiction. Let me add, however, if I had the time to sit down and make these over into a re-written book, rather than a revised book, I would

---

*"Princeton," *College Humor,* December, 1927.
†"What I Think and Feel at Twenty-Five," *American Magazine,* September, 1922.
**"A Short Autobiography," *New Yorker,* May 25, 1929.
††"The Crack-up" (February), "Pasting It Together" (March), and "Handle With Care" (April), all published in 1936.

devote that time to finishing Philippe. I simply can't afford to do it until I pull myself out of this pit of debt. Meanwhile, what do you think? I need advice on the subject.[79]

Ever yours,

Cambridge Arms,
Charles Street,
Baltimore, Maryland,
June 13, 1936.

Dear Max:

I am glad you agree with me about the Modern Library publishing "Tender Is The Night". There was no intention of asking them about it before letting you know and I thought the two letters had gone off in the mail at the same time.[80]

However, the subject has reminded me of the idea that I wrote you about last month, to wit: the practicability of collecting my articles into a book, even *without* unifying them as an auto biography. The new series for Esquire seems to have moved Gingrich so much that he has written me that the one that appears in the August issue (called "Afternoon of An Author") is the best thing he has published in six years of editing his sheet. I still think that if I could get an attractive title, that the book would have possibility. It would include very much the material I suggested before with the addition of these new Esquire pieces, and I would expect to do a certain amount of work on it in proof. Please reconsider the matter and let me know.[81]

My plans are still vague for the summer, but you can always reach me through the Cambridge Arms address.

Best wishes always,

Asheville, N.C., *
Sept. 19th, 1936

Dear Max:

This is my second day of having a minute to catch up with correspondence. Probably Harold Ober has kept you in general touch with what has happened to me but I will summarize:

I broke the clavicle of my shoulder, diving – nothing heroic, but a little too high for the muscles to tie up the efforts of a simple swan dive – At first the Doctors thought that I must have tuberculosis of the bone, but x-ray

*Fitzgerald had moved to Asheville to be close to Zelda who was in a sanitarium there.

230

showed nothing of the sort, so (like occasional pitchers who throw their arm out of joint with some unprepared for effort) it was left to dangle for twenty-four hours with a bad diagnosis by a young Intern; then an x-ray and found broken and set in an elaborate plaster cast.

I had almost adapted myself to the thing when I fell in the bath-room reaching for the light, and lay on the floor until I caught a mild form of arthritis called "Miotoosis," [myotosis] which popped me in the bed for five weeks more. During this time there were domestic crises: Mother sickened and then died and I tried my best to be there but couldn't. I have been within a mile and a half of my wife all summer and have seen her about half dozen times. Total accomplished for one summer has been one story – not very good, two *Esquire* articles, neither of them very good.

You have probably seen Harold Ober and he may have told you that Scottie got a remission of tuition at a very expensive school where I wanted her to go (Miss Edith Walker's School in Connecticut). Outside of that I have no good news, except that I came into some money from my Mother, not as much as I had hoped, but at least $20,000. in cash and bonds at the materi[a]lization in six months – for some reason, I do not know the why or wherefore of it, it requires this time. I am going to use some of it, with the products of the last story and the one in process of completion, to pay off my bills and to take two or three months rest in a big way. I have to admit to myself that I haven't the vitality that I had five years ago.

I feel that I must tell you something which at first seemed better to leave alone: I wrote Ernest about that story of his,* asking him in the most measured terms not to use my name in future pieces of fiction. He wrote me back a crazy letter, telling me about what a great Writer he was and how much he loved his children, but yielding the point – "If I should out live him – " which he doubted. To have answered it would have been like fooling with a lit firecracker. Somehow I love that man, no matter what he says or does, but just one more crack and I think I would have to throw my weight with the gang and lay him. No one could ever hurt him in his first books but he has completely lost his head and the duller he gets about it, the more he is like a punch-drunk pug fighting himself in the movies.

No particular news except the dreary routine of illness. . . .

As ever yours,

---

*"The Snows of Kilimanjaro," which, in its original version, had the hero thinking, "He remembered poor old Scott Fitzgerald and his romantic awe of [the rich] and how he had started a story once that began, 'The very rich are different from you and me.' And how someone had said to Scott, yes they have more money. But that was not humorous to Scott." In subsequent printings, the name was changed to Julian.

Sept. 23, 1936

Dear Scott:

If you are sure to get $20,000 in six months, doesn't this offer you your big chance? You have never, since the very beginning, had a time free from the necessity of earning money. – You have never been free from financial anxiety. Can't you now work out a plan to get at least eighteen months, or perhaps two years, free from worry by living very economically, and work as you always wanted to, on a major book? Certainly it seems to me that here is your opportunity. I am glad Scotty is doing so well. I know the school in Simsbury, once thought of sending our girls there. It is very good.

As for what Ernest did, I resented it, and when it comes to book publication, I shall have it out with him. It is odd about it too because I was present when that reference was made to the rich, and the retort given, and you were many miles away.

Always yours,

Oct 6, 1936

Dear Scott:

We have been talking here for a long time as a result of getting your telegram.[82] We have to have some business justification for the money we put out. With both Charlie* and me there is a strong personal element in the matter, but there is none, or hardly any, with others who do not know you and who cannot understand why your account should look as it does. How are we to explain it to them? We greatly want to help you and always have, but you do not half help us to do it. In this case, if we send you the two thousand, we should have some degree of justification if you could give us a guarantee from the administrator that this, and the earlier loan of two thousand for which we hold your note, would be paid on liquidation of the Estate. But we should feel much better about the whole thing, and about you yourself, if you could now, with the respite which this inheritance will give you, work out some plan by which you would be producing something upon which we might hope to realize, – and you would too. One successful book would clear the whole slate for you all round. Couldn't you now make a regular scheme by which you would produce a book? I am not at all sure but what that biographical book I urged upon you would not be the most likely one to do what is needed. But you will now have this interval of a year, and you ought to make the fullest use of the opportunity.

*Charles Scribner, President of Charles Scribner's Sons.

– If you only could tell us what you are planning, we should feel very much better about the whole matter, – and more on your account than on our own too.

Always yours,

Grove Park Inn
Asheville, N.C.
October 16, 1936

Dear Max:

As I wired you, an advance on my Mother's estate from a friend makes it unnecessary to impose on you further.

I do not like the idea of the biographical book. I have a novel planned, or rather I should say conceived, which fits much better into the circumstances, but neither by this inheritance nor in view of the general financial situation do I see clear to undertake it. It is a novel certainly as long as Tender Is The Night, and knowing my habit of endless corrections and revisions, you will understand that I figure it at two years. Except for a lucky break you see how difficult it would be for me to master the leisure of the two years to finish it. For a whole year I have been counting on such a break in the shape of either Hollywood buying Tender or else of Grisman getting Kirkland or someone else to do an efficient dramatization. (I know I would not like the job and I know that Davis* who had every reason to undertake it after the success of Gatsby simply turned thumbs down from his dramatist's instinct that the story was not constructed as dramatically as Gatsby and did not readily lend itself to dramatization.) So let us say that all accidental, good breaks can not be considered. I can not think up any practical way of undertaking this work. If you have any suggestions they will be welcomed, but there is no likelihood that my expenses will be reduced below $18,000 a year in the next two years, with Zelda's hospital bills, insurance payments to keep, etc. And there is no likelihood that after the comparative financial failure of Tender Is The Night that I should be advanced such a sum as $3,000. The present plan, as near as I have formulated it, seems to be to go on with this endless Post writing or else go to Hollywood again. Each time I have gone to Hollywood, in spite of the enormous salary, has really set me back financially and artistically. My feelings against the autobiographical book are:

First: that certain people have thought that those Esquire articles did me definite damage and certainly they would have to form part of the

*Playwright Owen Davis, who had done the dramatization of *Gatsby*.

fabric of a book so projected. My feeling last winter that I could put together the articles I had written vanished in the light of your disapproval, and certainly when so many books have been made up out of miscellaneous material and exploited material, as it would be in my case, there is no considerable sale to be expected. If I were Negly Farson* and had been through the revolutions and panics of the last fifteen years it would be another story, or if I were prepared at this moment to "tell all" it would have a chance at success, but now it would seem to be a measure adopted *in extremis,* a sort of period to my whole career.

In relation to all this, I enjoyed reading *General Grant's Last Stand,*† and was conscious of your particular reasons for sending it to me. It is needless to compare the force of character between myself and General Grant, the number of words that he could write in a year, and the absolutely virgin field which he exploited with the experiences of a four-year life under the most dramatic of circumstances. What attitude on life I have been able to put into my books is dependent upon entirely different field of reference with the predominant themes based on problems of personal psychology. While you may sit down and write 3,000 words one day, it inevitably means that you write 500 words the next.

I certainly have this one more novel, but it may have to remain among the unwritten books of this world. Such stray ideas as sending my daughter to a public school, putting my wife in a public insane asylum, have been proposed to me by intimate friends, but it would break something in me that would shatter the very delicate pencil end of a point of view. I have got myself completely on the spot and what the next step is I don't know.

I am going to New York around Thanksgiving for a day or so and we might discuss ways and means. This general eclipse of ambition and determination and fortitude, all of the very qualities on which I have prided myself, is ridiculous, and, I must admit, somewhat obscene.

Anyhow, that [thank] you for your willingness to help me. Thank Charlie for me and tell him that the assignments he mentioned have only been waiting on a general straightening up of my affairs. My God, debt is an awful thing!

Yours,

Heard from Mrs. Rawlings & will see her[83]

---

*American journalist and novelist, kmown primarily for his autobiographical books of adventure.

†By Horace Green, published by Scribners in 1936.

DEAR SCOTT / DEAR MAX

[*Oak Hall Hotel*]
[*Tryon, North Carolina*]
[*late in February, 1937*]

Dear Max:

Thanks for your note and the appalling statement. Odd how enormous sums of $10,000 have come to seem lately – I can remember turning down that for the serialization of *The Great Gatsby* – from College Humor.

Well, my least productive & lowest general year since 1926 is over. In that year I did 1 short story and 2 chaps. of a novel – that is two chaps. that I afterwards used. And it was a terrible story. Last year, even though laid up 4 mos. I sold 4 stories & 8 Esq. pieces, a poor showing God knows. This year has started slowly also, same damn lack of interest, staleness, when I have every reason to want to work if only to keep from thinking. Havn't had a drink since I left the north. (about six weeks, not even beer) but while I feel a little better nervously it doesn't bring back the old exuberance. I honestly think that all the prizefighters, actors, writers who live by their own personal performances ought to have managers in their best years. The ephemeral part of the talent seems when it is in hiding so apart from one, so "otherwise" that it seems it ought to have some better custodian than the poor individual with whom it lodges and who is left with the bill. My chief achievment lately has been in cutting down my and Zelda's expenses to rock bottom; my chief failure is my inability to see a workable future. Hollywood for money has much against it, the stories are somehow mostly out of me unless some new source of material springs up, a novel takes money & time – I am thinking of putting aside certain hours and digging out a play, the ever-appealing mirage. At 40 one counts carefully one's remaining vitality and rescources and a play ought to be within both of them. The novel & the autobiography have got to wait till this load of debt is lifted.

So much, & too much, for my affairs. Write me of Ernest & Tom & who's new & does Ring still sell & John Fox & The House of Mirth. Or am I the only best seller who doesn't sell?

The account, I know, doesn't include my personal debt to you. How much is it please?

. . . Please write me – you are about the only friend who does not see fit to incorporate a moral lesson, especially since the *Crack up* stuff. Actually I hear from people in Sing Sing & Joliet all comforting & advising me.

Ever Your Friend

235

March 3, 1937

Dear Scott:

In spite of the discouraging financial outlook, I thought your letter was fine. Maybe you really were the best diagno[s]tician of any, – maybe you best knew yourself. My urgency about doing the autobiographical book – which of course I thought would be extremely good and would sell – was part of one of my very cunning plots. – That is, I thought that if you wrote all about that period, and said your full say about it, you would get through with it all and step out into some fresh field without being directed back by the past. I do not think I am much of a psychologist, but maybe there was something in that side of the idea.

Hem was here last week, and on Saturday I saw him off for Spain on the Paris, along with Evan Shipman* and Sidney Franklin. I hope they won't all get into trouble over there. They seem to be quite bloodthirsty, although they are going strictly on business. Ernest has finished his novel,† but won't deliver it to us until June. He says he will be out of Spain by May first.

Tom is turning out volumes of manuscript, but he is terribly worried about his lawsuits. The landlady who sued him won't settle, at least for the present. She is too furious with him.[84]

Edith Wharton doesn't sell except with "Ethan Frome", and that excellently. Not "The House of Mirth" though, nor any of her other books. Nor does Ring sell to any extent. But John Fox does, and also Thomas Nelson Page.** We had an unusual experience with Marcia Davenport's novel, "Of Lena Geyer". Most books today succeed from the start or never. And even successes seldom carry into a new year. Marcia started out badly, with little advance sale, and none of the breaks. Not even good reviews, really. She has had no great sale yet, – about 20,000 – but almost half of that has come since Christmas. . . .

I see you have a story in the new Post.††

Always yours,

March 19, 1937

Dear Scott:

As for Ernest, I know he will cut that piece out of his story. He spoke to me a while ago about it, and his feelings toward you are far different from

---

*Poet and acquaintance of Hemingway.

† *To Have and Have Not*, published by Scribners in 1937.

**American novelist and diplomat, known primarily for his romantic stories of the post–Civil War South.

††"Trouble."

what you seem to suspect. I think he had some queer notion that he would give you a "jolt" and that it might be good for you, or something like that. Anyhow, he means to take it out.[85]

Ober told me about the Hollywood possibility,* and I hope it goes through; – and as he told you, I took the liberty of sending three hundred to the Baltimore bank myself, in view of the situation.

I hope the Hollywood thing goes, but even if it does not, don't get discouraged now because your letters are beginning to look and sound the way they used to.

Always yours,

[*Oak Hall Hotel*]
[*Tryon, North Carolina*]
[*ca. May 10, 1937*]

Dear Max:

Thanks for your letter – and the loan. I hope Ober will be able to pay you in a few weeks.

All serene here and would be content to remain indefinately save that for short stories a change of scene is better. I have lived in tombs for years it seems to me – a real experience like the 1st trip to Loudon County usually means a story. As soon as I can I want to travel a little – its fine not having Scottie to worry over, love her as I do. I want to meet some new people. (I do constantly but they seem just the old people over again but not so nice.)

Ever your Friend

Thanks for the word about Ernest. Methinks he does protest too much.

[*The Garden of Allah Hotel*]
[*Hollywood, Calif.*]
[*ca. July 15, 1937*]

Dear Max:

Thanks for your letter – I was just going to write you. Harold has doubtless told you I have a nice salary out here tho until I have paid my debts and piled up a little security so that my "catastrophe at forty" wont be repeated I'm not bragging about it or even talking about it. The money is budgeted by Harold, as someone I believe Charlie Scribner recomended years ago. I'm sorry that the Scribner share will only ammount to $2500

---

*Fitzgerald had written in his previous letter, that he was considering a Hollywood offer.

or so the first year but that is while I'm paying back Harold who like you is an individual. The seconde year it will be better.

There are clauses in the contract which allow certain off periods but it postpones a book for quite a while.

Ernest came like a whirlwind, put Ernest Lubitch [Ernst Lubitsch] the great director in his place by refusing to have his picture prettied up and remade for him a la Hollywood at various cocktail parties. I felt he was in a state of nervous tensity, that there was something almost religious about it. He raised $1000 bills won by Miriam Hopkins fresh from the gaming table, the rumor is $14,000 in one night.

Everyone is very nice to me, surprised & rather relieved that I don't drink. I am happier than I've been for several years.

Ever your Friend

[*Garden of Allah Hotel*]
[*Hollywood, Cal.*]
[*ca. August 20, 1937*]

Dear Max:
Have heard every possible version* save that Eastman has fled to Shanghai with Pauline.† Is Ernest on a bat – what has happened? I'm so damn sorry for him after my late taste of newspaper bastards. But is he just being stupid or are they after him politically. It amounts to either great indiscretion or actual persecution.

Thanks for my "royalty" report. I scarcely even belong to the gentry in that line. All goes beautifully here so far. Scottie is having the time of her young life, dining with Crawford, Scheerer ect, talking to Fred Astaire & her other heroes. I am very proud of her. And a *granddaughter.*** Max, do you feel a hundred?

Ever Your Friend

Aug. 24, 1937

Dear Scott:
Since the battle occurred in my office between two men whom I have long known, and for both of whom I was at the time acting as editor, I have tried to maintain a position of strict neutrality. – And I have said to every

---

*Of a scuffle in the Scribners offices between Hemingway and radical editor-critic Max Eastman, which is elaborately described in Perkins' letter of August 24th.

†Mrs. Ernest Hemingway.

**Perkins had recently become a grandfather.

newspaperman, and to everyone that I did not know very well, that the "altercation" was a matter entirely between them, and that I had nothing to say about it. But here, for your own self alone, is what happened:

Max Eastman was sitting beside me and looking in my direction, with his back more or less toward the door, talking about a new edition of his "Enjoyment of Poetry". Suddenly in tramped Ernest and stopped just inside the door, realizing I guess, who was with me. Anyhow, since Ernest had often told me what he would do to Eastman on account of that piece Eastman wrote,* I felt some apprehension. – But that was a long time ago, and everyone was now in a better state of mind. But in the hope of making things go well I said to Eastman, "Here's a friend of yours, Max." And everything did go well at first. Ernest shook hands with Eastman and each asked the other about different things. Then, with a broad smile, Ernest ripped open his shirt and exposed a chest which was certainly hairy enough for anybody. Max laughed, and then Ernest, quite good-naturedly, reached over and opened Max's shirt, revealing a chest which was as bare as a bald man's head, and we all had to laugh at the contrast. – And I got all ready for a similar exposure, thinking at least that I could come in second. But then suddenly Ernest became truculent and said, "What do you mean of accusing me of impotence?" Eastman denied that he had, and there was some talk to and fro, and then, most unfortunately, Eastman said, "Ernest you don't know what you are talking about. Here, read what I said," and he picked up a book on my desk which I had there for something else in it and didn't even know contained the "Bull in the Afternoon" article. But there it was, and instead of reading what Eastman pointed out, a whole passage, Ernest began reading a part of one paragraph, and he began muttering and swearing. Eastman said, "Read all of it, Ernest. You don't understand, – Here, let Max read it." And he handed it to me. I saw things were getting serious and started to read it, thinking I could say something about it, but instantly Ernest snatched it from me and said, "No, I am going to do the reading," and as he read it again, he flushed up and got his head down, and turned, and smack, – he hit Eastman with the open book. Instantly, of course, Eastman rushed at him. I thought Ernest would begin fighting and would kill him, and ran around my desk to try to catch him from behind, with never any fear for anything that might happen to Ernest. At the same time, as they grappled, all the books and everything went off my desk to the floor, and by the time I got around, both men were on the ground. I was shouting at Ernest and grabbed the man on top, thinking it was he, when I looked down and there was Ernest on his back, with a broad smile on his face. – Apparently he regained his

*"Bull in the Afternoon," *New Republic*, June 7, 1933.

temper instantly after striking Eastman, and offered no resistance whatever. – Not that he needed to, because it had merely become a grapple, and of course two big men grappling do necessarily fall, and it is only chance as to which one falls on top. – But it is true that Eastman was on top and that Ernest's shoulders were touching the ground, – if that is of any importance at all. Ernest evidently thinks it is, and so I am saying nothing about it.

When both Ernest and Eastman had gone, I spoke to the several people who had seen or heard, and all agreed that nothing would be said.

It seems that Max Eastman for some reason wrote out an account of the thing and that the next night at dinner, where there were a number of newspaper people and various others of that kind, read it aloud. Apparently he was urged to do it by his wife, and it was supposed that it would go no further. But of course it did go further, and reporters came to Eastman for it and he gave them his own story. His story appeared in the evening papers on Friday, and reporters were calling me up all day, and when, late in the afternoon, Ernest came in I told him this. The reporters represented the story as saying, as indeed it did imply, that Eastman had thrown him over my desk and bounced him on his head, etc. And Ernest talked to one of these reporters and then agreed to be interviewed by him, and then a number of others turned up. I was talking to different people outside all the time and did not know what Ernest said until I read it in the papers. He talked too much, and unwisely. It would have been better to have said nothing, but at the time it seemed as though Eastman's story should not appear without proper qualification. Ernest really behaved admirably the moment after he had struck the blow with the book. He then talked more the next day at the dock before he sailed. That is the whole story. I think Eastman does think that he beat Ernest at least in a wrestling match, but in reality Ernest could have killed him, and probably would have if he had not regained his temper. I thought he was going to.

I am glad everything is going well with you. In rather troubled times I often think of that with great pleasure, – and with admiration.

All this I am telling you about the fight is in strict confidence.

Always yours,

Metro-Goldwyn-Mayer Corp. Studios
Culver City, Calif.
Sept. 3, 1937.

Dear Max:
Thanks for your long, full letter. I will guard the secrets as my life.

I was thoroughly amused by your descriptions, but what transpires is that Ernest did exactly the same asinine thing that I knew he had it in him to do when he was out here. The fact that he lost his temper only for a minute does not minimize the fact that he picked the exact wrong minute to do it. His discretion must have been at low ebb or he would not have again trusted the reporters at the boat.

He is living at the present in a world so entirely his own that it is impossible to help him, even if I felt close to him at the moment, which I don't. I like him so much, though, that I wince when anything happens to him, and I feel rather personally ashamed that it has been possible for imbeciles to dig at him and hurt him. After all, you would think that a man who has arrived at the position of being practically his country's most imminent [eminent] writer, could be spared that yelping.

All goes well – no writing at all except on pictures.

Ever your friend,

The Schulberg book* is in all the windows here.

> Garden of Allah
> 8152 Sunset Boulevard
> Hollywood, California
> March 4th, 1938

Dear Max:

Sorry I saw you for such a brief time while I was in New York and that we had really no time to talk.

My little binge lasted only three days, and I haven't had a drop since. There was one other in September, likewise three days. Save for that, I haven't had a drop since a year ago last January. Isn't it awful that we reformed alcoholics have to preface everything by explaining exactly how we stand on that question?

The enclosed letter is to supplement a conversation some time ago. It shows quite definitely how a whole lot of people interpreted Ernest's crack at me in "Snows of K." When I called him on it, he promised in a letter that he would not reprint it in book form. Of course, since then, it has been in O'Brien's collection,† but I gather he can't help that. If, however, you are publishing a collection of his this fall, do keep in mind that he has promised to make an elision of my name. It was a damned rotten thing to do, and with anybody but Ernest my tendency would be to crack back.

---

* *They Cried a Little* by Sonya Schulberg.

† *The Best Short Stories 1937 and the Yearbook of the American Short Story*, edited by Edward J. O'Brien.

Why did he think it would add to the strength of his story if I had become such a negligible figure? This is quite indefensible on any grounds.

No news here. I am writing a new Crawford picture, called "Infidelity." Though based on a magazine story, it is practically an original. I like the work and have a better producer than before – Hunt Stromberg – a sort of one-finger Thalberg, without Thalberg's scope, but with his intense power of work and his absorption in his job.

Meanwhile, I am filling a notebook with stuff that will be of more immediate interest to you, but please don't mention me ever as having any plans. "Tender Is the Night" hung over too long, and my next venture will be presented to you without preparation or fanfare.

I am sorry about the Tom Wolfe business.* I don't understand it. I am sorry for him, and, in another way, I am sorry for you for I know how fond of him you are.

I may possibly see you around Easter.

Best to Louise.

Ever yours,

All this about The *Snows* is confidential.

March 9, 1938

Dear Scott:

I was mighty glad to get your letter. I'll bet you find the work out there very interesting. Don't get so you find it too interesting and stay in it. I don't believe anyone could do it better, and I should think doing "Infidelity" would be really worthwhile.

You know my position about Ernest's story "The Snows". – Don't be concerned about it. We do aim to publish a book of his stories in the Fall and that would be in it. His play† will presumably be put on in the Fall but I cannot find out definitely whether it has yet been arranged for. I think Ernest is having a bad time, by the way, in getting re-acclimated to domestic life, and I only hope he can succeed.

I am sending back the letter about Gatsby. – You might want to have it for some reason. What a pleasure it was to publish that! It was as perfect a thing as I ever had any share in publishing. – One does not seem to get such satisfactions as that any more. Tom was a kind of great adventure, but all the dreadful imperfections about him took much of the satisfaction out of it. I think that at bottom Tom has an idea now that he will go it

---

*Wolfe had left Scribners and was to have his future books published by Harpers.
†"The Fifth Column."

alone, doing his own work, and if he could manage that, it would be the one and only way in which he could really achieve what he should.

Scott, I ought not to even breathe it to you because it will probably never turn out, but I have a secret hope that we could some day – after a big success with a new novel – make an omnibus book of "This Side of Paradise," "The Great Gatsby," and "Tender Is the Night" with an introduction of considerable length by the author. Those three books, besides having the intrinsic qualities of permanence, represent three distinct periods. – And nobody has written about any of those periods as well. But we must forget that plan for the present.

I understand about your brief holiday, and thought it was justified, and greatly enjoyed seeing you the little I did. I wish you were to be here on April first when we are giving a party for Marjorie Rawlings, whose "South Moon" you liked. – She has written one called "The Yearling" which the Book of the Month Club has taken for April. – I planned the party before the Club did take it, though. They also took "South Moon" but that only sold about 10,000 copies even so, because it appeared on the day the bank holiday began.

Yours,

April 8, 1938

Dear Scott:

You know Ernest went back to Spain, and I think he did it for good reasons. He couldn't reconcile himself to seeing it all go wrong over there, – all the people he knew in trouble – while he was sitting around in Key West. It was a cause he had fought for and believed in, and he couldn't run out on it. So he went back for a syndicate, and he wrote me on his arrival in France ten days ago. He wrote from the ship, and in a quite different vein from what he ever did before, in apology for having been troublesome – which he hadn't been in any serious sense – and thanking me for "loyalty" and then sending messages to different people here, and also to you and John Bishop. In fact, his letter made me feel depressed all through the weekend because it sounded as if he felt as if he did not think he would ever get back from Spain. – But I haven't much faith in premonitions. Very few of mine ever developed. Hem seemed very well, and I thought he was in good spirits, but I guess he wasn't. I thought I would tell you that he especially mentioned you.

But the good news is that the play, which came right after the letter, is very fine indeed, and it shows he is going forward. At the end, after "Philip" has gone through all kinds of horrors and carried on an affair with a girl, Dorothy, who is living in a Madrid hotel writing trivial articles, he says to his side-partner, "There's no sense babying me along. We're in for fifty years of undeclared wars, and I've signed up for the duration. I don't exactly remember when it was, but I signed up all right."

And then later the girl, who has disgusted him by turning up with a silver fox cape bought for innumerable smuggled pesetas, tries to persuade him to marry her, or anyhow to go off with her to all the beautiful places on the Rivera and Paris and all that. And Philip says finally, "*You* can go. But I have been to all those places and I have left them all behind, and where I go now I go alone, or with others who go there for the same reason I go."

There isn't much to give you an idea from, but you have intuition, and you know Ernest. He has grown a lot in some way. I don't know where he is going either, but it is somewhere. But anyhow, I felt greatly moved by the play, but melancholy after his letter. One thing that worries him a lot is Evan Shipman who was in that foreign brigade, whatever they called it. Anything may have happened to him, and Ernest felt responsible about his being there. I hope everything will turn out all right, but I thought you would like to hear. Anyhow, the play is really splendid. It should be produced in September.

Always yours,

The Garden of Allah Hotel
Hollywood, Calif.
April 23, 1938

Dear Max:
I got both your letters and appreciate them and their fullness, as I feel very much the Californian at the moment and, consequently, out of touch with New York.

The Marjorie Rawlings' book fascinated me. I thought it was even better than "South Moon Under" and I envy her the ease with which she does action scenes, such as the tremendously complicated hunt sequence, which I would have to stake off in advance and which would probably turn out to be a stilted business in the end. Hers just simply flows; the characters keep thinking, talking, feeling and don't stop, and you think and talk and feel with them.

As to Ernest, I was fascinated by what you told me about the play, touched that he remembered me in his premonitory last word, and fascinated, as always, by the man's Byronic intensity. The Los Angeles Times printed a couple of his articles, but none the last three days, and I keep hoping a stray Krupp shell hasn't knocked off our currently most valuable citizen.

244

In the mail yesterday came a letter from that exquisitely tactful co-worker of yours, Whitney Darrow, or Darrow Whitney, or whatever his name is. I've never had much love for the man since he insisted on selling "This Side of Paradise" for a dollar fifty, and cost me around five thousand dollars; nor do I love him more when, as it happened the other day, I went into a house and saw someone reading the Modern Library's "Great Modern Short Stories" with a poor piece of mine called "Act Your Age" side by side with Conrad's "Youth," Ernest's "The Killers" because Whitney Darrow was jealous of a copyright.

His letter informs me that "This Side of Paradise" is now out of print. I am not surprised after eighteen years (looking it over, I think it is now one of the funniest books since "Dorian Gray" in its utter spuriousness – and then, here and there, I find a page that is very real and living), but I know to the younger generation it is a pretty remote business, reading about the battles that engrossed us then and the things that were startling. To hold them I would have to put in a couple of abortions to give it color (and probably would if I was that age and writing it again). However, I'd like to know what "out of print" means. Does it mean that I can make my own arrangements about it? That is, if any publisher was interested in reprinting it, could I go ahead, or would it immediately become a valuable property to Whitney again?

I once had an idea of getting Bennett Cerf to publish it in the Modern Library, with a new preface. But also I note in your letter a suggestion of publishing an omnibus book with "Paradise," "Gatsby" and "Tender." How remote is that idea, and why must we forget it? If I am to be out here two years longer, as seems probable, it certainly isn't advisable to let my name slip so out of sight as it did between "Gatsby" and "Tender," especially as I now will not be writing even the Saturday Evening Post stories.

I have again gone back to the idea of expanding the stories about Phillippe, the Dark Ages knight, but when I will find time for that, I don't know, as this amazing business has a way of whizzing you along at a terrific speed and then letting you wait in a dispirited, half-cocked mood when you don't feel like undertaking anything else, while it makes up its mind. It is a strange conglomeration of a few excellent over-tired men making the pictures, and as dismal a crowd of fakes and hacks at the bottom as you can imagine. The consequence is that every other man is a charlatan, nobody trusts anybody else, and an infinite amount of time is wasted from lack of confidence.

Relations have always been so pleasant, not only with you but with Harold and with Lorimer's Saturday Evening Post, that even working with the pleasantest people in the industry, Eddie Knopf and Hunt Stromberg, I feel this lack of confidence.

Hard times weed out many of the incompetents, but they swarm back – Herman Mankiewicz, a ruined man who hasn't written ten feet of continuity in two years, was finally dropped by Metro, but immediately picked up by Columbia! He is a nice fellow that everybody likes and has been brilliant, but he is being hired because everyone is sorry for his wife – which I think would make him rather an obstacle in the way of making good pictures. Utter toughness toward the helpless, combined with super-sentimentality – Jesus, what a combination!

I still feel in the dark about Tom Wolfe, rather frightened for him; I cannot quite see him going it alone, but neither can I see your sacrificing yourself in that constant struggle. What a time you've had with your sons, Max – Ernest gone to Spain, me gone to Hollywood, Tom Wolfe reverting to an artistic hill-billy.

Do let me know about "This Side of Paradise." Whitney Darrow's, or Darrow Whitney's letter was so subtly disagreeable that I felt he took rather personal pleasure in the book being out of print. It was all about buying up some second-hand copies. You might tell him to do so if he thinks best. I have a copy somewhere, but I'd like a couple of extras.

Affectionately always,

May 24, 1938

Dear Scott:

You know I wish you would get back to the Phillippe. – When you were working on that you were worn out, and I thought could not do it justice. – But if you could get at it now it would be different, and you could make a fine historical novel of that time, and the basic idea was excellent and would be appreciated and understood now better than when you were writing it. – But I must say I should think your present work would take all the time you have, pretty much. Does it ease off any in the summer?

You do the gentleman you particularly write about a wrong in regard to the short story. – That was not his fault, but that of A.H.S.* who was very much rooted in the past, as you know. He could not catch the new idea and felt as if the use of material we had published was always more or less of a robbery. In fact, W.D. wanted to do the book of stories we finally published in order rather to offset the decision in regard to the Modern Library. – But that too was based on a misunderstanding of the situation. For a short story in those days one could not do much of anything.

I am sure that to put the three books in one now would be hopeless. We

*Probably Arthur H. Scribner.

are really in as deep a depression as we ever saw, and you know how bad that was. It means books sell about a third of what they otherwise would, and we are mighty lucky in having "The Yearling". – It goes to the very tip top by the way, next week. And we have a splendid new first novel for the Fall too. But books in general do not get much of anywhere, and I would not want to waste the possibilities for this three-in-one volume in these adverse conditions. It would come to nothing and would merely spoil an opportunity for good. – What's more, I think it is a little too soon anyway. There comes a time, and it applies somewhat now to both "Para-dise" and "Gatsby," when the past gets a kind of romantic glamour. We have not yet reached that with "Tender Is the Night" and not to such a degree as we shall later even with "Paradise" I think. But unless we think there never will be good times again – and barring a war there will be better times than ever, I believe – we ought to wait for them. We shall lose nothing by it except that when one has an idea it is hard to postpone the execution of it.

I just had a letter from Ernest and he is about to come back. It was a fine and characteristic letter, and he wants to get back and write has plenty that is grand, he says. He has been right in it apparently, – says that "Nobody's got any social standing now who has not swum the Ebro at least once." He may have sailed by this time, but he wrote from Marseilles and was about to fly back to Madrid. I have seen dispatches of his from there. He was just going to look things over and then start for the U.S.A.

I had a mighty nice lunch with John Bishop. He gets better as he ages – he does age though for his hair is pretty white. I think he is now going to write a novel. – Its scene is to be Paris at the time when you were all over there, the post-war period. – It isn't really about that, but rather human relations of certain individuals. Bunny they say is very happy and I have always meant to get him and his wife over to New Canaan, but the trouble is that I have to do all my work at home. No one could do it here.

Always yours,

Sept. 1, 1938

Dear Scott:

I went over to see Harold Ober the other day and heard about you, what you are working on now, that you had a plan for a novel, that Scottie got safely into Vassar, etc. I hope something may bring you back this way again before long, but I suppose you will have to stay on that job for another year or eighteen months or so. I have a long letter from Elizabeth today, to tell about how she bought that church house on the place and made it all over and is just about getting it finished. – She is living in it now. She seems very happy, but it seems all wrong that she should be living alone.

Hem went through here like a bullet day before yesterday, to sail for France. He is going to take at least another look at Spain, but his real purpose was to work. I wish I could talk to you about him: he asked me about a plan he has, and I advised him quite vigorously, and yet had some doubts of the wisdom of it afterward. But I think it is right enough. I only would like to talk to someone who really would understand the thing. We are publishing, after a great deal of argument and frequent changes of plan which were made to meet Hemingway's wishes mostly, a book which is to be called "The Fifth Column and the First Forty-Nine Stories". It is the play, "The Fifth Column", the four new stories, and then all the old ones, in an omnibus volume. The play appears simply as if it were a story, and it can be read that way mighty well. – If later it is produced, we shall publish separately the version used, for there will be a demand for it in that form. – But here it appears as if it were one of his stories, you might say. There is a good introduction. One of the new stories is "The Snows of Kilimanjaro" and you are not in it. By the way, the O'Brien collection containing that, had nothing whatever to do with us, and I did not even know that that story was in it until the book was out. Hem was really in better shape and spirits than I have seen him in for years, and there were not so many people around, – all that rabble from Esquire has generally been hanging around recently, and I never really got a good chance to talk to him quietly. I did this time. I think his home problems are working out somehow or other, but having got into all this Spanish business, with all the partisanship there is around it, he could not work over here because so many people were bothering him to do things for this cause or that. – The communists seem to regard him as one of themselves now, and they keep pestering him for all kinds of reasons.

Couldn't you get time to write the old lone Wolfe? He went on an odyssey of the Northwest, not having seen it before, and after six or eight weeks of it, he found himself in Seattle, and mighty ill. – It turned out he had bronchial pneumonia and he is still far from well, and has a fever, though some seven weeks have passed. I think he came pretty close to death. He wrote me a very nice letter in answer to one I wrote him, and that apparently brought back his fever again. He needs support and encouragement now for I know he will begin to get into a panic about the time he is wasting. If this illness should result in his getting a really long rest, it would perhaps have been good fortune, and not bad, – for he has never rested a moment since I have known him hitherto. I think if he does what he should, he will go to California, and lay off for some months. – But I hope he won't go down your way, for then he would find too much that was exciting from Hollywood.

I am just sending you one book because it is so good. It is not in your line at all, and judged as a whole, it does not quite come off in a story sense. But really it is not a story. It is directly derived from experience, and it is excellent. It is a book you will remember pieces of for years. – But you do not have to read it if you haven't the time. It is called "The Captain's Chair".* It is too bad it had to be called that, and be presented as if it were a novel, but I could not contend against the English publishers, or do anything with the author when he was dealing with them first, – but I tried to get this man to write a book about this region twenty years ago, before he had ever done anything, and I still have in the safe thirty pages that he did bring in as an example of what he could do.

I think I have Louise moved back to Connecticut for good. – She may insist upon an apartment or a suite in a hotel, or something, for a month or two, but the house is filled up with children and grandchildren so that we cannot get back there, thank Heaven. I am glad to be a commuter again. – It is the way I began, and I never lost the habit. Zippy† has a magnificent boy with a Napoleonic head, and red hair. Peggy† is delighted with her job in Bergdorf Goodman, but just the same I told her plainly that if she did not watch her step she would find herself engaged. He is a very nice and attractive boy, but he has no money. Now she is getting an apartment on 78th Street.

Always yours,

Metro-Goldwyn-Mayer Corp. Studios
Culver City, Calif.
Sept. 29th 1938

Dear Max:
I feel like writing to you about Tom as to a relation of his, for I know how deeply his death** must have touched you, how you were so entwined with his literary career and the affection you had for him. I know no details. Shortly after I got your letter that he was in Seattle I read in the paper that he was starting East sick. This worried me and it seemed a very forlorn and desolate and grievous experience yet something which his great vitality would somehow transcend and dominate – and then the end at Baltimore and that great pulsing, vital frame quiet at last. There is a great hush after him – perhaps even more than after the death of Ring who had been moribund so long.

I would like to know something about the situation. You, as his literary

---

*A novel by Robert Flaherty, published by Scribners in 1938.
†Two of Perkins' daughters.
**Thomas Wolfe died on September 15th.

executor, are I suppose oddly enough more in control of his literary destiny than when he was alive. I don't suppose that his "million words" rounds out his great plan but I am not so sure that that matters because the plan must have been a mutating and progressive thing. The more valuable parts of Tom were the more lyrical parts or rather those moments when his lyricism was best combined with his powers of observation – those fine blends such as the trip up the Hudson in "Of Time And The River". I am curious to know what his very last stuff was like, whether he had lost his way or perhaps found it again.

With deepest sympathy for you and also for his family. Do you think it would do any good to write them a letter and to whom should I address it?[86]

Ever, your friend –

. . . . .

Metro-Goldwyn-Mayer Corp. Studios
Culver City, Calif.
December 24, 1938.

Dear Max:

Since the going-out-of-print of "Paradise" and the success (or is it one?) of the "Fifth Column" I have come to feel somewhat neglected. Isn't my reputation being allowed to let slip away? I mean what's left of it. I am still a figure to many people and the number of times I still see my name in *Time* and the *New Yorker* ect. make me wonder if it should be allowed to casually disappear – when there are memorial double deckers to such fellows as Farrel[l] and Stienbeck.

I think something ought to be published this Spring. You had a plan for the three novels and I have another plan, of which more hereafter, for another big book; the recession is over for awhile and I have the most natural ambition to see my stuff accessible to another generation. Bennet Cerf obviously isn't going to move about *Tender* and it seems to me things like that need a spark from a man's own publisher. It was not so long ago that "Tender" was among the dozen best of a bad season and had an offer from the Literary Guild – so I can't be such a long chance as say, Callaghan. Either of the two books I speak of might have an awfully good chance to pay their way. A whole generation now has never read "This Side of Paradise". (I've often thought that if Frank Bunn at Princeton had had a few dozen copies on his stands every September he could have sold them all by Christmas).

But I am especially concerned about *Tender* – that book is not dead. The *depth* of its appeal exists – I meet people constantly who have the same exclusive attachment to it as others had to *Gatsby* and *Paradise*, people who identified themselves with Dick Diver. It's great fault is that the *true* beginning – the young psychiatrist in Switzerland – is tucked away in the middle of the book. If pages 151–212 were taken from their present place and put at the start the improvement in appeal would be enormous. In fact the mistake was noted and suggested by a dozen reviewers. To shape up the ends of that change would, of course, require changes in half a dozen other pages. And as you suggested, an omnibus book should also have a preface or prefaces – besides my proposed glossary of absurdities and inaccuracies in *This Side of Paradise*. This last should attract some amused attention.

The other idea is this:

A Big collection of stories leading off with *Phillipe* – entirely rewritten and pulled together into a 30,000 word novelette. The Collection could consist of:

1. Phillipe

2. Pre-war (Basil & Josephine)

3. May Day

4. The Jazz Age (the dozen or so best Jazz Stories).

5. About a dozen others including Babylon.

The reason for using *Phillipe* is this: He is to some extent completed in the 4th story (which you have never read) and in spite of some muddled writing, he is one of the best characters I've ever "drawn". He should be a long book – but whether or not my M.G.M. contract is renewed I'm going to free-lance out here another year to lay by some money and then do my modern novel. So it would be literally *years* before I got to *Phillipe* again – if ever.

In my work here I can find time for such a rewrite of *Phillipe* as I contemplate – I could finish it by the first of February. The other stories would go in to the collection unchanged. Unlike Ernest I wouldn't want to put in *all* the stories from all four books but I'd like to add four or five never published before.

I am desperately keen on both these schemes – I think the novels should come first and, unless there are factors there you haven't told me about, I think it is a shame to put it off. It would not sell wildly at first but unless you make some gesture of confidence I see my reputation dieing on its feet from lack of nourishment. If you could see the cards for my books in the public libraries here in Los Angeles continually in demand even to this day, you would know I have never had wide distribution in some parts of the country. When *This Side of Paradise* stood first in the *Bookman's Monthly List* it didn't even appear in the score of the Western States.

You can imagine how distasteful it is to blow my own horn like this but it comes from a deep feeling that something could be done if it is done at once, about my literary standing – always admitting that I have any at all.

Ever your friend,

Dec. 30, 1938

Dear Scott:

I have had the same problem on my mind right along, but the first thing to remember is that in books a unit is always better than a collection. Besides, I do not think that so large an undertaking as the three novels in one could be done until you have written a major book (that seems to be the current phrase nowadays) and even then it would make a difficult problem. I hope it may some day be done though.

I think the prohibitive thing in the case of the Modern Library was that the three books are too different in typography to be printed from the existing plates. – The Modern Library tries to avoid resetting. They rent plates from the publisher, and I think they are less inclined to do anything afresh nowadays than ever.

Then you propose Philippe and the various stories, – that is, a collection. What I think we ought to do, and I would be mighty glad if it could be done, would be to publish the Philippe, a unit, in the Summer. I know the book had good, deep qualities in it and popular ones too, and I think that that historical sort of book is fitted better to these days than to those in which you wrote it. It might go well. It is as long as "The Great Gatsby". And anyhow, it would do what we want by publishing a book by you and keeping you on the map. – You may think you are more off it than you are, for when you do a book it will have attention. This book might do very well indeed, and it will get attention, and somewhat of a special sort, as being a different kind of book by you. Can this be done? We might have someone like Shenton do decorations for it.

What you say about the public library demand is true also in New Canaan. It is a curious thing that books do not keep on when they are so much in demand that way. I do not understand it altogether. I have noticed it through years because my girls have brought home copies of your books all read to pieces through the last thirteen years from the New Canaan library.

Ernest's book sold between nine and ten thousand to date, but there are quite a large number on consignment that may have been sold. We cannot tell until the latter part of January. But then the book should go on selling as a kind of stock book, containing stories that cannot be got anywhere else. It should get to 15,000 within the next year. We wanted to publish the play separately, and I believe we would have sold as many of the stories without it, and some thousands of the play as well. There too, comes in the element of the unit. The play by itself would have seemed more attractive than it ever did in this collection. – But Ernest was convinced it was the other way. Anyhow, when the play is produced, we can publish it alone in the form in which it appears, and it should have a considerable sale to the audience that always buys plays on the stage.

Jane* tells me about Scottie once in a while. She is very popular, and Jane has a notion that she is coming out all right as a student too. I hope it is true.

I have a lot of things I would like to write you about but whoever called these days the Holidays must have been a master of sarcasm.

I am sending you a little book about the War. I just thought it would interest you, – it tells of some curious happenings.

Always yours,

P.S. Did you read John Bishop's piece on Tom Wolfe in the Kenyon Review? It is mighty interesting.

Metro-Goldwyn-Mayer Corp. Studios
Culver City, Calif.
January 4, 1939.

Dear Max:

Your letter rather confused me. I had never clearly understood that it was the Modern Library who were considering doing my three books as a giant volume. I thought it was an interprise of yours. If they show no special enthusiasm about bringing out "Tender" by itself, I don't see how they would be interested in doing a giant anyhow. You spoke of it last year as something only the recession kept you from doing.

What I don't like is the out-of-print element. In a second I'm going to discuss the Philippe business with you, but first let me say that I would rather have "This Side of Paradise" in print if only in that cheap American Mercury book edition than not in print at all. I see they have just done Elliot Paul's "Indelible". How do you think they would feel about it? And what is your advice on the subject?

Now about *Philippe*. When I wrote you I had envisaged another year of steady work here. At present, while it is possible that I may be on the Coast

---

*Perkins' daughter, who was a student at Vassar with Fitzgerald's daughter.

for another year, it is more likely that the work will be from picture to picture with the prospect of taking off three or four months in the year, perhaps even more, for literary work. Philippe interests me. I am afraid though it would have to be supported by something more substantial. I would have to write 10,000 or 15,000 more words on it to make it as big a book as "Gatsby" and I'm not at all sure that it would have a *great* unity. You will remember that the plan in the beginning was tremendously ambitious – there was to have been Philippe as a young man founding his fortunes – Philippe as a middle-aged man participating in the Captian founding of France as a nation – Philippe as an old man and the consolidation of the feudal system. It was to have covered a span of about sixty years from 880 A.D. to 950. The research required for the second two parts would be quite tremendous and the book would have been (or would be) a piece of great self-indulgence, though I admit self-indulgence often pays unexpected dividends.

Still, if periods of three or four months are going to be possible in the next year or so I would much rather do a modern novel. One of those novels that can only be written at the moment and when one is full of the idea – as "Tender" should have been written in its original conception, all laid on the Riviera. I think it would be a quicker job to write a novel like that between 50 and 60,000 words long than to do a thorough revision job with an addition of 15,000 words on "Phillipe". In any case I'm going to decide within the next month and let you know.

Thanks for your letter. I wish you'd send me a copy of the Tom Wolf article because I never see anything out here. John wrote about me in the Virginia Quarterly, too.*

Ever your friend,

P.S. I hope Jane and Scottie see a lot of each other if Scottie stays in, but as I suspected, she has tendencies toward being a play-girl and has been put on probation. I hope she survives this February.[87]

> 5521 Amestoy
> Encino, California
> February 25, 1939

Dear Max:
I was sorry that a glimpse of you was so short but I had a hunch that you had wanted to talk over something with your daughter and that I was rather intruding. How pretty she was – she seemed a little frightened of me for some reason, or maybe it was one of my self-conscious days.

*"The Missing All" by John Peale Bishop, Winter, 1937.

One of the things I meant to tell you was how much I enjoyed the book "Cantigny" by Evarts, whom I gather is a cousin of yours – or is that true? It seemed to me very vivid. It reminded me of one of the best of Tom Boyd's stories in "Point of Honor" though the attitude was quite satisfactorily different.

No doubt you have talked to Harold in regard to that life insurance business.* Of course, he thinks I am rash, but I think it would be morally destructive to continue here any longer on the factory worker's basis. Conditions in the industry somehow propose the paradox: "We brought you here for your individuality but while you're here we insist that you do everything to conceal it."

I have several plans, and within a day or so will be embarked on one of them. It is wonderful to be writing again instead of patching – do you know in that "Gone With the Wind" job I was absolutely forbidden to use any words except those of Margaret Mitchell, that is, when new phrases had to be invented one had to thumb through as if it were Scripture and check out phrases of her's which would cover the situation!

Best wishes always.

P. S. I am, of course, astonished that Tom Wolfe's book did what you told me. I am sure that if he had lived and meant to make a portrait of you he would at least have given it a proper tone and not made you the villain.† It is astonishing what people will do though. Earnest's sharp turn against me always seemed to have [a] pointless childish quality – so much so that I really never felt any resentment about it. Your position in the Wolfe matter is certainly an exceedingly ironic one.

Feb. 27, 1939

Dear Scott:

I am glad you spoke of "Cantigny" because it will please Jerry, who is a cousin. He cut out one of his very best stories, and I never understood why.

I only know what your plan is in a rough way, but I hope it will work out well. Of course the kind of thing you have to do in Hollywood is extremely unattractive in the ways you say. If only it were not for the Department of Infernal Revenue, you would have been all squared up already, and a free man.

---

*Fitzgerald had gotten Harold Ober to pay $750 so that his life insurance policy, which had been assigned to Scribners during a low period in his fortunes, could be reassigned to him.

†Wolfe portrayed Perkins not altogether flatteringly as Foxhall Edwards in *The Web and the Rock* (1939) and *You Can't Go Home Again* (1940).

I have been talking to Spivak* about the possiblity of putting out an edition of "This Side of Paradise". He thinks it dates, which of course in one sense it does, and ought to. – But he is making some investigation of the library demand, etc. I hope something may come of it, and I shall keep in touch with him.

The trouble with Jane is she is shy, – at any rate when I am around. She showed great interest in you after you had gone. I think I gave you the wrong impression about Tom. I just hate to be written about on any account, and it seemed odd that with all the designs he had upon Scribners, the only part that he wrote that fits into the book – and it's pretty long – should be about me. There is poetic justice in it too, since I had backed him up so strongly, and all his writings were about real people. And as executor, and the man who had backed him, I ought to take it. – But what is written does not present me as a villain. I have skimmed around in it. The trouble is it has no resemblance to me. In reading some of it I even thought if I really were like that man, I would be quite proud of myself.

Always yours,

5521 Amestoy Avenue
Encino, California
May 22 1939

Dear Max: –
Just had a letter from Charlie Scribner – a very nice letter and I appreciated it and will answer it. He seemed under the full conviction that the novel was about Hollywood and I am in terror that this mis-information may have been disseminated to the literary columns. If I ever gave any such impression it is entirely false: I said that the novel was about some things that had happened to me in the last two years. It is distinctly *not* about Hollywood (and if it were it is the last impression that I would want to get about.)

It is, however, progressing nicely, except that I have been confined to bed for a few weeks with a slight return of my old malady. It was nice getting a glimpse of you, however brief – especially that last day. I caught the plane at half past four and had an uneventful trip West.

I have grown to like this particular corner of California where I shall undoubtedly stay all summer. Dates for a novel are as you know, uncertain, but I am blocking this out in a fashion so that, unlike "Tender", I may be able to put it aside for a month and pick it up again at the exact spot factually and emotionally where I left off.

*The publisher of Mercury Books.

256

Wish I had some news, but what I have seen lately is only what you can see outside a window. With very best to all – and please do correct that impression which Charlie seems to have.

Ever your friend,

May 25, 1939

Dear Scott:

Don't worry a bit about any idea of your writing a Hollywood novel getting out. I think Charlie just jumped at a conclusion. I never knew what the novel was, and I don't believe I ever said anything to indicate it was about Hollywood not myself knowing. I am mighty glad that you got going on it, – and I won't bother you with inquiries all the time. – You know I am anxious to hear any news whenever you can tell it.

If you read "Grapes of Wrath" tell me what you think of it. I have only read part of it, but I don't much believe in that chap, i.e. the author. He will probably be very successful though.

I am glad you are O.K. again, and perhaps it was a good thing you did have to lay up for awhile.

Always yours,

July 26, 1939

Dear Scott:

You asked my opinion of a good agent and so I'll give you the name of Brandt & Brandt, 101 Park Avenue, of whom you will have heard. I think Carl Brandt is an extremely shrewd, and an agreeable chap, if perhaps a little bit slick. Maybe I am doing him an injustice. I like him anyhow. But, Scott, I think that Harold Ober is one of the very best and most loyal friends you have in the world.[88] I hope to God you will stand by him. I don't know what misunderstanding you may have had, but I do know what he thinks of you, and that he has always been absolutely true to you in every sense. I do not think a man has any business to interfere in relations between other people, but if you will allow me in this case, I should say that something very serious would have to have happened before you would think of turning away from Harold.

Anyhow, I am mighty glad things are looking up, and that you are able to go to work, and I hope you will be in fine shape before long, and that you will forgive me for talking about things that are not my business.

Always yours,

257

5521 Amestoy Avenue
Encino, California
October 20 1939

Dear Max: –

I have your telegram but meanwhile I found that Collier's proposition was less liberal than I had expected.* They want to pay $15,000. for the serial. But (without taking such steps as reneging on my income tax, letting go my life insurance for its surrender value, taking Scottie from college and putting Zelda in a public asylum) I couldn't last four months on that. Certain debts have been run up so that the larger part of the $15,000. has been, so to speak, spent already. A contraction of my own living expenses to the barest minimum, that is to say a room in a boarding house, abandonment of all medical attention (I still see a doctor once a week) would still leave me at the end not merely penniless but even more in debt than I am now. Of course, I would have a property at the end, maybe. But I thought that I would have a property when I finished "Tender Is The Night"! On the other hand, if I, so to speak, go bankrupt, at least there will not be very much accumulating overhead.

However, if Collier's would pay more it would give the necessary margin of security and it would give me $2,000. in hand when I finish the novel in February. I feel quite sure that if I wasn't in such a tight spot Collier's would not figure that $20,000. was exorbitant for such a serial.

The further complication of money to get started with – to take me through the first ten thousand words, was something I hope you might be able to work out between you. Certainly there is no use approaching Harold with it in any way. I would have to pay the piper in the end by paying him a cut on a deal on which he has done nothing. He is a stupid hard-headed man and has a highly erroneous idea of how I live; moreover he has made it a noble duty to piously depress me at every possible opportunity. I don't want him to know *anything about the subject of the novel.*

Meanwhile I have sold in the last few months ten short stories to *Esquire,* at the munificent sum of $250. a piece. Only two of these were offered to another magazine because when you're poor you sell things for a quarter of their value to realize quickly – otherwise there wouldn't be any auctioneers.

Have you talked to Charlie Scribner or mulled over the question further? If you come to any decision which is possibly favorable, would you put it in the form of a night letter? I am enclosing a letter to Kenneth Littauer which will keep you up with the situation at present.

Ever yours,

---

*Fitzgerald had written Kenneth Littauer of *Collier's Magazine* about the possibility of serializing his new novel. Through Perkins, Littauer had expressed guarded interest.

Nov. 30, 1939

Dear Scott:

I had meant to write you right after I wired you, but was too terribly rushed. I thought the book had the magic that you can put into things.* The whole transcontinental business, which is so strong and new to people like me, and to most people, was marvellously suggested, and interest and curiosity about Stahr was aroused, and sympathy with the narratress. It was all admirable, or else I am no judge any more. I think Littaur had a preconception.† He had not read "Tender Is the Night" and he was thinking that it was way back to Gatsby since you last wrote. Anyhow he is wrong, – though for all I know he may be right as to serialization.

I sent you $250 because Littaur told me – and I hope you won't mind this – that you had wanted it. And I thought you might need it badly. I spoke of a thousand more. Before the first of January I ought to receive a small bequest. I need most of it to pay off a small debt that I got into by going on a man's note. – I didn't do it like a fool, but because he had to have the help at the time, and I realized he almost certainly would not ever be able to meet it himself. But anyhow, I shall be left with a thousand which is what they used to call "velvet" and you are welcome to it if it will help with this book. I can believe that you may really get at the heart of Hollywood, and of what there is wonderful in it as well as all the rest.

I got your telegrams and I called up Leland Hayward[89] so as to try to arrange to show him the outline. – But although it is a quarter of three, he has not yet come in. I shall follow instructions though, and I hope you will push on with courage, for you have a right to. I also sent the manuscript to Braun.** I'll give you any pertinent news as it comes along.

Shut your eyes and ears to the war if you can, and go ahead.

Always yours,

Dec. 7, 1939

Dear Scott:

I don't want to keep bothering you but I do want you to know how deeply interested I am in this book. I think what you have done is most excellent, and if anyone thinks differently, he is wrong. I am not interested in it only

---

*Fitzgerald had sent Perkins the first part of his new novel (posthumously published, unfinished, as *The Last Tycoon*), and on November 29th Perkins had wired, "A beautiful start. Stirring and new."

†Littauer had decided that he needed to see more of the novel before deciding and Fitzgerald broke off negotiations with *Collier's*.

**Joe Braun of the *Saturday Evening Post*, in the hope that he might want to serialize it.

for Scribners or even only for you, but because I want to see what you have in you justify itself. – So any time you have a chance to tell me how things go on, do it as briefly as you please.

Always yours,

5521 Amestoy Avenue
Encino, California
December 19 1939

Dear Max: –

The opinion about the novel seems half good and half bad. In brief, about four or five people here like it immensely, Leland likes it and you like it. Collier's, however, seems indifferent to it though they like the outline. My plan is to just go ahead and dig it out. If I could interest any magazine, of course it would be a tremendous help but today a letter from the Post seems to indicate that it is not their sort of material. The plan has changed a bit since I first wrote the outline, but it is essentially as you know it.

Your offering to loan me another thousand doallars was the kindest thing I have ever heard of. It certainly comes at the most opportune time. The first thing is this month's and last month's rent and I am going to take the liberty of giving my landlady a draft on you for $205., for January 2nd. This with the $150. that you have already sent me is $355. For the other $645., will you let me know when it is available?[90]

I am not terribly in debt as I was in 1935–7, but uncomfortably so. I think though my health is getting definitely better and if I can do some intermittent work in the studios between each chapter of the novel instead of this unprofitable hacking for Esquire, I shall be able to get somewhere by spring.

Max, you are so kind. When Harold withdrew from the questionable honor of being my banker I felt completely numb financially and I suddenly wondered what money was and where it came from. There had always seemed a little more somewhere and now there wasn't.

Anyhow, thank you.

Ever your friend,

c/o Phil Berg Agency
9484 Wilshire Blvd.
Beverly Hills, Calif.
May 20, 1940

Dear Max: –

I've owed you a decent letter for some months. First – the above is my best address though at the moment I'm hunting for a small apartment. I am in the last week of an eight week movie job for which I will receive $2300. I couldn't pay you anything from it, nor the government, but it was something, because it was my own picture *Babylon Revisited* and may lead to a new line up here. I just couldn't make the grade as a hack – that, like everything else, requires a certain practised excellence –

The radio has just announced the fall of St. Quentin! My God! What was the use of my wiring you that Andre Chamson has a hit when the war has now passed into a new stage making his book a chestnut of a bygone quiet era.

I wish I was in print. It will be odd a year or so from now when Scottie assures her friends I was an author and finds that no book is procurable. It is certainly no fault of yours. You (and one other man, Gerald Murphy)* have been a friend through every dark time in these five years. It's funny what a friend is – Ernest's crack in *The Snows*, poor John Bishop's article in the Virginia Quarterly (a nice return for ten years of trying to set him up in a literary way) and Harold's sudden desertion at the wrong time, have made them something less than friends. Once I believed in friendship, believed I *could* (if I didn't always) make people happy and it was more fun than anything. Now even that seems like a vaudevillian's cheap dream of heaven, a vast minstrel show in which one is the perpetual Bones.

Professionally, I know, the next move must come from me. Would the 25 cent press keep *Gatsby* in the public eye – or *is the book unpopular*. Has it *had* its chance? Would a popular reissue in that series with a preface *not* by me but by one of its admirers – I can maybe pick one – make it a favorite with class rooms, profs, lovers of English prose – anybody. But to die, so completely and unjustly after having given so much. Even now there is little published in American fiction that doesn't slightly bare my stamp – in a *small* way I was an original. I remember we had one of our few and trifling disagreements because I said that to anyone who loved "When Lilacs last – " Tom Wolfe couldn't be such a *great* original. Since then I have changed about him. I like "Only the Dead" and "Arthur, Garfield etc.", right up with the tops. And where are Tom and I and the rest when psychological Robespierres parade through American letters elevating such melo as "Christ in Concrete"† to the top, and the boys read Steinbeck like they once read Mencken! I have not lost faith. People will *buy* my new book and I hope I shan't again make the many mistakes of *Tender*.

---

*Gerald Murphy and his wife, Sara, had been close friends of the Fitzgeralds since meeting them in the south of France during the Twenties and, to some extent, served as models for Nicole and Dick Diver in *Tender Is the Night*.

†A novel of 1939 by Pietro Di Donato, which was a very great popular success.

Tell me news if you have time. Where is Ernest and what doing? . . .
Love to all of you, of all generations.

Dear Scott:

I am mighty glad to have an address again. I wanted to write you. . . .

Your letter sounds sombre but good. There are a few straws of good news in the paper today to grasp at. I am terribly pessimistic, and I think I am naturally an optimist. Anyway they give me a little cheer to work with. As for your position, it is a mighty high one. I never see an editor or writer, hardly, but they ask about you. It shows what you did, for think of all the writers who were thought to be notable and whose output has been much larger, who have simply vanished without a trace. But we knew the Gatsby was a truly great book. – I don't think there is much use in the 25¢ publishing though. You know that you are in almost all the school anthologies. I hope you are able to press on with this book that begins with such promise.

Ernest is still finishing a novel, but he is to be up here on the 10th of June. Ernest's "Fifth Column" was a notable success in its revised form, – I suppose you have heard about all that. And now I understand there is to be a sale of movie rights at any moment.

. . . It must be mighty interesting, and a happy event, to work on the production of your own story in a movie. Of course you couldn't be one of the regular hacks, and you don't want to become a professional at it.

I follow Scottie's career with great interest. In spite of what you once said, there must be a very large proportion of Scott in her. There is certainly courage and enterprise. Jane tells me of her whenever she comes down, – of the play she wrote and produced up there, and of the club, MGIMA, My God It's Monday Again. Maybe I haven't got it just right. By the way, Thomas Wolfe has Jane in his book, – a sort of combination of Jane and Nancy, but physically Jane at the age of fourteen, – says she entered the dining room as silently and swiftly as a ray of light. I'll write you more later.

At the "sales conference" about the fall books, the salesmen were all anxious to know what you were doing.

Always yours,

This should have
been recopied but
no facilities at the moment
   S.*

1403 Laurel Avenue
Hollywood
California
(new address)
June 6, 1940

Dear Max:

Thanks for your nice long letter, and for the book – or did I thank you for
the book?† I was fascinated, not only by the excellent coverage of the
battles (though the man's extreme bias and the necessity of compression
threw some of them out of focus), but by the curious philosophic note
which began to run through it, from the discussion of Pharsalla on.

The note was reminiscent, exultant and dumb, but not until I found the
name Spengler did his psychology become clear to me. Up to then I had
thought: "What a wide range for a military man!" Then the truth became
plain. Poor old Spengler has begotten Nazis that would make him turn
over in his grave, and Fuller makes his own distortion. Spengler believed
that the Western world was dead, and he believed nothing else but that
– though he had certain ideas of a possible Slavic re-birth. This did *not*
include Germany, which he linked with the rest of western Europe as in
decline. And that the fine flower of it all was to be the battle of Vitorio
Veneto and the rise of Mussolini – well, Spengler's turn in his grave must
have been like that of an aeroplane propeller.

In his last four chapters Fuller begins to get ridiculous. I wonder how
he feels now when that *admirable* Mr. Franco is about to batter down
Gibralter. This of course does not detract from the interest of the book,
especially through the Napoleonic era. Did you ever read Spengler –
specifically including the second volume? I read him the same summer I
was writing "The Great Gatsby" and I don't think I ever quite recovered
from him. He and Marx are the only modern philosophers that still manage to make sense in this horrible mess – I mean make sense by themselves
and not in the hands of their distorters. Even Mr. Lenin looks now like
a better politician than a philosopher. Spengler, on the other hand, prophesied gang rule, "young peoples hungry for spoil," and more particularly "The world as spoil" as an idea, a dominant supersessive idea.

Max, what becomes of copyrights when a book goes out of print? For
example: in the case of "Flappers." For the sake of possible picture rights
and so forth should I renew that copyright now? I haven't an idea about
this.

How does Ernest feel about things? Is he angry or has he a philosophic

---

*This note, in Fitzgerald's handwriting, appears above the salutation.
† *Decisive Battles: Their Influence Upon History and Civilization* by J. F. C. Fuller.

attitude? The Allies are thoroughly licked, that much is certain, and I am sorry for a lot of people. As I wrote Scottie, many of her friends will probably die in the swamps of Bolivia. She is all right now, by the way. I got what I wanted a year ago last Fall a year ago. I kept her out of New York while she was sixteen and kept her in Vassar, through an interview with the Dean in which the Dean told her that she had only *twenty-five per cent chance* of staying in. This stiffened her back bone and did the work. All this time that wretched Mrs. Ober was buying her party dresses for New York, and putting me in the awful humor I was in that day you mention. She (Scottie) is a very different person now, Vassar has done wonders for her (sorry I didn't get a chance to talk to Jane that day) This wasn't meant to be parenthetical – the typist put it in the wrong place. Excuse the messy letter* and I feel a proper paternal pride. It was close going there for a while. I finished the "Babylon Revisited" and may do a revise next week.

Do let me know about the copyright business,[91] and I would be interested in at least a clue to Ernest's attitude.

Ever your friend,

1403 Laurel Avenue
Hollywood, California
August 15 1940

Dear Max:

I suppose the pilgrims are on their way across the country by this time.† I was sorry I didn't get to see them again but there was nothing in the studios that week to attract them back – that is nothing I could have arranged by myself with Sheilah** gone. Unless someone goes around with them the guides simply show them the outsides of the sets and that's no fun. As usual, I was in bed during the whole time they were in California except for the one day I got up and had dinner with them. I'm glad that at least Jane and one other had a glimpse of the real thing.

I finished the job for Shirley Temple, working the last weeks without pay on a gamble. But it may possibly bring enough money to let me get back to the novel.

I feel rather lost out here now. What do people in the East say? Why

---

*These two sentences, in Fitzgerald's hand-writing, appear at the bottom of the letter, with an arrow inserting them in the text at this point.

†Perkins' daughter Jane and four of her friends had visited Fitzgerald on their cross-country motor tour.

**Hollywood columnist Sheilah Graham, who had become Fitzgerald's constant companion.

aren't the isolationists mobbed and hung to lamposts? It all seems so mysterious from here, like people living in a dream. What about Ernest? What does he think? The only cheerful thing is the game scrap the British are putting up.

Ever your friend,

August 20, 1940

Dear Scott:

I was mighty grateful for all you did for Jane, and I never gathered from all that she wrote that you weren't up and about. Also Sheilah couldn't have been kinder. I hope you will come on some day again with her and that Louise and I can thank her personally, because she plainly went to a great deal of trouble. I'd write you all I think and hear about the war, etc. except that Miss Wyckoff* is away and almost everyone else, on account of vacations. People hereabouts are very much alive to the war and anxious we should get prepared and should help England in all ways "short of war" in the meantime.

As for Ernest you know how he is situated at the present. Pauline, I think, is out your way, somewhere in California. Hem has quite a large house on a hill and is very happy. Martha† is with him (though this is supposed to be a secret). He has just finished, or all but finished, a novel and we hope to publish it in the fall. Ernest was up here some three weeks ago and in very good form, better than in years. I could write you a great deal about the novel** – it is a magnificent one – also about one that Bunny Wilson is doing etc. but I had better wait until Miss Wyckoff is here to do it.

. . . . .

Always yours,

Sept. 19, 1940

Dear Scott:

I was delighted by what John O'Hara told me yesterday over the telephone, – that you had actually written about 25,000 or more words, and that they were extraordinarily expressive words. I had no idea you had got that far. As this was to be a short book too, you are probably half through it. He didn't tell me much more than just that, and in fact I would rather

---

*Irma Wyckoff (Mrs. Osmer Muench), Perkins' secretary.

†Martha Gellhorn, who became Hemingway's third wife late in 1940.

** *For Whom the Bell Tolls.*

not know any more than I do know from having read the first chapter and a little beyond it. But it is splendid you have done it, and especially in the circumstances, with other things to do and having been ill too.

I called up Scottie and everything was O.K. and her voice sounded like it used to. Isn't it odd that she has turned out to be so much of a scholar in a way, and determined to finish her course and pleased with the Harvard summer school. I asked her about her stories and she told me what she had done. I'll now hear of her occasionally through Jane who went back for her senior year.

I suppose you have heard of the good fortune that has befallen Ernest. "For Whom the Bell Tolls" has been taken by the Book of the Month Club. – The stamp of bourgeois approval. He would hate to think of it that way, and yet it is a good thing, practically speaking. I'll send you a copy of the book as soon as we get one, which will be early in October, but I won't say any more about it now. You know, I guess, that Pauline and he are to be divorced, and presumably he will marry Martha Gellhorn. – This is so well known about that you must have heard of it, but otherwise it ought to be regarded as strictly confidential.

Bunny Wilson is working on a novel that we are to publish. – John* was to try to do another novel, but he doesn't seem to have got forward with it, and one of the people who has visited him says he fears John is too deeply occupied with dogs and children, and too much under the surveillance of his wife. Maybe he will master the situation somehow.

Anyway, Scott, I am awfully glad you have been able to make all that progress, and it may have magnificent results.

Always yours,

1403 N. Laurel Avenue
Hollywood, California
October 14 1940

Dear Max:
I'm finishing up a job here at Twentieth Century and hope then to be able to turn again to the novel. I wish I could work on it steadily from now to the first of February. It seems too much to hope for but it is just possible if this producer sells the Shirley Temple story for any decent sum.
. . . . .

It will be odd to think of Ernest married to a really attractive woman. I think the pattern will be somewhat different than with his Pygmalion-

*John Peale Bishop.

like creations. I think Bunny Wilson's book* is magnificent and I think he's had a dirty deal from that slick and superficial Fadiman and a rather stupid review from Malcolm Cowley who should know better. They seem to have expected a sort of Vincent Sheehan burst of prophecy. My God, why shouldn't he start with the philosophy of history? That's where Marx started. Most of these ignorant bastards seem to think that Das Kapital is a sort of refutation of Adam Smith.

Ever your friend,

Oct. 16, 1940

Dear Scott:

I have got to get at Bunny's book. I was only afraid that a certain inconclusiveness and perhaps inconsistencies in it – which might well make it a much better book in reality – would hurt its sale. I only gathered that it did have these supposed defects, in common with some of the greatest books in the world, from several reviews I saw. I don't think Cowley does good reviews anyhow. – By the way, I think Bunny is back with us now for all his work. I told you that we had contracted for a novel which he says is going beautifully, and he is a good critic of his own writings. But before that, should come a book somewhat in the nature of "Axel's Castle" to be called "The Wound and the Bow" which will examine certain writers including Dickens, which was in the Atlantic, and Kipling which will be, and – which fills me with apprehension – Hemingway. This book was contracted for by W.W. Norton, but we have all but taken it over from him. – I had lunch with Bunny not long ago to discuss these matters, and I was mighty glad to talk to him again. You were right about him. He has a most unusual intellect, and great integrity. – But he despises publishers.

Ernest wrote me to send him your address, and so I did. – I am sure he will be sending you a copy of the "Bell" and so I am not doing it. There is a great stir among the movie people over it, and its success as a book seems absolutely certain.

In writing Jane the other day, I asked her to let me know how Scottie seemed if she took any courses with her, or saw her. But Scottie now assured me of the greatest interest in scholarship, and so here she will have got through the discipline of Vassar, which I judge to be greater than that of either Princeton or Harvard, at a very early age. Even if she only gets the advantage of that, it will be something of value to her.

Well, here's hoping that the story you have been working on does bring enough to let you give your whole time to the novel. – I told you what John

* *To the Finland Station,* published by Harcourt, Brace.

267

O'Hara said about it. He isn't talking "poor old Scott" nor anything like it.

Always your friend,

[*1403 North Laurel Ave.*]
[*Hollywood, Calif.*]
December 13 1940

Dear Max:

Thanks for your letter. The novel progresses – in fact progresses fast. I'm not going to stop now till I finish a first draft which will be some time after the 15th of January. However, let's pretend that it doesn't exist until it's closer to completion. We don't want it to become – "a legend before it is written" which is what I believe Wheelock* said about "Tender Is the Night". Meanwhile will you send me back the chapters I sent you as they are all invalid now, must be completely rewritten etc. The essential idea is the same and it is still, as far as I can hope, a secret.

Bud Shulberg, a very nice, clever kid out here is publishing a Hollywood novel with Random House in January.† It's not bad but it doesn't cut into my material at all. I've read Ernest's novel and most of Tom Wolfe's and have been doing a lot of ruminating as to what this whole profession is about. Tom Wolfe's failure to really explain why you and he parted mars his book but there are great things in it. The portraits of the Jacks (who are they?) [and] Emily Vanderbilt are magnificent.

No one points out how Saroyan has been influenced by Franz Kafka. Kafka was an extraordinary Czchoslovakian Jew who died in '36. He will never have a wide public but "The Trial" and "America" are two books that writers are never able to forget.[92]

This is the first day off I have taken for many months and I just wanted to tell you the book is coming along and that comparatively speaking all is well.

Ever your friend,

P.S. How much will you sell the plates of "This Side of Paradise" for? I think it has a chance for a new life.

---

*Scribners editor John Hall Wheelock.
† What Makes Sammy Run.

Notes

1. F. Scott Fitzgerald's association with Charles Scribner's Sons began on May 6, 1918, when Shane Leslie, an Irish novelist and critic whom Fitzgerald had met through Father Sigourney Webster Fay of the Newman School (the prep school Fitzgerald had attended), sent Charles Scribner the manuscript of *The Romantic Egotist*, a novel which Fitzgerald had written while he was in the army. Scribners returned the manuscript to its author in August. The cover-letter, according to Fitzgerald biographer-critic Arthur Mizener, "was almost certainly written by Maxwell Perkins." It contained considerable encouragement but noted "a governmental limitation on the number of publications" and admitted "we are also influenced by certain characteristics of the novel itself." The letter concluded with a number of detailed suggestions, urging Fitzgerald to make them and resubmit the novel. Fitzgerald made the revisions and sent the manuscript back to Scribners, which in October, 1918, rejected the book finally, with only Maxwell Perkins favoring its publication. Perkins, in fact, liked the book so much that he unsuccessfully tried to interest two other publishers in it.

   After his discharge from the service, Fitzgerald went to New York, worked as an advertising copy writer during the day, and wrote fiction at night. Between April and June, 1919, he wrote nineteen short stories, but they were all turned down by magazine editors, including, in several instances, Robert Bridges of *Scribner's Magazine*. On July 4, 1919, Fitzgerald returned to his family's home in St. Paul to rewrite *The Romantic Egotist*, so that he could become the famous novelist he yearned to be and so that he could win the hand of Zelda Sayre, the beautiful and ambitious southern belle from Montgomery, Alabama, with whom he had fallen in love while he was in the army. By the end of July, he had finished the revision.

2. In a letter dated September 24th, Perkins replied, "We are not for illustrations. As a matter of fact, while they are necessary in novels of adventure, they are not used as a general thing to-day in novels of this kind."

3. On August 23, 1921, Perkins wrote Fitzgerald that he had just read *McTeague* "with great rapidity and interest."

4. On June 30th, Perkins had reported that William Collins, Sons & Co., Ltd. of London, had expressed interest in publishing an English edition of *This Side of Paradise*.

5. In his letter of August 12th to Charles Scribner, Fitzgerald explained: "My new novel, called 'The Flight of the Rocket concerns the life of one Anthony Patch between his 25th and 33rd years (1913–1921). He is one of those many with the tastes and weaknesses of an artist but with no actual creative inspiration. How he and his beautiful young wife are wrecked on the shoals of dissipation is told in the story. This sounds sordid but it's really a most sensational book & I hope won't dissapoint the critics who liked my first one."

6. With a letter dated November 9th, Perkins had enclosed the $1500 and indicated that the total sales to date of *This Side of Paradise* were 33,796.

7. On September 12th, Fitzgerald had asked for $650 and Perkins had wired on September 15th that he had deposited it.

8. Perkins answered Fitzgerald in a letter dated October 20th. He explained that the "table of works" to which Fitzgerald referred (which Perkins called "the card plate") was always inserted by the publisher "at the last minute" and thus was not in the proof the author had seen. On the question of publishing the novel in February, Perkins said that he would have to rely on the advice of the Wholesale Department and their estimate of the book's sales prospects. Finally, he reported that he had that morning deposited $1000 in Fitzgerald's account in the Chatham & Phoenix Bank.

9. On November 22nd, Perkins wrote that he had looked into the *Who's Who* matter and discovered that no payment was required. On the contrary, he explained, "they pride themselves on their entire independence in the matter," adding that he had written the publisher of the volume, presumably advising him to include Fitzgerald in the next edition.

    During this period also, on October 28th, Fitzgerald wrote Perkins that Zelda "had a girl day before yesterday. Both are doing excellently well." Perkins replied on November 1st, offering his congratulations and observing, "I know Zelda will be delighted about the sex and perhaps you will, but if you are like me you will need some slight consolation and having had great experience with daughters – four of them, I can forecast that you will be satisfied later on." Also during the first week of November, Fitzgerald asked for an additional $700 toward his advance on the novel, and Perkins, on November 10th, deposited the money.

10. Perkins wrote, on December 20th, that he was "glad" that Fitzgerald had changed Maury's speech, but admitted that "my comments were not properly expressed." He added, "I always want you to speak out your mind on things and I am glad you did it in this case."

11. On December 23rd, Fitzgerald had wired that Zelda thought *The Beautiful and Damned* should end "with Anthony's last speech on ship. She thinks new ending is a piece of morality. Let me know your advice." Fitzgerald replied,

on December 28th, to Perkins' December 27th letter, that everything beginning with the phrase "That exquisite heavenly irony" should be cut.

12. On January 6th, Perkins noted that the general public, while being "hugely
    entertained" by Fitzgerald's writings, had not "regarded them as having the
    literary significance to which they are entitled." He added, "We ought to try
    to impress this – to get away altogether from the flapper idea."

13. Earlier in the month, Fitzgerald had written Perkins, "I am writing an awfully
    funny play that's going to make me rich forever. It really is. I'm so damned
    tired of the feeling that I'm living up to my income."

14. In a reply dated January 23rd, Perkins explained that he could not adopt
    Fitzgerald's suggestion about the wrap because it was already printed; but he
    added, "we did better than simply to speak of 'Eight of the Best Stories.' " He
    also told him that the date of publication was March 3rd.

15. Fitzgerald had written Perkins late in January expressing hope that review
    copies of *The Beautiful and Damned* would not be sent too early. On February
    1st, Perkins had replied that there was "an advantage in getting a book of this
    kind into the reviewers hands a long time before the book comes out besides
    that of a prompt review. These men . . . are not only writers, but they are
    talkers. They are the center from which interest and appreciation of books is
    diffused. Each one is the center of a little circle. Whatever they say about a
    book is to its advantage and that talk which they do after seeing and reading
    a book, among themselves, and with other people, counts for a great deal."

16. On February 3rd, Perkins had written that he didn't like "Sideshow" as a title:
    "It does not seem to me to have much life. . . . It suggests something of
    secondary importance which I suppose a collection of stories is really; but we
    do not want to emphasize the fact."

17. Perkins had inquired, on February 8th, about *The Love Legend* by Woodward
    Boyd, about which the St. Paul *Daily News* had reported that Fitzgerald was
    enthusiastic. On February 9th, Fitzgerald replied by telegram that the book
    was "a good first novel somewhat on the style of Rose McCauley [Macaulay]
    and better than Edna Ferber," it was "too talky and needs some revision," but
    it would soon be sent to Scribners for their consideration.

18. Late in February, Fitzgerald had written asking for $1000, which Perkins, on
    March 2nd, wrote that he had deposited for him.

19. Fitzgerald is probably referring to the extended appreciative summary of the
    book which appeared on the back of the dust jacket and which expressed
    sentiments very much like those in the second paragraph of Perkins' letter of
    August 3, 1921.

20. *The Beautiful and Damned* was dedicated to Shane Leslie, Nathan, and Perkins
    "in appreciation of much literary help and encouragement."

21. In a letter written about April 10th, Fitzgerald had said, "I deduce from your
    retiscense on the subject of the B.&D. that it is still a disappointment."

22. Perkins had reported, in a letter of May 8th, that at a meeting of the Scribners
    book salesmen "there were loud and precipitous criticisms of the title, 'Tales
    of the Jazz Age'. They feel that there is an intense reaction against all jazz

and that the word whatever implication it actually has, will itself injure the book."

23. Perkins had asked, on May 26th, whether Fitzgerald was "thinking any more about a new novel," adding, "I suspect the next book will be a wonder."

24. In an undated letter, written late in July, Fitzgerald had confirmed the fact that several of the proof sheets of *Tales of the Jazz Age* had never reached him and asked Perkins why this was so.

25. Although unsigned, this "Comment" is probably by Perkins. On December 26th, he wrote Fitzgerald, "I wrote out some comments on the play [later published as *The Vegetable*] and I would like to see you about them."

26. In an undated reply to this analysis, Fitzgerald agreed that "Jerry's political enemies should *not* despise him – they should think of the poor ineffectual egg as a dangerous, vicious man – letting the audience themselves discover this is harmless."

27. Between January and April, Fitzgerald, living in Great Neck, Long Island, worked on his novel. On April 1st, Perkins asked if he had decided on a title so that advance publicity material could be prepared. The title which Fitzgerald proposed was "Among the Ash Heaps and Millionaires," but Perkins, on April 7th, opposed this, noting that "The weakness is in the words 'Ash Heaps' which do not seem to me to be a sufficiently definite and concrete expression of that part of the idea."

28. Between 1917 and 1923, Lardner had published eight books with Bobbs-Merrill (*Gullible's Travels, etc.; My Four Weeks in France; Treat 'em Rough; Own Your Own Home; The Real Dope; The Young Immigrunts; Symptoms of Being 35; and The Big Town*) and two (*Say It With Oil* and *You Know Me Al*) with George H. Doran.

29. On October 28th, Perkins had wired, asking when he could expect the novel. On the same day, Fitzgerald replied, also by telegram, that he had sent it but was undecided about the title.

30. Early in February, Fitzgerald wrote, "I've thought it over & decided the Tom & Myrtle episode in Chap. III isn't half as rough as lots of things in the B.&D. and should stand."

31. On March 7th, Fitzgerald had wired, "Is it too late to change title[?]" Perkins replied, also by cable, on March 9th, "Title change would cause bad delay and confusion."

32. Fitzgerald cabled, on March 19th, "Crazy about title 'Under the Red[,] White and Blue.' What would delay be[?]" Perkins cabled back, on the same day, "Advertised and sold for April tenth publication. Change suggested would mean some weeks delay, very great psychological damage. Think irony is far more effective under less leading title. Everyone likes present title. Urge we keep it." On March 22nd, Fitzgerald, by telegram, agreed.

33. Ruth Hale's review, in the April 18th Brooklyn *Eagle*, found not "one chemical trace of magic, life, irony, romance or mysticism in all of 'The Great Gatsby.' " The unsigned brief review in the New York *World* on April 12th was headlined, "F. Scott Fitzgerald's Latest a Dud."

34. On April 29th, Fitzgerald had cabled, "If you could please deposit one thousand it will be absolutely the last." On the same day, Charles Scribner wired back, "Gladly done Scott."

35. This is a reference apparently to a rumor that Fitzgerald was leaving Scribners and joining Boni & Liveright. Perkins' "letter in longhand" does not survive. Fitzgerald's wire, dated June 1st, read, "Liveright rumor absurd." Perkins replied by telegram on June 10th: "Grateful for previous cable."

36. *The Redbook* had accepted "The Rich Boy" and Scribners was concerned that the story should appear well in advance of its book publication in *All the Sad Young Men*. It eventually appeared in two parts in the January and February, 1926, issues, thus delaying the publication of the book until the Spring of 1926.

37. Perkins had written, on August 6th, that "The Bell Syndicate . . . is hot to syndicate 'The Great Gatsby'. . . . What do you say?"

38. On July 27th, Perkins had sent Fitzgerald the contract for *All the Sad Young Men*, with the terms as they had been for *Gatsby*, despite Fitzgerald's request that the terms be adjusted, in Scribners interest.

39. In a reply dated September 28th, Perkins explained, "I do not know whether Capes saw 'The Great Gatsby'. Your suggestion did not come to us until an arrangement had been made."

40. In a second letter on the subject, written early in October, Fitzgerald observed, "*Gatsby* is just the sort of book which the English say that Americans can't write. . . ." In March, 1926, Perkins, sending Fitzgerald two reviews of the English edition, noted, "There is a dash of Gatsby in ever so many men just as there is a dash of Hamlet," but he added, "there is so much in this book that is so utterly American" that a good comprehending review deserved "almost as much credit" as an utterly uncomprehending and bad one.

41. On October 7th, Perkins had given Fitzgerald the current sales figures on Lardner's *How to Write Short Stories* (18,764) and *What of It?* (7,688) and Boyd's *Through the Wheat* (10,300) and *Points of Honor* (1,545). He also remarked, "This is perhaps the first time in history that a publishing house ever gave a statement of sales to anyone but the author without at least doubling it."

42. Fitzgerald's cable, dated January 8th, had read, "You can get Hemingway's finished novel provided you publish unpromising satire. Harcourt has made definite offer. Wire immediately without qualifications." The reply, dated the same day, read, "Publish novel at fifteen percent and advance if desired. Also satire unless objectionable other than financially." A later telegram, dated January 11th, from Scribners, read, "Confidence absolute. Keen to publish him."

43. Dated January 18th and addressed to Zelda Fitzgerald, Perkins' telegram had read, "Please cable about Scott. Disturbed by report of illness." Fitzgerald's cable in reply, dated January 19th, read, "Rumor unfounded." The rumor was apparently based on a news item which Perkins had seen.

44. Early in February, Fitzgerald had written that he was considering "collecting in one volume the best stories from my 3 books, to be published by you in

about two years but to be published in England next year perhaps, instead of publishing *All the Sad Young Men.* "

45. Fitzgerald had gone to Hollywood early in January to write movie scenarios, wiring Perkins to that effect on January 4th and urging him to keep his whereabouts confidential.

46. On September 24th, Perkins had deposited $600 for Fitzgerald; on December 2nd, $250; and on December 7th, $150.

47. Stories centering around the character of Basil Duke Lee. The three referred to are probably "The Scandal Detectives" (*Saturday Evening Post,* April 28, 1928), "A Night at the Fair" (*Saturday Evening Post,* July 21, 1928), and "The Freshest Boy" (*Saturday Evening Post,* July 28, 1928).

48. Soon after his arrival in Paris, Fitzgerald had assured Perkins that he was "on the absolute wagon and working on the novel, the whole novel and nothing but the novel. I'm coming back in August with it or on it."

49. Early in July, Fitzgerald had advised Perkins to obtain the translation rights to Chamson's *Les Hommes de la Route,* noting that the author was "young, not salacious, and apparently . . . destined by all the solid literary men here to be the great novelist of France."

50. On August 7th, Fitzgerald wired, "Knopf wants André Chamson. If you don't please wire before Friday." Perkins' reply read, "Want Chamson. Making offer. . . ."

51. Scribners had refused Random House permission to use a Fitzgerald story in a planned anthology, because, as Perkins explained in a letter of February 25th, the royalty proposed (one-half cent) "seemed like robbery." He added that Scribners was planning their own similar anthology and that they would pay "2¢ apiece royalty."

52. During the summer of 1929 in Paris, Fitzgerald had acted as unofficial time-keeper for a boxing match between Hemingway and Callaghan. He became so fascinated with the action of the match that he forgot to keep track of the time and only ended the round when Callaghan dropped Hemingway with a wild swing. Hemingway at first accused Fitzgerald of deliberately prolonging the round so that he could be beaten; but, according to Callaghan, all ended in an amicable drink at a nearby bar. Caroline Bancroft's account, in the Denver *Post,* inaccurately portrayed the match as the result of Hemingway's having spoken slightingly of Callaghan's knowledge of boxing. This same version was printed in the New York *Herald Tribune* Sunday *Books* Section by Isabel M. Paterson, on November 24, 1929.

53. This agreement was terminated when Knopf dissolved their London house.

54. Zelda Fitzgerald had submitted her story, "A Couple of Nuts," to *Scribner's Magazine.* Dashiell had rejected it, writing Fitzgerald on October 16th that "the story itself is so encrusted with figures of speech that it is obscure and in some places it seems that the really dramatic parts of the story are dodged."

55. Fitzgerald had gone to Hollywood late in November to write for the movies and had offered to do an article for *Scribner's Magazine* on his experiences there. He never finished the piece, explaining to Dashiell late in September, 1932,

that he had written "about twenty pages" of it but was now immersed in his novel and couldn't finish the article.

56. Late in August, 1932, Perkins wrote Zelda, "However things come out with this book, I think from everything of yours I have seen, that you should go on with writing because everything you do has an individual quality that comes from yourself, and no one else can duplicate it. And each thing you do, it seems to me, shows a growing skill in expression."

57. In a letter of reply, dated September 27th, Perkins said that he hoped to put the first fourth of the novel into the January number of the magazine, "and therefore to finish by about the 20th of March, and we could publish on the day we finished." Failing that, they would begin it in the February issue and publish by April 20th. On the book club matter, he explained that a number of serialized books had been taken by clubs. He also reported that he had talked to Bennett Cerf of Random House about issuing *Gatsby* in the Modern Library and "we will do all we can to help that along."

58. *Scribner's Magazine* finally agreed to publish *Tender Is the Night* (the title which Fitzgerald decided on for his novel) in serial form, paying the author $10,000, $6,000 of which was applied to reduce his debt to Scribners and the remainder in cash.

59. On October 7th, Fitzgerald declined Perkins' invitation because he was too busy and suggested Gilbert Seldes as the editor. He also outlined the direction the collection ought to take, observing that it should be organized very carefully so that it would present "the story of a whole period, not up to the present, for toward the end he [Ring] was a sick man and did not record very well; but during the period in which Ring functioned rationally he 'got' everything that was going and that might be of interest to many people." The volume should be "a sort of Ring's history of the world," not "spotted like Lears nonsense but . . . organized like Carroll's nonsense."

60. Fitzgerald apparently showed the novel to a psychiatrist at Johns Hopkins, for, in a letter to Dashiell written on December 25th, he reported that the doctor had said that "not only is the medical stuff in [Section] II accurate but it seems the only good thing ever written on psychiatry. . . ."

61. On January 5th, Perkins sent Harold Ober a check for $2,000, with the understanding that the sum was a "loan at 5% to be repaid upon the sale of movie rights to 'Tender Is the Night'; – but in the event that no sale is possible, this amount becomes a charge against Mr. Fitzgerald's general account."

62. Cerf eventually agreed to publish *Gatsby* in the Modern Library, giving Fitzgerald a $500 advance and a fee of $50 for writing an Introduction to the new printing which was set directly from Scribners plates and published in 1934.

63. In an earlier letter, dated February 1, 1934, Fitzgerald had said, "Oh God, it's hell to bother you about all this but of course the book is my whole life now and I cannot help this perfectionist attitude."

64. The sixteen listed were: "The Scandal Detectives," "The Freshest Boy," "He Thinks He's Wonderful," "The Perfect Life," "First Blood," "A Woman With a Past," "Crazy Sunday," "Two Wrongs," "Jacob's Ladder," "Majesty,"

"Family in the Wind," "A Short Trip Home," "One Interne," "The Last of the Belles," "A New Leaf," and "Babylon Revisited."

65. The titles Fitzgerald suggested were: "Basil, Josephine and Others," "When Grandma Was a Boy," "Last Year's Steps," "The Salad Days," "Many Blues," "Just Play One More," and "A Dance Card." Perkins wrote on June 11th that the best of these was the first, but that "it would be better to have some phrase which suggested the general character of the whole collection."

66. On June 18th, Perkins had written, suggesting that Fitzgerald add "The Captured Shadow" and possibly "A Nice Quiet Place" or "A Night at the Fair."

67. Perkins, in a letter on June 19th, had remarked, "You might call the book, 'Babylon Revisited: Stories by Scott Fitzgerald.'"

68. On August 19th, Fitzgerald had wired that he was sending two O'Mara manuscripts and advised Perkins to "give them your best eye as he is the white headed boy hereabouts and already has fine work to his credit."

69. Fitzgerald had gone again to Middleburg, Virginia, to visit Elizabeth Lemon, and in a letter on October 26th, Perkins had remarked, "Tom [Wolfe] went down to Welbourne over the weekend, and came back with legends of your doings thereabouts."

70. Perkins had written, on October 31st, explaining that the legends about Fitzgerald at Welbourne "related mostly to the fact that the telephone down there apparently is one that everybody can listen in on, and one was that you represented yourself as the author of 'Anthony Adverse', and another about something you telephoned to Elizabeth when you were dining with Mary Rumsey."

71. On December 21st, Fitzgerald wrote that he was now uncertain about including "The Night Before Chancellorsville" because he had intended originally to make it a longer story and was afraid it was now "too spare." He asked for Perkins' advice. Perkins replied, on December 26th, that he was "very much for" including the story, adding that two people at Scribners who had read it, besides himself, also favored including it. The story was included in the collection, but under the title "The Night of Chancellorsville."

72. On December 3rd, Fitzgerald had expressed surprise at receiving a second set of galleys and warned Perkins that it would "slow up the completion of the book," for, he explained, "a proof is to me as a covey of partridges to Ernest Hemingway. I can't let it alone." That Perkins had trouble in getting proofs back from at least one other of his authors is made clear in his letter of December 6th in which he reported that he finally had to give Thomas Wolfe "an ultimatum, – that we would send back twenty galleys a day whether he read them or not."

73. Fitzgerald had wired on February 12th that the title "seems increasingly meaningless" and suggested four possible alternatives: "Last Night's Moon," "In the Last Quarter of the Moon," "Golden Spoons," and "Moonlight in My Eyes."

74. Perkins replied, on February 27th, that Boyd had died of a brain tumor which he had had, unbeknownst to his doctor, for some time.

75. The dedication read:

TO
MAXWELL EVARTS PERKINS

> A great editor and a brave and honest man, who stuck to the writer of this book through times of bitter hopelessness and doubt and would not let him give in to his own despair, a work to be known as "Of Time and the River" is dedicated with the hope that all of it may be in some way worthy of the loyal devotion and the patient care which a dauntless and unshaken friend has given to each part of it, and without which none of it could have been written.

76. Probably the day of the Preakness Stakes, an annual horserace run at Pimlico Race Track in Baltimore.

77. Fitzgerald's daughter had been staying with the Obers and plans to have her spend some time with the Perkins family were cancelled when Nancy, the youngest Perkins daughter, became ill.

78. Perkins replied, on March 20th, that he had "always been interested" in McHugh ever since Scribners had "most reluctantly" declined *Sing Before Breakfast* "about which I was very enthusiastic." He assured Fitzgerald that he would help McHugh in any way he could and that he would read anything McHugh wrote "with great interest."

79. In his reply, dated April 8th, Perkins reiterated his feeling that the book would not be wise unless it were unified and revised into a volume of reminiscence. To publish the book Fitzgerald proposed, he pointed out, would "injure the possibilities of a reminiscent book at some later time."

80. Fitzgerald had wired Donald Klopfer and Bennett Cerf of the Modern Library, suggesting that they publish *Tender Is the Night*. Klopfer had replied on May 19th that he was personally interested in the book but that he would have to await Cerf's return from England before a final decision could be made. On June 3rd, Perkins had written Fitzgerald that he too approved the idea.

81. On June 16th, Perkins replied in much the same vein as his earlier response of April 8th, but he ended the letter, "we shall do it [the book Fitzgerald proposed] if you think well of it, and do our best for it."

82. Fitzgerald had asked for $2,000. On October 6th, Perkins wired that he was sending $300, but added, "If we advanced more could you have administrator legally guarantee repayment[?]"

83. Perkins, in a letter of October 2nd, had told Fitzgerald that Marjorie Kinnan Rawlings was nearby in North Carolina and was very interested in meeting him. Perkins recommended her highly as "a great deal of a person, both in intelligence and in personality," and urged Fitzgerald to see her.

84. Late in 1936, Scribners and Wolfe had gotten into a $125,000 libel suit brought on the allegation of a woman who claimed that she had been slanderously portrayed in Wolfe's short story "No Door" and was identifiable. The suit was eventually settled out of court.

85. Fitzgerald had written a few days earlier that when he had asked Hemingway

to remove his name from "The Snows of Kilimanjaro," Ernest "answered, with ill grace, that he would – in fact he answered with such unpleasantness that it is hard to think he has any friendly feeling to me any more. Anyhow please remember that he agreed to do this if the story should come in with me still in it."

86. Replying on October 3rd, Perkins said, "If you could find time to write to his [Wolfe's] mother, who really was wonderful in her courage and fortitude on the day of the operation in Baltimore, and at the funeral, I think it would be a great thing to do."

87. Concluding his letter of January 18th, Perkins observed, "I do hope Scottie gets through those mid-years. You will probably know about it soon. But I cannot get very much alarmed about probation, having been the first man in my class to be on it. And you were on it too."

88. On July 3rd, Fitzgerald had wired Perkins that "Ober has decided not to back me though I paid back every penny and eight thousand commission." On July 24th, he asked Perkins for the names "of the two or three best agents in New York – just in case this difculty with Harold gets too hard to handle."

89. Fitzgerald had wired Perkins to show producer Hayward the outline of the novel in the hope that Hayward "might make a deal with the studios to finance the writing of such a picture." After Hayward's visit, Perkins reported, on December 1st, that Hayward was of the opinion that "nothing in a movie way could be done until after the book was out (or the serial)," although "he did seem to be really *impressed* by the outline."

90. Replying on December 21st, Perkins indicated that "any time after January 1st" would be all right. "Or in fact, if important to you, any time after December 26th." On December 26th, Fitzgerald proposed that, after Perkins sent him $372.66, he, Perkins, could then pay $150 for a back rent owed and $122.44 for a long overdue telephone bill, making the total of $645. This Perkins did.

91. On July 8th, Perkins reported that it made no difference as to copyright whether or not a book was out of print. The copyright still held and Scribners would renew when it expired.

92. Replying on December 17th, Perkins said he was returning the manuscript of the novel but he didn't think that Schulberg's book would interfere with it. He admitted that he knew nothing about Kafka but would look him up. His last words to Fitzgerald were: "Well, I hope that 'some time after January 15th' will come soon." Fitzgerald died of a heart attack, in Hollywood, on December 21st.

Index

281

Radiguet, Raymond, 76, 78, 104, 117, 152
Rascoe, Burton, 79, 108, 109, 111
Rawlings, Marjorie Kinnan, 7, 13, 180, 192, 193, 194, 234, 243, 244
Reynolds, Paul R., 24–25, 34–36, 41, 50, 81, 87, 93, 119, 121, 135, 142, 161
Rhinelander, Mrs. Leonard K., 125
Rice, Grantland, 185
Rimmer, William, 6
Rinehart, Mary Roberts, 19
Robertson, George, 7
Robinson, James Harvey, 55
Ross, Cary, 163
Rothstein, Arnold, 89
Rylee, Robert, 223

Sayre, Zelda. *See* Fitzgerald, Zelda
Scheerer, Norma [Shearer], 238
Schulberg, Sonya, 241
Scopes trial, 118
Scott, Cecilia Ashton, 5
Scribner, Arthur H., 246
Scribner, Charles, 1, 8, 22, 34, 77, 78, 80, 83, 89, 91, 93, 105, 108, 121, 147, 151, 153, 169, 207, 232, 234, 237, 256, 257, 258
Seabrook, William B., 228
Seldes, Gilbert, 76, 77, 101, 104, 108, 116, 228
Shakespeare, William, 48, 61, 63, 115, 138
Shaw, George Bernard, 22, 46, 47, 57, 58, 73
Sheehan, Vincent, 267
Sheldon, Edward, 222
Shelley, Percy Bysshe, 7, 71, 72
Sherman, Stuart P., 95, 96
Sherman, William T., 5
Shipman, Evan, 236, 244
Shulberg, Bud [Schulberg, Budd], 268
Sinclair, Upton, 57
Smith, T. R., 107, 114
Spengler, Oswald, 139, 263
Spiegal, Doris, 217
Stallings, Laurence, 78, 103, 105, 126, 161
Stein, Gertrude, 73, 76, 78, 79, 81, 90, 91, 104, 108, 111, 126, 159, 186, 214, 227, 228
Steinbeck, John, 250, 261
Stendahl, 73
Stewart, Donald Ogden, 124, 135
Strater, Mike, 165, 219

Stromberg, Hunt, 242, 245
Suckow, Ruth, 90, 106, 110, 123, 126
Sullivan, Mark, 138, 139, 171
Sykes, Gerald, 162

Tarkington, Booth, 19, 62, 111, 196, 199
Temple, Shirley, 264, 266
Thalberg, Irving, 173, 242
Thomason, John W., 139, 140, 145, 204
Tolstoy, Leo, 4, 7, 48
Train, Arthur, 73, 124, 136, 137, 171
Troy, William, 219
Turnbull, Andrew, 5
Turnbull, Bayard, 177
Twain, Mark, 6, 7, 46, 47, 49
Twysden, Lady Duff, 144

Vanderbilt, Emily, 268
Van Loon, Hendrik Willem, 95
Van Vechten, Carl, 9, 77, 108, 126, 154
Vidor, King, 152, 161
Voto, Bernard de, 171, 172
Voltaire, 47

Walpole, Hugh, 27
Weaver, John V. A., 75, 104
Wells, H. G., 22, 57, 105
Wescott, Glenway, 10, 98, 111, 133
Wharton, Edith, 13, 39, 111, 116, 126, 236
Wheelock, John Hall, 4, 6, 268
Wilder, Thornton, 152, 162
Williams, Blanche Colton, 62
Williams, Jesse, 113
Wilson, Edmund, 1, 8, 13, 35, 45, 53, 66, 86, 106, 108, 154, 157–59, 177, 221, 226, 247, 265–67
Wolfe, Thomas, 1, 2, 4, 7, 8–11, 13, 158, 168, 169, 174, 202–4, 209, 213, 217–23, 235, 236, 242, 244, 246, 248–50, 253, 254, 255, 256, 261, 262, 268
Woollcott, Alexander, 197, 198
Wordsworth, William, 203
Wright, Willard Huntington, 167
Wyckoff, Irma, 153, 265
Wylie, Elinor, 80, 96, 98, 128

Young, Brett, 104, 110

Ziegfeld, Florenz, 141
Zola, Émile, 109, 111